The Year-Round Messier Marathon Field Guide

With complete maps, charts and tips to guide you to enjoying the most famous list of deep-sky objects

Harvard C. Pennington

Published by:

Willmann-Bell, Inc. T.M.

Publishers and Booksellers Serving Astronomers Worldwide Since 1973
P.O. Box 35025   Richmond, Virginia 23235

Dedication . . .

To all those who also work in their head: My sympathies.

First Edition
Fifth Printing Decemer 2003

Telrad is a trademark of Steve Kufeld, Huntington Beach, CA 92647

Library of Congress Cataloging-in-Publication Data

Pennington, H.C. (Harvard C.)
  The year-round Messier marathon field guide : with complete
maps, charts and tips to guide you to enjoying the most famous list of
deep-sky objects / Harvard C. Pennington.
       p.   cm.
   Includes bibliographical references and index.
   ISBN 0-943396-54-9
   1. Astronomy--Observers' manuals. 2. Astronomy--Charts, diagrams,
etc. 3. Galaxies--Charts, diagrams, etc. 4. Stars--Clusters-
-charts, diagrams, etc. 5. Nebulae--Charts, diagrams, etc.
6. Messier, Charles. Catalogue des nébuleuses et amas d'étoiles.
I. Title.
  QB64.P46 1997   97-18168
  523.8--dc21   CIP

Printed in the United States of America

Acknowledgements

I **have received** invaluable data and information from Don Machholz — one of the originators of the Messier Marathon — and Joe Neu in the form of various written materials they have prepared for their own use and for which I am most grateful.

Perhaps the most valuable contributions have come from Dave Thompson and John Gossett of the Pomona Valley Amateur Astronomers. It was Dave's insistence on having a Messier Marathon that planted the seed for this project. It was John Gossett's simple instructions on how to find M81 and M82 that sparked the idea that I could successfully complete, in one night, what I could not do in almost three years — which in turn, led to this book. Thank you, Dave. Thank you, John.

I am deeply grateful to Jackson Wang and Jim Degner, who, in the beginning, provided silent but necessary and valuable assistance by making the most advanced computer equipment and software available to me for the production of this book.

Charley Trapp, my good friend, has endured and suffered and persevered silently as this project has moved from wild-eyed conjecture to finished product.

My fellow Pomona Valley Amateur Astronomy club members have given me assistance by testing, making suggestions, proofing the charts, methods and text. They are many, and space is limited. Thank you all, especially the following: Jim Bolton, Curtis Byrom, Brian Cox, David Chandler, Billie Darrah, Bob Diaz, Gene Fair, Gary Fick, Bill Garcia, Pete Gurtson, Mike Hill, John Kerns, John Liebiez, Ray Magdziarz, Ahmed Miloud, Tony Molina, Bob Oliver, Marilyn Oliver, Mike Peters, Dave Phelps, Jacob Meunier, Chuck Rader, Jerry Rosenblatt, Jeff Schroeder, John Seaton, Don Shad, Steve Siedschlag, Steve Simon, Alice Smith, Elihue Stanback, Barry Thompson, Keith Thompson, Amelia Tremblay, Ernie Williams, Mike Whiteside, Dorothy Woodside, John Yard, and Jesse Yin.

Finally, I would like to thank Perry Remaklus, who interrupted his nap on a warm May afternoon after an "all-nighter" at the 1988 Riverside Telescope Maker's Convention at Big Bear Lake to listen to an insistent nut. Me.

Harvard C. Pennington
Walnut, California

Contents

Preface

by
Perry W. Remaklus

I **first met** Harvard Pennington at the 1988 Riverside Telescope Makers Convention at Big Bear Lake, California. Somehow Harvard had found out that I would be there, and he came prepared to convince me to publish his book. As I had been up most of the night before, "doing Riverside," I was taking a much needed nap.

Pointing to me in my sleeping bag Harvard asked, "Is that Perry Remaklus?" My traveling companions took one look at Harvard with his black top hat complete with the ace of spades jauntily jutting out of the hat band and gleefully said "Yes, indeed, it is he." I now opened my eyes to see Harvard in his Mad Hatter outfit—straight out of *Alice in Wonderland*. *Oh boy*, I thought, *this is going to be a great dream.*

As soon as Harvard saw my eyes open, he started right into his pitch. "Do you know that most of the people here have never seen all the Messier Objects?" *Hum . . . I* thought, *he looks strange but he doesn't talk like the Mad Hatter.*

"You are probably right," I heard myself saying. "I've been at this for more than 30 years and I still have not seen them all—just never got around to it."

"Well, you can do it in a single night and it can be a blast—if you use my methods."

"Look here at this book." And with that he began to flip through the manuscript. Normally, authors have no problems with the words but cannot draw, but what I saw flipping by was pretty slick art.

"How did you do that?" I asked.

"Well, when I was a kid I worked for one of the studios here in California doing animation. Then when desktop computers came in, I gravitated to them. In fact I wrote a bunch of books on the subject, but my downfall was when I bet that the Radio Shack TRS80 would bury the IBM-PC. That turned out to be a big mistake. So now I have an IBM-PC and am working as a programmer."

"Looks as if you have figured out how to draw using a computer," I said.

"Yes, I did it all in PageMaker 3"

After our meeting in 1988, Harvard found little free time to complete this book. Most years we would meet at RTMC, but very little progress would be made. Then at the 1993 RTMC, Harvard advised that he had been making progress and expected to finish the book soon. Three days later he suffered a massive heart attack and died. Harvard's friends pulled together his computer files and sent them to me. Fortunately I had a pretty good idea from our meetings over the years what he intended to produce; this knowledge has been the guide used to finish the book you are now holding in your hands.

Besides being a tightly orchestrated book for doing a Messier Marathon, this book fills an even more important and long-standing need—it is a great beginner's book! Beginners need early success. Nobody knows how many people have tried to get into astronomy and given up after a series of frustrations. As hobbies go, observational astronomy can be pretty intimidating. Take a look at pages 51 and 52, you'll see that Harvard also had this problem, but through luck and sheer persistence he hit upon a method for locating deep-sky objects that all of us can immediately understand—locate a pattern of stars near or around the object and then use the illuminated reticle of a one-power finder superimposed on those stars to pinpoint that object. Success breeds success. If a beginner uses this book on practically any clear night during any month of the year he or she will almost certainly see *at least* 25 or 30 deep sky objects *before* midnight! So rather than being useful for a few days in the spring, this Messier Marathon handbook can be used on clear nights throughout the year.

Take a minute now and flip through the last 50 pages to this book. You'll see a nearly foolproof method for locating the Messier Objects. Maps, descriptions, drawings of the objects as they appear in the eyepiece and verbal descriptions.

The sketches were made by George R. Kepple. Maps were checked by Wil Tirion and errors and omissions were corrected. Wil also created the "Signpost" charts in Chapter 5 and several other illustrations found throughout the book. I am indebted to Richard Berry for his insight and assistance over a period of several months to fine tune the manuscript.

Don Machholz, Tom Reiland, Tom Hoffelder and Dorthy Woodside took time to explain various things and to provide pictures. Craig Crossen, Harold R. Suiter, Tom Polakis, Brent A. Archinal, Brian Skiff and Tom Reiland read and commented on this manuscript. Their comments have in many seen and unseen ways made this a better book. Errors that remain are my responsibility and I would appreciate their being brought to my attention so that they can be corrected in future printings.

Perry W. Remaklus
President and Publisher
Willmann-Bell, Inc.

Introduction

by
Harvard Pennington

Bob Stevens, Ken Thulowhite, Larry Warner, Lance McKay and I were the "Oildale Astronomers." Only Lance had a telescope. It was a huge 8 or 10-inch equatorially mounted Newtonian with a tarnished silvered mirror that was, as I recall, in need of collimation. At 13 or 14, none of us had a car, so we used the telescope in his backyard. We were an "astronomy club" with only one telescope, so Bob organized "meteor watches." For two years we dutifully charted meteors. We did a pretty good job of it, too; Bob would gather the data into a bundle and send it off to someone who would use it.

In time the "Oildale Astronomers" drifted apart, but I always maintained my interest in astronomy. In 1969, I bought a used Sesi 80mm refractor from a friend. Over the years I would occasionally do some casual "duffer style" observing, but I always entertained the thought that one day I would become involved in amateur astronomy again and be serious about it.

That day came in the spring of 1985. I hauled out the old 80mm refractor, went through the bearings, cleaned it up, got out my collection of astronomy books and bought the current magazines.

Charley Trapp, my good friend, had a pained look on his face — I sensed that he didn't want to get involved in, or with, another of my adventures. Charley had only a very slight passing interest in astronomy, but I conned him into spending a few evenings in the backyard with me and the telescope.

It wasn't long before aperture fever set in and I was the proud owner of a Celestron C8-Plus and a lot of trinkets to go along with it. By this time Charley was a little more interested, and I made him an offer he couldn't refuse on the 80mm refractor — he wasn't hooked yet, but the deal was good enough that it made having the scope worthwhile. The C8 didn't cure my aperture fever, and I bought *Shamu*, a 17½-inch Coulter Dobsonian. Now I had two telescopes: one for photography and another for visual observing.

In August of 1986, I joined The Pomona Valley Amateur Astronomers (PVAA). Between August and December I attended only one meeting and none of the star parties. Then I decided to "get serious" about getting serious and became active in club affairs.

I had heard and read of the Messier Marathon, but assumed that I was not advanced enough to attempt it. In February of 1987, Dave Thompson, the PVAA secretary and newsletter editor, suggested that we have a Messier Marathon. Here was an opportunity to learn a lot in a short time. I had 30 days to get ready.

I had personally located fewer than forty of the Messier objects. I was unable either to locate them or to identify them if I could find them! Obviously, I had a lot of homework to do and time was short.

How successful was I on my first try? One hundred eight out of one hundred ten Messier objects. I missed M74 in the evening twilight and M30 in the dawn twilight. If someone had only told me of the difficulties I would have with these two objects and how to find them in the twilight, I believe I could have gotten all 110 objects on my first try. On that particular night, finding all 110 objects was possible as some had located M74 in the evening twilight, and one person located M30 in dawn's twilight, although no one person got all 110 objects. Two of the marathoners made use of my first crude charts and methods for a solid 97 and 99 objects on their first try. Like me, neither had located, on their own, more than forty of the Messiers, and neither knew the sky any better than I did. I'm embarrassed to tell you how little I knew when I decided to tackle my first marathon—but it was a wonderful experience.

With this book I will take you through every step and every detail that you will need to complete your first March Messier Marathon successfully, and I hope you will feel the same thrill and sense of accomplishment that I felt.

What about my friend Charley? Well, he got a little dose of aperture fever, too. Now he owns a 10-inch Coulter Dobsonian in addition to the 80mm refractor. He is pretty pleased with himself after getting 99 Messiers in his first Marathon. I'm pleased, too.

1 | What is a Messier Marathon?

The best definition of a Messier Marathon that I know of was proposed by members of the Amateur Astronomers of Pittsburgh. They called it " . . . an informal competition to locate the most Messier objects by a single observer during a dusk-to-dawn Marathon." You can do a Messier Marathon with any telescope, with any number of observers, at any time of the year, and it's always lots of fun. Sure, you'll fight bugs and wind and cold, but you'll soon know the sky better than you ever thought you could.

The Messier objects are 110 prominent deep-sky objects discovered by the great French comet hunter Charles Messier (pronounced Mess-ee-ay). For over 200 years, countless amateur and professional astronomers have observed and studied them. Generations of amateur astronomers have cut their observing teeth on them, although it has often taken new observers years to see them all. An amateur who has seen all the Messier objects, or even most of the Messier objects, is generally regarded as an "advanced" observer. Just between you and me, it doesn't take years to see the Messier objects, and you don't have to be advanced. All you need is basic smarts, determination, and this book!

Now, you may be scratching your head a little, wondering how finding over 100 deep-sky objects in a single night could be of any value. After all, you're probably thinking, *I won't have a moment to look at the objects I find!* There might be a grain of truth to that assertion—but I have found that even in the midst of the busiest Messier Marathon, I can spare a good solid 60 seconds to study each object before moving on and still see as many objects as the night and the time of year allow me to see. Sixty seconds doesn't seem long, but if you try it, I think that you will agree that in 60 seconds of careful study you can see a lot.

So why run the Marathon? First and foremost, nothing motivates an observer like a real goal—to see as many Messiers as possible—and a real deadline—dawn. With a few hours of study and preparation, anyone that can set up a telescope without assistance and identify a dozen constellations can successfully complete a Messier Marathon with over 90 objects and, more likely, over 100 objects. For the beginner this is powerful stuff — instead of the usual two or three discouraging years it takes to see fewer than half of the Messier objects, the beginner masters the skill of locating deep-sky objects in one night! Instead of observing a paltry few of the easy Messier objects over the next year, his new-found skills enable him to observe and study scores, if not hundreds, of faint NGC galaxies, planetaries and nebulas.

Second, the Marathon forces you to hone your skills. Sure, there's an element of competition, but a Messier Marathon is more like batting practice than it is like a baseball game. You are competing against yourself to improve your knowledge and skill. Unlike sports competitions, where there is only one winner, everyone who runs the Messier Marathon wins.

Third, running the Messier Marathon teaches you to locate and identify deep-sky objects quickly. After a Marathon night you have time to study, observe, and develop the techniques necessary to "run" through a Marathon. At the next Marathon you will find that you can locate objects in seconds that used to take you many minutes or even hours. This means that during regular observing, you will have more time for study and observing instead of hunting and searching. It also builds confidence — after a Marathon night, you will *know* that you can locate those more difficult objects that you have always wanted to see but have avoided because you didn't want to spend the time trying to find them.

Finally, the March Messier Marathon is kind of like Christmas. You wait all year for that magic month of March to roll around. As it gets closer, you prepare by studying your charts, refining your order list, checking the lunar phases as you plan the date, and selecting a site.

As the date you have set draws near, you'll find yourself looking at the night sky while driving or while walking to the car after a movie — all the while reviewing the more unfamiliar constellations in preparation for Marathon night. You'll check the paper for the long-range weather charts, noting the fronts moving down from Canada. Will the night be cloudy, cold, or windy? Will there be a lot of dust in the air? Or will it be a night that's crystal clear from dusk to dawn?

At long last the night arrives. It is like a wonderful gift that opens itself as the twilight creeps across the sky and gradually reveals the night and the jewels embedded in its soft dark fabric. It is a night you will talk about for the next year and the year after that.

Ordinary, Maxi, and March Messier Marathons

I have said that a **Messier Marathon** can be run at any time of the year, and that is true. If you go to a dark-sky site with a good horizon, whatever the time of the year, you will always be able to find at least 90 Messier objects if you observe from dusk to dawn, and often you can find at least 95 objects. January, June, July, August, September, and December are the **Ordinary Messier Marathon** months.

Of course, some times of the year are better than others. During the dark of the moon in February, March, April, May, October, and November, you should be able to locate 100 or more of the Messier objects. Whenever the sky offers you an opportunity to see 100 or more Messier objects, that's a **Maxi Messier Marathon**.

The best month for seeing Messiers is March, when under dark, clear skies all 110 objects can be located in a single night. This annual opportunity to sweep the sky of Messier objects is called the **March Messier Marathon.** Some people go Marathoning *only* in March and spend the rest of the year indoors talking about how great last March was and how great next March is going to be. That is silly. The very next dark of the moon is the best time for you to run your first Messier Marathon.

Why You're Running the Marathon

In this competitive world, a race in which everybody is a winner might seem a little strange. But if this is indeed a "race," it is a race against the clock, and *everybody* who enters can be a "winner." It is a race in which your skill and ability will win the day. Of course, the obvious objective of a March Messier Marathon is to locate and identify all 110 Messier objects in one night. But a Messier Marathon is not a contest or a competition against your fellow amateurs. Rather, it is a personal accomplishment. With that thought, let's take a brief look into the reason (or reasons) you got into amateur astronomy in the first place.

There is probably not just one reason — I can think of at least five, and all of them are equally compelling:

- It looks like fun.
- Astronomy is interesting.
- You like learning new things.
- You like gadgets, especially ones that you can look through.
- You want to see the splendors of the deep sky for yourself.

I'm sure you have reasons of your own. Anything that satisfies one or more of these reasons is reason enough. Especially the fun part.

The objective, then, is to find and identify as many Messier objects as you can, regardless of your experience level. You will learn, you will have fun, and you will get to put your telescope to good use.

If you are only able to locate and identify 25 objects, that's 25 more than you would have seen had you stayed home. If it is 50 or 80, so much the better. Next time, maybe you'll get even more.

Weight lifters practice weight lifting, baseball players go to batting practice, and golfers hit buckets of balls. By doing the Marathon, you are practicing your astronomical skills of location, identification and verification. Each Marathon in which you participate will increase your confidence, skill level and general knowledge of the sky. With these improved skills you will find that you will be able to spend more time at the eyepiece instead of at the charts and finder. You will be able to share your knowledge with others and teach them how to locate and identify the more difficult and hard-to-find objects. You will know that if there is something out there and your optics are capable of resolving it, you can find it. After the Messier Marathon, you will be better equipped to go after the really dim deep-sky objects.

Why You Need to Know the Sky

I have heard a number of very skilled amateur astronomers remark that they don't believe their participation in a Marathon is a worthwhile use of their "valuable" observing time: "Yeah, I did it for a few years, but now it's so easy I would rather spend my time on something more interesting." It is my observation that when the old timers get involved then the newcomers give it a try. And when they try, they make the critical breakthroughs which lead to new skill levels and confidence. In an astronomy club, the more participation, the more fun it is for everyone.

So, regardless of your current skill level or the number of times you have done it before, there is a compelling reason to participate in a Messier Marathon. Novices, beginners, or others who have not yet mastered the skills of location and identification look to the more experienced for motivation, instruction, and guidance. Your enthusiasm will provide the necessary energy and confidence that the less-skilled need in order to progress. Regular Messier Marathons give everyone something to look forward to. It is an excuse to get out there and try. It is without a doubt a major motivating force for newcomers to study, practice, and subsequently enjoy the hobby all the more.

If you are a newcomer or consider yourself a beginner or novice, this book will provide you with all the information, techniques and motivation I can put on a printed page. If you do your homework, you can master the Marathon regardless of your present skill level.

One last point. Since the Messier Marathon began way back in the now dim 1960s, there has been a veritable electronic revolution in astronomy. Today, it is quite common to see digital setting circles and computerized telescopes. When they are working correctly these electronic marvels are a joy to use. In fact, they are so good that many of the old timers have upgraded to this technology even though they are perfectly capable of finding what they want to see the "old fashioned" way. However, on more than one occasion I have seen this technology fail. The entire night was lost because there was no "Plan B."

One of these events remains etched in my mind. The observer was obviously successful at his chosen occupation — he had the very latest equipment and when it was working he could "zoom" from object to object. About one hour into his observing session the system "crashed." Unlike crashing an airplane or car nothing mechanical was damaged — but his telescope just would no longer "zoom" from object to object.

He tinkered with this and that, became frustrated, and was about to pack up and leave when this kid (maybe 13 or 14) asked what the problem was. The guy replied the telescope was broken and he could not find such and such. The kid looked at the sky, moved the telescope slightly, peered through the finder, "tweaked" the fine adjust knobs, and then said, "Take a look." As I walked away I could hear the guy ask the kid, "How did you do that?" and the kid reply "Well, it's like this..."

I later heard that they both stayed up until dawn using that "broken" telescope.

The point of this little story is that it is nice to have the benefits of technology, but a basic understanding of the night sky and how to find things in it is an invaluable skill. As we will see in this book, it is not all that hard to learn.

2 | Messier and Messier Marathons
The Ferret of Comets Meets the Twentieth Century

Charles Messier (Mess-ee-ay) was a French astronomer (1730–1817) whose lifelong goal was to discover as many comets as possible. He was so successful at discovering comets that King Louis XV gave him the nickname "The Ferret of Comets."

Figure 2-1 In addition to compiling his famous catalog, Charles Messier discovered over 50 comets during his lifetime. Photo courtesy of Owen Gingerich of the Harvard Smithsonian Astrophysical Observatory.

The telescopes that Messier used were small by today's standards — even for amateur astronomers. In his early years, his favorite was a Gregorian telescope with a speculum (a metal alloy) mirror with an aperture of about 7½ inches. Later he used a slightly larger Newtonian reflector, also with a metal mirror, of about 7¾ inches. Eventually he used several achromatic refractors by the famous English optician Peter Dollond. The Dollond instruments were all of about 3½ inches aperture (90 mm) and 43 inches (1100 mm) in focal length, very similar in size to the popular 80 mm telescopes of Meade, Orion, Celestron and others, although these modern amateur instruments will outperform Messier's telescopes thanks to advances in optical design, coatings, and glass.

While observing a comet in the constellation Taurus in 1754, Messier recorded the first object for his famous catalog, M1, the famous Crab Nebula. This nebula had appeared so much like a comet, as other objects had, that he decided to make a catalog of objects that might be confused with comets. He presented his first list of 45 objects to the French Academy in 1771. In 1774 it was published, but with some of the southern objects missing. Messier went on to publish several supplements to his catalog. He might even have thought they had importance in their own right beyond his comet hunting interests.

Many of the Messier objects had been discovered prior to Messier's time, and some of the later discoveries were made by Messier's associate and friend, Pierre Méchain. Messier never attempted to hide this fact since his only purpose was to offer a complete catalog of objects that might appear to be comets—regardless of who discovered them.

Messier died on April 12, 1817, at the age of 86, after suffering through the French Revolution and being reduced to poverty. He was finally restored to prominence as a member of the Academy of Sciences and Bureau des Longitudes after the revolution had run its course.

Today's Messier Catalog is actually a combination of four catalogs that were published about 200 years ago. Between them, these catalogs contain 103 deep-sky objects: clusters, nebulae, open clusters, globular clusters, asterisms, and, of course, a few errors. Over the years, the errors have been accounted for to almost everyone's satisfaction.

Recently, seven additional objects have been added to bring the total count of Messier objects to 110. These seven "new" Messier objects were apparently observed by Messier, but not included in his catalog.

Since the time of Messier, several new catalogs of deep-sky objects have been compiled. Most notable of these were the *General Catalog* (GC), the *New General Catalog* (NGC), and the *Index Catalogs, I and II* (or just IC), which were published as an addition to the NGC. As a result, virtually all of the Messier Objects have an NGC or IC or some other catalog number (or numbers) in addition to their Messier (M) number.

Ironically, Messier wished to be known for his cometary discoveries, but it is his list of objects that are *not* comets that has earned him immortality.

Fast-Forward to the 1960s . . .

For a century and half after Messier's death, no one seemed to realize that it is possible to observe every object in his famous catalog in one night. In fact, prior to the first Messier Marathon, most amateur astronomers probably would have maintained that it takes at least six months to see all the objects in the Messier Catalog. But times have changed. The first group known to be working with the Marathon idea was a group of observers in Spain during the late 1960s. Although they did not achieve very high counts, it was a beginning that would be improved upon.

In the mid-1970s Tom Reiland, Tom Hoffelder and the Amateur Astronomers Association of Pittsburgh also independently invented the Messier Marathon in Pennsylvania. This group started the Marathon as, "...an informal competition to locate the most Messier objects by a single observer during a dusk-to-dawn Marathon."

Tom Reiland, a long time observer, surmised that it might be possible to observe all the Messier objects in a single springtime evening and mentioned it to Tom Hoffelder, who worked out how one might go about it. Tom Hoffelder moved to Ohio and then to Florida, where he led a small group of observers in implementing the idea, and they began to hold Messier Marathons each year.

While this was going on in the East and South, the Messier Marathon idea occurred to yet another independent inventor: Don Machholz of San Jose, California. In the September, 1978 San Jose Amateur Astronomer's newsletter, he wrote an article in which he suggested the Marathon. Don was not aware of the Marathons being conducted in Pittsburgh or Florida or of the earlier Marathons conducted in Spain; as with the others, it just seemed to him like a good idea, and he got the ball rolling with his local group. Don suggested that a weekend in March would be a good time to conduct the Marathon because his research on the subject indicated that the maximum number of Messier objects (110) could be seen at this time. The idea was beginning to take root. The Astronomical Association of Northern California learned of the Marathon as a result of Don's newsletter article and also endorsed the idea.

There were now at least four independent groups conducting Messier Marathons in the U.S. — and with the exception of the two California groups, none was aware of what the others were doing.

In 1979, the cat finally got out of the bag. In the March, 1979 issue of *Sky & Telescope*, Walter Scott Houston wrote of the work done by Hoffelder in Florida and Reiland and the Pittsburgh observers in Pennsylvania. Houston reported that Ed Flynn had found 97 objects in one night with an 80 mm refractor and that Tom Hoffelder bagged 101 objects using a 10-inch f/5 reflector. By the time this article appeared, it was too late to spur much activity for the March Marathon in 1979.

However, the San Jose Astronomical Association conducted its first Marathon that year. It resulted in a record turnout for the club's star party. Several of the SJAA members scored extremely well that first try: Gerry Rattley and Don Machholz located 108 Messier objects, and three others located over 100.

Between March, 1979, and March, 1980, many articles were published about the Messier Marathon. One by Don Machholz appeared in the August, 1980 issue of *Astronomy*. With his usual skill and care, Don compiled a Messier order list and atlas chart cross-reference for the *Skalnate Pleso Atlas of the Heavens*. He also included some hints on conducting a Marathon. Now the Marathon idea really began to take hold. Don's article brought requests for more information on the Messier Marathon from would-be Marathoners around the world.

In March of 1980, Marathon madness was on a roll — in that year Don observed 109 of the 110 Messier objects, one better than the previous year. Don also began keeping a record of the Marathon results of others. Since there is no *Messier Marathon Central* to collect results, Don culls them from magazine articles, newsletters, personal contacts and, on occasion, from the correspondence of those who write to thank him for compiling the *Astronomy* article. According to Don, the first U.S. Marathoner to

observe all 110 Messier objects in one night was Gerry Rattley on the night of March 23–24, 1985 from Dugas, Arizona. The second 110-object entry is by Rick Hull, on the same night, from a location in Anza, California. No one knowns how many people have participated in Messier Marathons since those first Marathons in the mid-70s, but it now probably numbers in the many thousands. Probably many people have observed all 110 objects in one night, but no one has maintained any sort of national record, save for the records that Don has collected.

Each year more groups and individuals get caught-up in the Marathon Madness of March and April. Each year more people discover that the Messier Marathon is not a competition between "advanced" amateurs — rather, it is an exercise to sharpen the skills of deep-sky observing. It is for the greenest greenhorn and the most advanced amateur alike.

Although the charts in the back of this book are organized to help you find all 110 Messier objects in a single night in March, I don't want you to think for even one moment that March is the only time of year you can run the Messier Marathon. There is never any dark of the moon when you can see fewer than 90 of the Messier objects, and during seven of the thirteen New Moons each year, you may be able to score 100 or more Messier objects. After all, the idea is to build your skills, compete against yourself, and have a lot of fun—and that you can do all year round.

Figure 2-4 Walter Scott Houston first reported on Messier Marathon activities in the March, 1979 issue of *Sky & Telescope* magazine. "Scotty" wrote a regular monthly column for *S&T* for more than 50 years.

3 | Messier Marathons All Year Long
An Observational Prospectus

Charles Messier's catalog is by today's standards short, incomplete, and disjointed, but it is a convenient and easily remembered reference to some of the more prominent objects, and it is in wide use by amateurs and professionals around the world. The catalog is arranged more or less in the order in which he found the objects. He made no effort to list the objects in order of right ascension or to use some other scheme which would place them in a logical order of size, position or class. He had planned to do so, but died before he accomplished the task. Actually, I believe Messier only talked about this project, as there seems to be no record of any work on an "improved" catalog.

If you arrange the Messier Catalog in order of right ascension, you will see that the objects are spread around the entire span of right ascension. Of course, all the Messiers are northern hemisphere objects, the most southern being M7 at a declination of −34° 49" (epoch 2000.0). This is not surprising since Messier's observations were made from Paris, which is at about 45° north latitude.

However, there are two remarkable concentrations in Messier's catalog. The first occurs in the vicinity of 12 hours right ascension, in the Virgo cluster of galaxies. In a small region you can cover with an outspread hand lie no less than 14 galaxies. During the month of September, when the sun shines in front of the stars of Virgo, all these objects are lost in the solar glare. The other, much broader concentration lies in the winter constellations Orion, Canis Major, and Puppis that serve as backdrop to the sun in June and July. Thus, during June, July, and September, far fewer Messier objects can be seen than any other time of year.

Aside from these considerations, it would seem to the casual observer that the best viewing times would be during the months with the longest period of darkness — possibly late December or early January, also two of the coldest months. Fortunately, the only time of year in which all 110 Messier objects can be seen in one night is during the milder months of March and April—and then only between about +40° North and −20° South Latitude — M110 is too elusive outside this range. It is true that late December has the longest period of darkness, from about 5:30 p.m. to 6:15 in the morning, 12 hours and 45 minutes. Because the Messier objects are not evenly distributed over the entire sky, during the nights of longest duration the southernmost objects are just setting at darkness and do not rise again until after dawn's twilight. In fact, even in March, you will be searching for the last object at dawn's first light.

Besides the duration of darkness there are two other factors to be considered — one is working for you, and one against. The fact that a number of circumpolar objects are up virtually all night definitely works *for* you. That an object which is more southerly than another with the same right ascension will set first definitely works *against* you. Of course, both of these propositions are true throughout the year, but while doing the Marathon, they acquire some importance and fix the date of the Marathon "observing window." Furthermore, they influence the order in which the objects must be located on Marathon night.

The period between March 5th and April 12th is the only time of year that all 110 objects can be seen in one night. The very best nights occur between March 30th and April 3rd. However, there are other considerations which might make your best night for a Marathon earlier or later than this optimum date.

How Many Messiers Can I See this Month?

Any time of the year is a "good time" for a Marathon, it's just that some times are better than other times. Although March is definitely the richest month for running the Marathon, you can hold a "Marathon" any time of the year. In fact, the idea of having a Marathon at any time of the year except March (for those of you located in areas were the weather is particularly bad in March) is a pretty good one. Another advantage of year-round Messier Marathons is that they will give you a chance to get out there and practice your location and identification skills.

If you make Marathons a club activity, you will find that they will substantially add to the club's participation level. Marathons will bring out many of your armchair members. Marathons will give the novices an activity with a goal. Marathons will give your advanced members more contact with the new members. Marathons can be a source for many programs and presentations. The participation and energy level a Marathon can create for a club is incredible.

An ideal time for a high-participation Marathon is mid-July. The warm temperatures and fair weather, coupled with a potential 100 to 103 objects at 20° north latitude, and 93 to 95 objects at 40° north latitude, makes July a favorable time to hold a Marathon. The summertime Milky Way objects set early and the Virgo galaxies rise late.

The middle of October or the beginning of November is another good time. If you live in one of the more southerly climes, say, 20° north latitude, you will have almost as good a shot at a Marathon, in terms of the number of objects, as in March—with a potential 105-plus Messier objects!

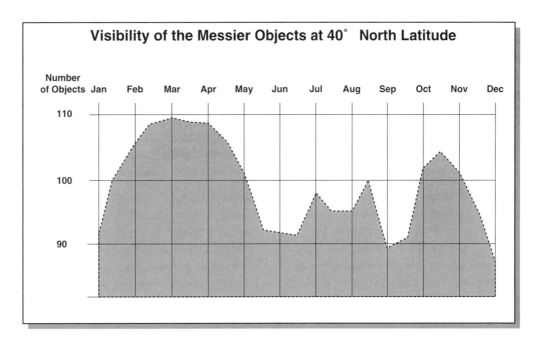

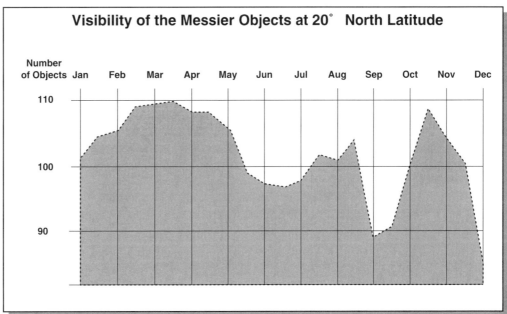

The graphs on this page are adapted from tables prepared by Don Machholz for his "The Visibility of the Messier Objects Throughout the Year," a paper which he sends on request. One is for 40° north latitude and the other for 20° north latitude.

The charts contained in this book can be used on any night of the year. It is only when you have spent some significant time observing each and every one of these objects that you will develop the observational skills to appreciate the feast the night sky spreads out before you.

4 | Messier Strategy and Tactics

Seeing As Many Messier Objects As You Can

A t 40° north latitude, twilight lasts about an hour and twenty-five minutes during late March. You will have to catch some objects during the twilight hours if you are going to get them all. This is challenging, but not impossible if you are prepared.

You have probably figured out that the objects that will set first have to be observed first, but after the first couple of objects, what should be the order of battle?

Generally, the order of objects proceeds from west to east and south to north. You must realize that if there are two objects on the same right ascension, the more southerly will set first. As a practical matter, simply using the setting times to determine the order does not work very well because you would be zigzagging all over the sky when you could have seen several objects in the same general area.

Fortunately, I have already done this homework for you. The charts in this book are arranged in "March Marathon order." Except for the first six and last three or four objects, the exact order isn't important. What you must do, however, is to locate all the objects shown on a chart before moving on to the next chart. Do this as long as you can stay on schedule or fairly close to it.

You must start trying to locate the first object at the first possible moment. Even if you know the sky like the back of your hand, you have only a short time to catch the first objects before they set, as this will be your only opportunity to locate them. Failure to locate the first few objects means that you will be unable to get to the maximum number possible regardless of your ability. As a consequence, part of your grand strategy must be to arrive at the observing site early so that you will be set up and have every little detail taken care of before sunset.

My dad, who was in sales, always told me to make the easy ones first — this is pretty good advice for the Marathon too. Locate and identify the easy objects within the *finder constellation* locale first. Then, proceed to the ones you are less familiar with. With the exception of the objects that must be found before they set, this procedure works well. The reasoning is this: if you are familiar with an object and its location, and you can find and identify it quickly, do it — you'll have more time for those that remain within the current locale.

The final facet of the strategy is to maintain a schedule. After you have moved on from your dead-run, locating the objects that will set early in the evening, you will find that you can *stroll* through most of the sky until you come to the Virgo cluster "clutter" and the Scorpius-Sagittarius "snarl." These areas require that you stop "strolling" and begin "jogging" in order to be finished with all the objects that are up at the time and to be ready for the sunrise sprint. If you fall behind during the stroll, you won't make the maximum number of identifications possible — remember, on Marathon night the task is to locate and identify as many of the Messier objects as possible.

To stay on schedule, you must set a limit to how far behind you will allow yourself to fall. When you reach that limit, you simply skip the objects on which you have fallen behind and immediately move to the point on the schedule where you should be. If you get ahead, go back to the point you left off, and, moving from west to east and south to north, pick up the objects you skipped. Be warned: keep an eye on the clock so that the minute you run out of "makeup" time, you can resume the schedule.

Here is a recap of the tactics that make up the strategy:

- Set up early.
- Move west to east and south to north.
- Begin during twilight.
- Locate easy objects first.
- Locate the objects in the finder constellation locale before moving on.
- Stay on schedule.

Find a Good Site

For your Marathon to be successful, your observing site will need to have an unobstructed horizon. For each fifteen degrees that the surrounding terrain rises above the true horizon, the objects will set an hour earlier or rise an hour later. This is important at the beginning of the Marathon because you will need to catch some objects during the twilight, just before they set. If you do not locate them at that time, you will not be able to see them again because they will not rise until 12 hours later — after daylight. For the same reason, it is important to have a low horizon for those objects that you'll have to

Figure 4-1 This "strip photo" of the Pomona Valley Amateur Astronomers' desert observing site was assembled from individual photos. This certainly is not a professional quality panoramic photograph, but it is more than adequate as a planning aid. The club's Messier Marathons were held at this location 65 miles northeast of Los Angeles for many years.

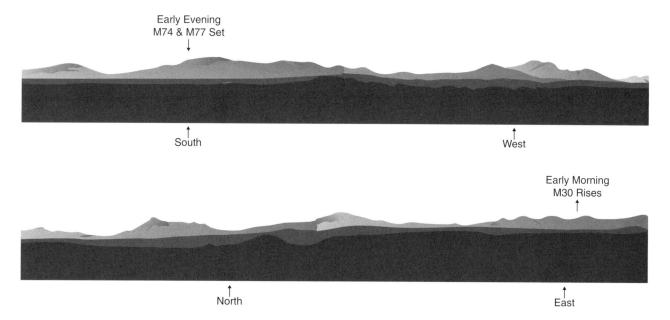

Early Evening
M74 & M77 Set
↓

↑
South

↑
West

Early Morning
M30 Rises
↑

↑
North

↑
East

Figure 4-2 A horizon plot of the Pomona Valley Amateur Astronomers' desert observing site. Note the hill which will obstruct M30 when it rises. Also note the horizon at the points M74 and M77 will set.

Figure 4-3 Sky glow and light pollution from Los Angeles, over 65 miles southwest from the PVAA desert observing site. Local communities also contribute to the pollution.

observe just before dawn's twilight — a 15-degree horizon means that they will rise above the obstruction an hour later and will be impossible to see.

A horizon that extends much above 8 degrees (approximately one-half hour, in terms of time) will seriously affect your ability to complete the list of objects that are near the horizon before they set. Conversely, objects that rise just before dawn twilight will not clear the surrounding horizon before daylight makes them invisible.

If at all possible, try to find a site with a horizon near 0 degrees— especially to the east and west. Therefore your objective should be to select an observing site that has a low (not over 6 or 8 degrees of elevation) horizon in all quadrants. For every degree you can reduce your horizon you will gain about 4 minutes time.

The next consideration is light pollution at the site. Quick identification and easy recognition of the constellations requires relatively dark skies. Even small towns can create a fair amount of light pollution. Some of the tougher areas of the sky are toward the south, as the constellations in this area will not rise very high before they begin to set (Sagittarius, Scorpius, etc.). You need to avoid a site with any light pollution in that sensitive area if you can. Another light sensitive area is to the east — where the last Marathon objects will rise in the morning.

Another phenomenon of a population center is that it generally has a pall of smog and other pollutants hanging over it. The explanation is simple: cities have a "bubble" (imagine that it looks like an inverted salad bowl) of warm air over and around them. This bubble of warm air acts like a container that holds the pollutants that hang in the air immediately over the city. The lights of the city bounce off the fine particles suspended in this bubble and create a warm glow in the sky above the city — a kind of terrestrial reflection nebula. This nebula is very bright compared to some of the objects you will be looking for and will make finding them difficult if not impossible. Fortunately, the light pollution from most cities and towns diminishes after 2:00 A.M. However, large cities and towns with smokestack industries can create light and air pollution that hangs on throughout the night.

The next consideration is the general wind condition at the site. Don't pick a site where there is constant wind. This can be difficult to reconcile with your desire to get a low horizon from a hill top. For purposes of the Marathon, turbulence will not affect the images to any appreciable degree: we only need to identify them, not study them. But a constant wind makes for a cold, miserable and uncomfortable night. Sites that are located near mountain passes are notorious for being windy at all times of the year. Beware of long narrow valleys (even those with a low horizon) and isolated mountain peaks. About the only way you can make a judgement about a new site is to find local residents who can tell you what kind of general weather prevails during the time you want to observe. Forest rangers, county firemen, sheriffs who patrol the lonely back roads and farmers can give you more reliable information than anyone else. If you live in brush country, you can get a great deal of useful information about winds from the county fire departments as they constantly monitor wind conditions.

Air turbulence affects the imaging quality of your telescope. Fortunately, deep-sky objects such as those in the Messier Catalog won't suffer the apparent image degradation that planetary images suffer with even the slightest turbulence. Even gentle breezes make planetary images dance, jitter, and "breathe" in the eyepiece. Deep-sky images are less apparently affected. Wind and gentle breezes also make a cool night seem colder than a thermometer would indicate. Check the site for the general wind conditions before you commit to an all-night session.

Figure 4-4 Select a site that is off the beaten path—lest this happen to you!

Observing sites near roads have a life of their own: there you are, trying to find some tough object and stay on schedule when a passing motorist (coming from a session at one of the local taverns) spots your telescope and decides to investigate. Of course, he is probably going too fast to make a smooth dustless stop, so he slams on the brakes. A huge cloud of dust rolls around the car and overhead as his locked wheels finally lose forward momentum. Blazing headlights are, of course, shining directly into your eyes as he has maneuvered the car so that he can get a better look. "Hey, is that there a telescope?" the question remains unanswered as you try to shield your formerly dark-adapted eyes from further insult. "How far can you see with that thing anyway? My cousin has a telescope. Can you see the moon?" I won't tell the rest of the tale as I have sufficiently made the point — pick a spot away from casual passers-by. On this night you won't regret it.

There is one last observing site consideration: How dangerous is the site? Is there any possibility of fire (especially if you live in the western states)? If there is an accident, can you get to some sort of emergency facility within a reasonable time? Certainly amateur astronomy does not carry any of the connotations of danger associated with mountain climbing, hunting, skin diving and other leisure pursuits, and there lies the danger — there might be possibilities you have not considered because of the genteel nature of the hobby. Consider all of the possibilities. Don't forget the buddy system. Have spare warm clothing, water, and food. If at all possible, take a friend or two along (I always recommend inviting guests). If your site is very remote, leave a map and word with someone before leaving. Such precautions might save you from considerable discomfort later on.

Marathon at New Moon

You cannot control the moon as a source of light pollution, but you can allow for it. Regardless of the optimum date for a Messier Marathon, you will have to take into consideration the dates on which the moon will be up. However, just after the new moon, when it is a small crescent in the southwestern portion of the sky at sunset, is an acceptable time for successful observing. For the most part, it is out of the way and will set in an hour or two, anyway. This will give you a couple of extra days to consider when picking a date. The perfect time is during the new moon, but more than two days before or after a new moon, M72, M73 and M74 will be washed out.

You can get the current rise and set times from almost any current almanac at the corner bookstand. Some calendars also show the rise and set times. Of course, if you have an ephemeris, you can get the information you need by consulting the tables or a computer planetary program.

Watch the Weather

The weather is the one variable that cannot be predicted. If your observing site is located a great distance from your home, you will not even be able to judge the weather at the site based on what it is like where you live.

Figure 4-5 The crescent moon low on the horizon at sunset. This condition is acceptable for Messier Marathon night.

In my own case, I live near Los Angeles, California. One of my favorite observing sites is on the high desert about 65 miles away. I have seen the most miserable weather at home extend to within twenty miles of the observing site while at the site the conditions have been close to perfect.

If you're into the Internet, you can call up the latest satellite photo and see what the sky was like an hour earlier. Or you can watch the Weather Channel and try to figure out the cloud patterns. I will modestly concede that we Californians get more clear nights than folks in New England and the Midwest, but you know your weather and can plan for it, too. Wait for one of those Canadian highs to come rolling down from the north, and a couple clear nights are guaranteed—well, maybe.

You just never know what it is going to be like until you get wherever you are going. Be prepared for the worst and expect that it will be different at the site. In any case, if you can't have a *star* party, you can always have a party, if you have made adequate preparations.

A good weather strategy during the Marathon time-frame is to plan at least one alternate date so that if the weather isn't cooperating, you'll have another shot at it. So far I have only covered the observing aspects of the weather; there is also the consideration to be made for your own comfort. My best advice is dress for the coldest possible conditions — ice, snow, sleet, wind — and pray for nice weather.

Learn the Finder Constellations

One of the things you will notice about the charts in this book is that quite a few objects are shown with constellations other than the one in which they are actually located. For instance, M50 (located in Monoceros) and M46, M47, and M93 (located in Puppis) are shown on the Canis Major chart (Marathon Chart 8 and 9) along with M41, the only Messier object which is actually located *within* the official boundaries of Canis Major.

There are three reasons for using a finder constellation rather than the actual constellation:

1. Depending on your experience level, the actual constellations might be hard to see and/or identify.
2. The object you are looking for is actually nearer a brighter or more prominent grouping of stars or a constellation that is easier to locate and identify.
3. You might not know the sky all that well anyway—why not make things as easy as possible?

I cannot stress enough the idea of locating the easy objects first. Although it seems obvious, you will be tempted to locate that one fairly nearby object out of sequence or to go for a hard one in order to save the easy ones for dessert. If you want to maximize the number of identifications, don't do it. Another problem is likely to occur when you do things out of order: it is easy to forget to do the objects that were skipped over.

Keep in mind that 50 is better than 25, 75 is better than 50, and so on. Your success with this Marathon will prepare you for the next one, but it is

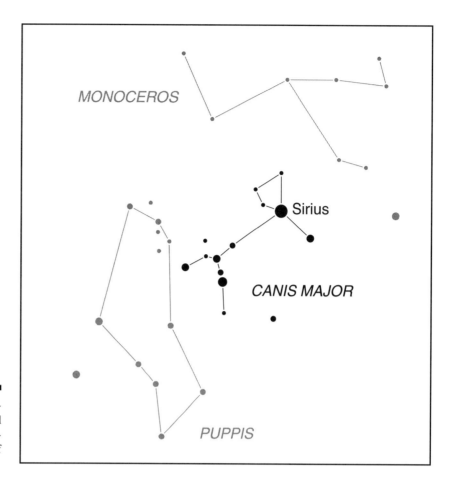

Figure 4-6 Using a *"finder constellation"* instead of the actual constellation in which an object is located. Canis Major, as well as parts of Puppis and Monoceros, is shown.

not necessary to come up short because "you didn't know," or because you "didn't have any experience" — that is what this book is for, to prepare you by providing the knowledge and experience you don't have yet.

Chapter 5 is devoted to helping you learn the constellations.

Know Your Telescope

Your telescope is a window on the sky, and a rather small window at that. In order to locate and identify Messier objects, you need to know how much of the sky you are seeing when you look through the eyepiece, through your finder telescope and through a one-power finder such as the Telrad. Learning how much sky you see with each of these is a process I call calibration—you're calibrating your eye to know in advance what the telescope will see. Chapter 6 is devoted to calibrating your telescope.

Learn to Find Sky Objects

Of the various methods that you can use to locate the Messier objects, my vote is for the geometric method using a one power finder. It is an easy, low-cost, low-tech method. With the *geometric method* you first locate the finder constellation, then place cross-hairs or Telrad circle at the geometric position that is at the correct angle and distance from the identifiable stars or groupings of stars of the finder constellation. It is as simple as it sounds. This method, in my opinion, offers the best chance for someone, especially someone unfamiliar with setting circles, eyepiece fields or polar alignment to locate successfully and identify as many objects as possible in one night, regardless of skill level. I have real-life examples of people who have used this method with success; I am one of them. Chapter 7 is devoted the "geometric method."

The other techniques are *starhopping* and the *right angle method*. Starhopping is exactly what the name implies — an easily identified star near the object to be located is centered in the finder scope. Then, you "hop" from star to star until you arrive at the location of the object for which you are searching.

The right angle method is exclusively for equatorially mounted telescopes, with or without setting circles. First, the telescope must be reasonably well polar aligned. Second, just like the starhopper method, you locate a star near the object to be located — this is the "reference star." This star is centered in the eyepiece. You then move the telescope a specified number of degrees in right ascension and declination. If you have setting circles, they are set to zero hours and zero degrees when the "reference star" is centered, and the telescope movements are made by reference to the setting circles. If you do not have setting circles, the movements are made by gauging the distance movement in each axis by noting the movement of the field stars shown in an eyepiece of a one degree true field.

Plan for Success

Once you have taken all of the above considerations into account, you will need to begin planning the date and location. Certainly, there are things which you cannot plan for, but you should make every effort to plan for that which is possible. The best bet is to make a *Plan A*, a *Plan B*, and possibly a *Plan C*.

Hypothetical site and date planning tables are given on the opposite page. As you can see from the site planning table, Mt. Gigantic is the best all around observing site if there is no snow. Even then it might still be best; it will just be cold. The second best site is Desert 1. This site has the best horizon. Both sites are about the same driving time. Lake Green is not suitable for the Messier Marathon because of its high horizon.

In the date planning table you can see that there are only two Saturdays that will qualify for a Marathon night. On March 16th the Moon will be four days into its last quarter. It will rise at 4:07 — about two hours before sunrise. That's not great, but it might be acceptable on Marathon night. On the twenty-third the new moon will be three days old and will set at 20:41 (8:41 p.m. Standard Time) — not bad, considering the other available Saturday). Of course, if you can afford the time off, you could pick a weekday on the dark of the moon.

From these tables, the best date would be March 16 (fairly close to the optimum date), and if the moon is too bright (it should be okay), or the

Site Planning Table for Messier Marathon

Location	Driving Time	Wind Conditions	Maximum Altitude	Typical Cloud Cover	Horizon
Mt. Gigantic	1:45	0-6 mph	5500	0	+8 degrees

Usually clear this time of year. Wind conditions are usually zero after sunset. Horizon is 8° high from 020° to 120° and 6° high from 210° to 280°. Can have snow into late April.

Desert 1	1:30	0-12 mph	1400	0	+6 degrees

Usually clear this time of year. Wind is usually zero after 9 p.m. Best horizon of three sites.

Lake Green	2:10	0-5 mph	3500	1/10	+18 degrees

Usually some cloud cover to the east and south. Sometimes there is fog over the lake. Has the worst horizon of the three sites. Horizon is 8° from 080° to 270° and 18° from 290° to 300°.

Date Planning Table for Messier Marathon

Saturday Dates	Days Past Phase		Phase	Moon Rises	Moon Sets	Sun Sets	Sun Rises
March 9	1	○	Full	21:41	06:40	18:11	06:29
March 16	4	◑	Last Quarter	04:07	13:45	18:18	06:19
March 23	3	●	New	07:20	20:41	18:24	06:08
March 30	2	◐	First Quarter	11:58	02:30	18:31	05:57
April 6	2	○	Full	20:32	06:39	18:38	05:46
April 13	3	◑	Last Quarter	01:15	10:33	18:44	05:36

weather unsuitable, try again on the twenty-third. That would give you two shots at finding all 110 objects. If you make it on the first try, then you could help someone else on the twenty-third. If you don't get them all, it will be a wonderful practice session for the next try on the twenty-third.

The sunrise and sunset times are listed so that you will know how many hours of darkness you'll have. You will also have to figure the twilight hours after sunset and before sunrise to really get an accurate estimate of the number of dark hours. Twilight times vary depending on your latitude. The farther north you are, the longer twilight will last.

You will of course need to make a table that is accurate for the current year.

If you are not rained-out, snowed-in, blown away with an unseasonable hurricane, covered over by clouds, and if there is no moon or very little moon, and your boss doesn't want you to work overtime on the weekend, and your car is not in the shop, and no relatives are coming to visit, you just might make it.

5 | Learning the Night Sky
Constellations as Celestial Signposts

The purpose of this book is not to teach the sky in detail; there are other books that do a terrific job of that. The problem is how to get the *necessary* knowledge now, not six months or two years from now. What you need is *some level* of knowledge — not a detailed knowledge of the three thousand or so stars you can see on a clear dark night and all the constellations visible from the northern hemisphere, but just enough so that you can locate the Messier objects and get started on your quest for more knowledge.

Learning the constellations is not much different from learning a new neighborhood or town. At first you are lost. Then you find out where the 7-11 is, then a convenient service station and a shopping mall. Little by little, you learn the byways and highways, using each new discovery as a *signpost* to locate the next until you can go anywhere at any time. The sky is like that too. There are a few constellations you already know, and you can use that knowledge as a starting point.

You can learn some key constellations, then learn how to locate those you don't know by using those you do know. In a short time you will know enough to be able to locate any Messier object in a few minutes, if not seconds. The following is an outline of the method that I used to learn the sky. If it worked for me, I know that it will work for you. I call it the *signpost method*.

Before we proceed, I need to define a word with which you might be unfamiliar: *asterism*. An asterism is a recognizable grouping of stars that is not necessarily a constellation or even part of a single constellation. For instance, the *Big Dipper* is an asterism as it is only part of the constellation of Ursa Major (Great Bear). The *Teapot* is only part of the constellation Sagittarius. The *Summer Triangle* is a huge equilateral triangle that is part of three different constellations — all of these are asterisms. Actually, any recognizable grouping of stars is an asterism. You can even create your own asterisms.

One of the best tools you can use to assist you in learning the sky is a planisphere. This is a small circular device whose origins can be traced back to antiquity. It has a star map and a movable "window" to show what is visible. Early astronomers used a device called an astrolabe, which is an ancestor of the planisphere. The early astronomers relied on these devices, as they did not have computers, calculators, and the wealth of information that we have in this day and age.

You may think this is strange, but planispheres are almost always found at major observatories; they are used by professional astronomers as well as the greenest beginner. The reason is simple — a large number of professional astronomers never learn the sky; they rely on assistants and setting circles to find celestial objects. When push comes to shove and they need to know if an object is *up* or find something visually (a rare occurrence), they will dig out the planisphere. As an interesting sidelight, I had an opportunity to tour Palomar Mountain — a real "hands-on" tour. I noticed that the bookshelf next to the telescope's control console included a well used copy of *Peterson's Field Guide to the Stars and Planets* (Houghton Mifflin Company) as well as a planisphere. At the end of this section you will

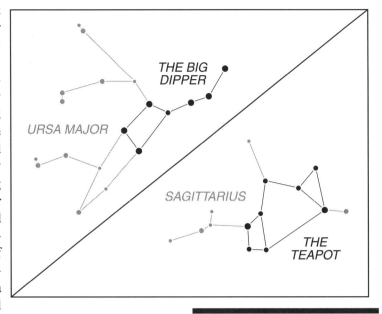

Figure 5-1 *Asterisms* in Ursa Major and Sagittarius. Although Ursa Major is actually supposed to depict a bear, the Big Dipper *asterism* is much more familiar. The Teapot *asterism* is more easily recognized than the archer in Sagittarius. *Asterisms* are shown with solid lines.

find a set of six signpost maps arranged like a planisphere to get you started. For many people these charts and the others provided in this book could be all that is needed in the way of "finder" and "star accumulator" to do the Marathon.

Another tool you can use to learn quickly the night sky is a pair of 7x35 binoculars. With or without binoculars, a few minutes a night studying the constellations will take you a long way toward gaining the necessary knowledge for a successful Marathon.

The following is my list of *signpost* stars and constellations. Learn these, and you will be able to find the rest of the constellations with little or no trouble. There are 17 stars and 17 constellations that you should know fairly well. After learning those, the rest is easier than you can imagine.

Signpost Stars:					
Arcturus	**Spica**	**Antares**	Deneb	**Vega**	Altair
Enif	Fomalhaut	Mirach	**Capella**	Aldebaran	Rigel
Pollux	Procyon	**Sirius**	**Regulus**	**Polaris**	

Signpost Constellations:				
Leo	**Ursa Major**	Boötes	Corvus	**Hercules**
Scorpius	**Cygnus**	**Sagittarius**	Cepheus	Pegasus
Cassiopeia	Andromeda	**Auriga**	**Orion**	Gemini
Canis Major	Lyra			

Note that within this list some of the names are in bold face. These are the *signposts to the signposts*, something which we will take up in detail in a few paragraphs.

What makes this method so easy is the fact that the *signpost* constellations bracket the entire sky, and any constellation you don't know is always next to or between one or two that you do know. Let's suppose you want to find Cancer — not one of the signpost constellations. It is directly between Leo and Gemini, two of the *signpost* constellations. You should also note that the stars *Regulus* in Leo and *Pollux* in Gemini are two of the *signpost* stars. What is important to realize is that it is not necessary for you to know everything, but only for you to know enough to *find* things quickly.

Remember, you will need fairly dark skies to see all the stars of the constellations and even parts of some of the prominent ones. Trying to find or see the constellations from the suburbs of Los Angeles, Chicago, Detroit, New York or any large population center will be trying. However, you will be able to see *all* of the signpost stars I have listed above, even from badly light-polluted areas. The main thing is to be persistent — don't give up and don't let a few failures at first discourage you.

I am sure that some will make the argument that I should have picked a different set of prominent stars and constellations and that they have a better method or that I have ignored some of the more prominent ones. That may be, but if you will learn these, you will learn to *find* the others in record time.

Some of the stars and constellations in this list are easier to find than others, and a few are so much easier that they can be used as signposts to find the other signposts. The reason that these are so easy is that they are bright and unmistakable in appearance or location. That is not to say that the others are not easy, but these are so unique in appearance or position that you can learn to find and identify them in a few minutes.

Which should you learn first, some prominent stars, or some prominent constellations, or both at the same time? Learning both at the same time is my recommendation, but it is messy to explain both of them at the same time. To solve the problem here is what I want you to do:

1. Read the rest of this chapter without going outside or using any other aids or references to give an overview of the task at hand and the objects you are going to identify.
2. Come back to this point and, using Signpost Maps 1 through 6 at the end of this chapter, find each star and constellation on the maps. Now you will have a good general idea of what you are looking for and its approximate location.
3. Go to a relatively dark site if you can; otherwise, your backyard is good enough for starters. Use the Signpost Map Selector Tables to select the Signpost Map that best matches the date and time. With this book in one hand and a red-filtered flashlight in the other, locate and identify each *signpost* star and constellation (bold type) that is above the horizon.
4. Once you have identified these *signposts to the signposts*, go back to the list above and identify *all* of the signpost stars and constellations that are visible.
5. Take a deep breath, and begin locating Messier objects.

Signpost Stars

Polaris: The North Star (Figure 5-2). From the northern hemisphere, Polaris is visible every hour of every night — it never sets. Although it is a relatively bright bluish star (magnitude 2.0), it is not nearly as bright as the other *easy* stars listed. However, it is conspicuous because of its position, the lack of other bright stars around it, and its relationship to the *Big Dipper*. The first step to making a positive identification of Polaris is to locate the pan of the Dipper (see *Ursa Major*, below). The two stars that define the end of the pan (called the "Pointer Stars") point approximately to Polaris; the only bright star in line with the pointers is Polaris. The stars that create the constellation *Ursa Minor* (the Little Bear) are hard to see from areas with light-polluted skies.

Use one of the Signpost Maps (that begin on page 34) or the simplified chart in Figure 5-2 to identify Polaris. Of course, the stars cross the sky from east to west during the night, so you will need to pick the Signpost Map that best matches the date and time you go outside to look at the stars. For example, the map that shows the stars as they appear in November at about 9:00 p.m. is Signpost Map 1 (page 34).

Arcturus: The most prominent bright yellow-orange star in the northern sky — magnitude 0.0. After the first time you identify it, you will be able to recognize it instantly. Starting with the Dipper handle, at the point where it joins with the pan, sight down your arm and it swing it along an arc following the handle of the Dipper. At the end of the handle, continue the arc and "arc to Arcturus." It will be the first bright star you will come to. Arcturus is the brightest member of the constellation Boötes. Unfortunately there are no Messier objects in this constellation. Arcturus is useful as a signpost reference star, and Boötes is a signpost constellation to locate other stars and constellations.

Spica: Following your arc along the line of the Dipper handle to Arcturus, you next "spike to Spica," a blue-white star of magnitude 1.0 in the constellation Virgo. An easy way to "spike to Spica" is to point, with your arm extended, at the base of the handle of the Dipper where it joins the pan. Sighting along your arm, move along the arc of the handle and beyond until you come to Arcturus; then continue the arc until you come to a bright blue star.

This star is prominent because of the lack of other nearby bright stars. I have not used Virgo as one of the primary *signpost* constellations, although it is certainly an important constellation, as you will discover on Marathon night. However, simply being able to identify Spica is sufficient at this point. Presuming that you are reading this at a time of the year in which you can see Spica and Arcturus, you will have established two additional signposts. From here on the process becomes easier. Arcturus and Spica are in the springtime evening sky.

Vega: Almost due east of Arcturus you will find an extremely bright (magnitude 0.0) pure white star. It is in the constellation Lyra, and it is very nearly as bright as Arcturus, but of a pure white color which makes it stand out from its surroundings. There is no other white star in the northern part of the sky that even comes close to Vega in appearance. Only Arcturus rivals it in brightness. Like Sirius (the next *signpost* star), its color reminds me of an electric spark. Vega dominates the evening summer sky.

Sirius: Sirius is the brightest star in the night sky, magnitude –1.5. Located in the constellation Canis Major, it is a blue-white color. This star is so brilliant that it is almost impossible to mistake it for any other star or planet. Finding it is simply a matter of facing southward and looking for an extremely bright blue-white star. If it is above the horizon (it is a winter star), you will immediately recognize it. The only mistake that a novice will make is to mistakenly identify Sirius as Venus, Jupiter or possibly Saturn, or vice-versa. However, remembering that Sirius is south of the ecliptic (the path of the planets) should preclude misidentification.

One way to eliminate the confusion between the planets and stars is to remember that stars tend to twinkle while planets do not. Jupiter is yellow-white,

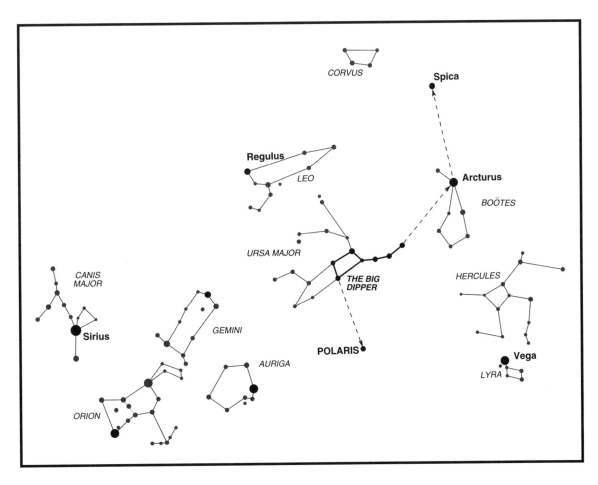

Figure 5-2 Start from the Big Dipper asterism to locate other signpost stars and signpost constellations. For example, the two stars that form the end of the Big Dipper point to Polaris. The last star in the Big Dipper's handle points to Arcturus which in turn leads you to Spica.

Venus is almost pure white, and Saturn tends to be orange-white, while Sirius is a blue-white color.

The spring skies are shown best on Signpost Map 3 (page 36). These are the stars that you see at 9:00 p.m. in March. By 11:00 p.m., Signpost Map 4 shows how the sky will look. As summer approaches, you will see these stars earlier and earlier in the evening sky. By mid-May, they are lost in the evening twilight.

Signpost Constellations

Ursa Major: The Big Dipper — Ursa Major, the Great Bear — is the master key for all the locks, so to speak. Almost everyone is familiar with this constellation to some degree. I will use this constellation as the *signpost* from which to locate all the others. Although we have already become familiar with this constellation from the discussion of the *signpost* stars above, because it is so important, I will review it.

The Big Dipper is an asterism within the constellation Ursa Major. The Big Dipper's huge handle swings through the night sky like the hour hand of a big clock, and it can actually be used to tell time. The handle of the Big Dipper arcs from the dipper pan outward and away from the North Pole. Continuing the arc of the handle will lead you to the bright yellow-orange star, Arcturus, which we discussed above.

To find the Big Dipper, face north. Tilt your head back slightly and study

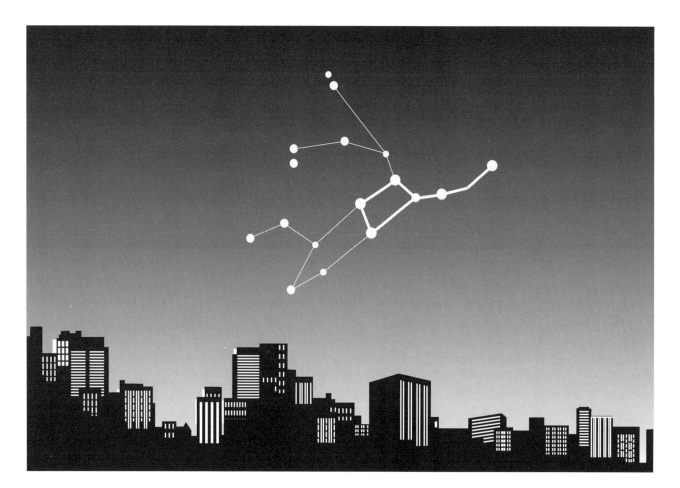

the sky. Unless it is grazing the horizon, you will almost always spot it, even from an area with considerable light pollution. Its appearance is unmistakable. If you possibly can, find it at different times of the night and notice how it swings around the sky, following a circular path about the North Star, Polaris.

At latitudes above 32 degrees, most or all of the Dipper is visible all night. Below that latitude, at the very minimum, some part of it is usually visible at every hour somewhere along its circumpolar path. Find the Dipper on one of the Signpost maps and study its path and the times at which it is visible. Notice that the Dipper circles around Polaris. Then, go outside and find the real thing.

Orion: Orion, the Hunter, is a "winter" constellation — meaning that it is highest in the winter months. The center of the constellation is right on the line of the celestial equator. All of the main stars are bright, and two of them are very bright — Betelgeuse (magnitude 0.5) and Rigel (magnitude 0.1). Orion's appearance is unique. It looks like a belted figure, and even with heavy light pollution Orion shines through brilliantly.

Signpost Map 5 (page 38) shows the stars you see in the predawn hours in March, but these same stars are overhead at midnight in June and emerge from evening twilight by mid-summer. Look to Signpost Map 6 (page 39) or Figure 5-5 to learn the signpost stars of summer.

There are three closely spaced stars in a line that make up the "belt" of the Hunter. As you can see from Figure 5-4, this constellation is near Sirius, to the east. The easiest way to find it for the first time is to look for the belt. Once you see those three stars in a straight line, the rest of the constellation will leap out of the sky.

Figure 5-3 Even from a modern city some star patterns, like the Big Dipper, stand out. While you would not like to observe under these conditions, you can learn the signpost stars and constellations from practically anywhere. Of course the Big Dipper at certain times of the year is hard to see from low latitude. Also, depending on the local horizon and light pollution conditions it also can be hard to see from mid northern latitude, when at lower culmination.

Figure 5-4 (Right) This chart shows the relationship of Polaris to Arcturus, Regulus, Capella, Pollux, Sirius, Aldebaran, and Rigel.

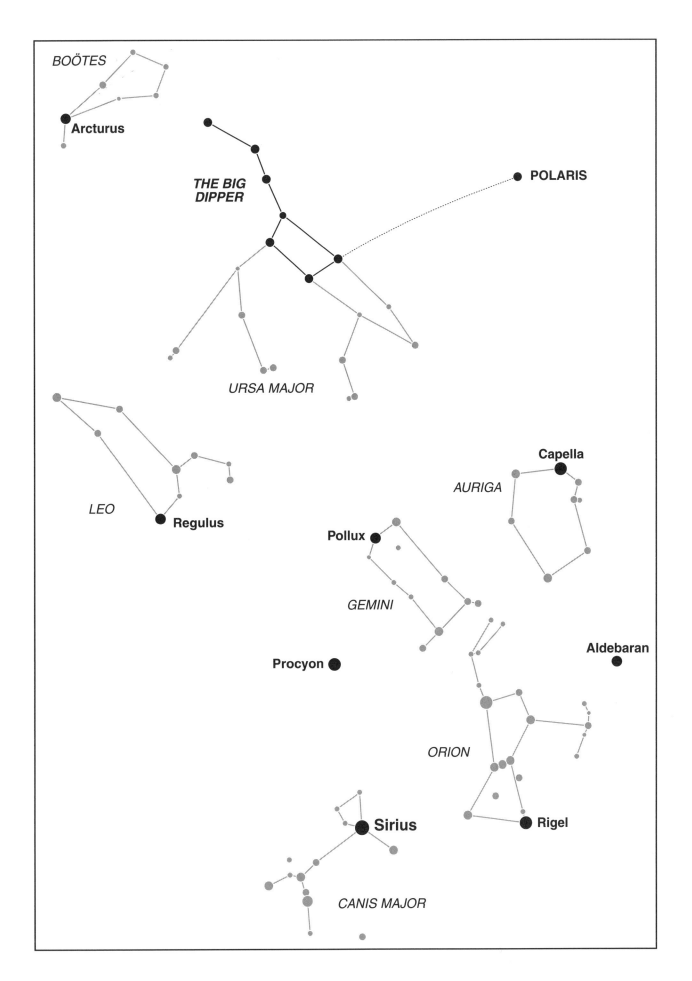

BOÖTES

Arcturus

THE BIG DIPPER

● POLARIS

URSA MAJOR

LEO

Regulus

Capella

AURIGA

Pollux

GEMINI

Procyon ●

Aldebaran

ORION

Sirius

Rigel

CANIS MAJOR

Boötes: (Boh'teez) Starting with the Dipper handle from the point where it joins with the pan, arc along the handle and "arc to Arcturus." Although Arcturus is considered a "spring and summer" object, it can be seen at mid-northern latitudes near the horizon into late fall at early evenings and mornings.

Arcturus is the alpha star (the brightest star of the constellation) of the constellation Boötes. There aren't any Messier objects in this constellation, but our purpose here is to find the signposts from which we will learn the sky.

Boötes is described as appearing like a "necktie," "kite," or a "ice-cream cone." Arcturus is at the knot-end of the necktie or the tail-end of the kite. The lower end of the necktie points generally north. The stars in this constellation are somewhat dimmer than those of the Dipper, and it might not be possible to see all of them from an area with heavy light pollution.

Hercules: Hercules is almost in the center of a straight line drawn between the bright stars Arcturus and Vega, two of the signpost stars we discussed above. It is slightly closer to Vega.

The main feature of Hercules is the asterism called the "Keystone," which is four stars forming a box that is slightly tapered at one end like the top stone of an arch. There are two Messier objects in Hercules, one of which is the largest and most brilliant globular cluster in the northern hemisphere: M13.

Cygnus: Cygnus, the Swan, contains the asterism called the "Northern Cross." Unlike the Southern Cross which points to the south celestial pole, the cross in Cygnus does not point to the north celestial pole. Strangely enough, this constellation is easier for novices to identify from areas with a little light pollution because it is embedded in the Milky Way, which is so rich that under dark sky conditions the proliferation of stars can make identification somewhat difficult.

The bright star at the top of the cross (the tail of the Swan) is Deneb. This brilliant blue-white star (magnitude 1.3) is just east and north of Vega. The cross-like appearance of Cygnus is unique.

Scorpius: The Scorpion is an unmistakable constellation with a prominent bright red-orange star, Antares (magnitude 1.0). When Arcturus is directly overhead, the tail of the Scorpion is just above the southern horizon, and Antares is about 30 degrees above the southern horizon.

Antares, one of the signpost stars and the most prominent star in the immediate neighborhood, is so colored (red-orange) that you will immediately know that you have found it. It is possible for a novice to mistake one of the planets for Antares because (and unlike Sirius) it is almost on the ecliptic, and frequently there are bright planets nearby. However, once you have identified it correctly and noted the color, you will not confuse it for anything else.

From Antares, the head and tail of the Scorpion are quite easy to trace out. Antares is in the body of the Scorpion. Above and to the right is the head, three stars almost in a line. Below Antares a string of stars gently arc to the right and then curl sharply to the left, clearly defining the tail of the Scorpion.

Figure 5-5 (Right) *The relationship of Polaris to Deneb, Vega, Altair, Arcturus, Antares, and Spica.*

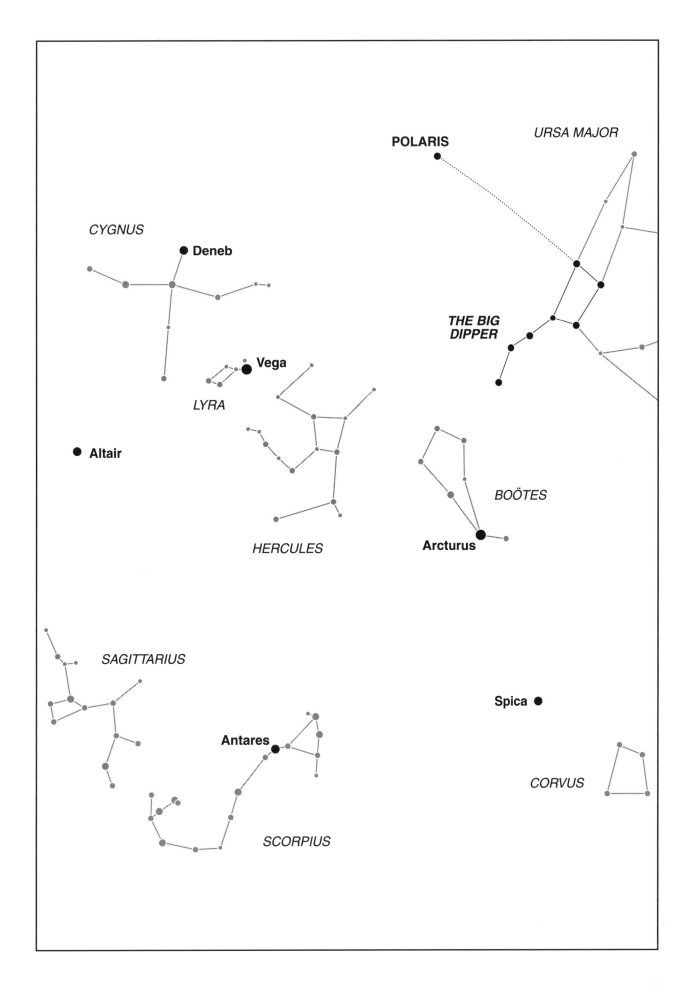

POLARIS

URSA MAJOR

CYGNUS

● Deneb

THE BIG
DIPPER

Vega

LYRA

● Altair

BOÖTES

HERCULES

Arcturus

SAGITTARIUS

Spica ●

Antares

CORVUS

SCORPIUS

Signpost Map 1

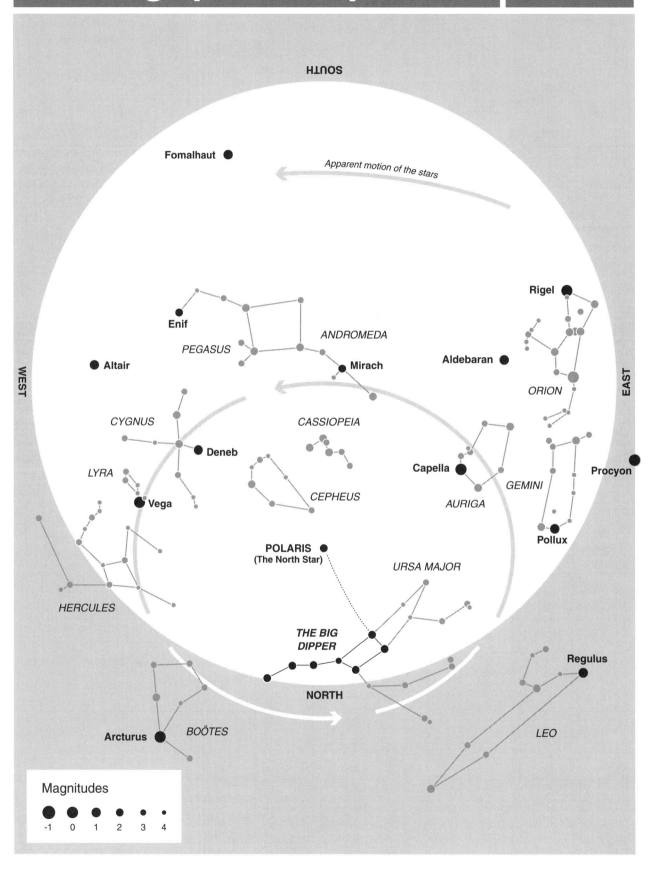

SOUTH

Fomalhaut ●

Apparent motion of the stars

Rigel ●

Enif ●

ANDROMEDA

Aldebaran ●

PEGASUS

● Mirach

ORION

● Altair

WEST

EAST

CYGNUS

CASSIOPEIA

Capella ●

Procyon ●

● Deneb

GEMINI

LYRA

CEPHEUS

AURIGA

● Vega

Pollux ●

POLARIS
(The North Star) ●

URSA MAJOR

HERCULES

*THE BIG
DIPPER*

Regulus ●

NORTH

BOÖTES

LEO

Arcturus ●

Magnitudes

● ● ● ● · ·
-1 0 1 2 3 4

The Year-Round Messier Marathon Field Guide

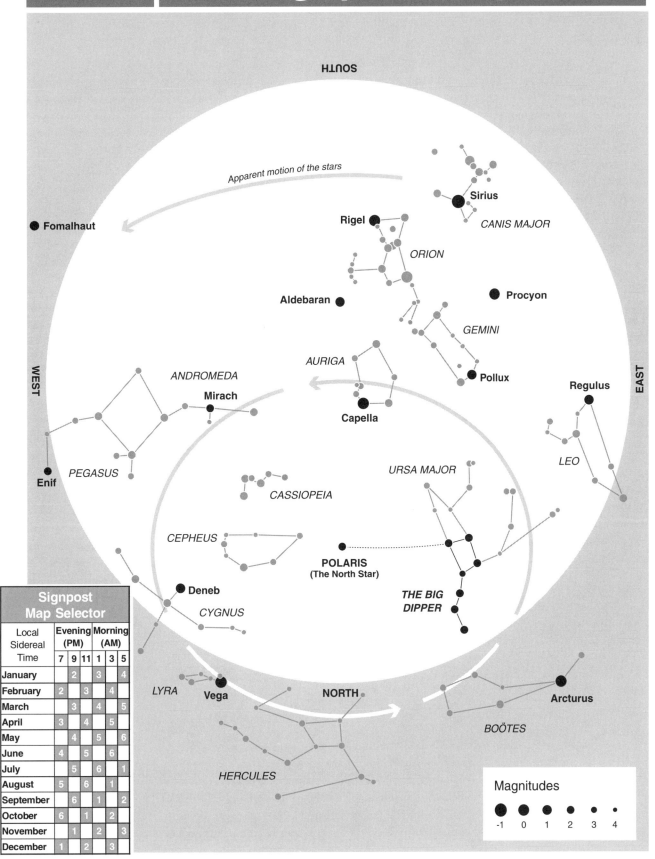

SOUTH

Apparent motion of the stars

Fomalhaut

Sirius

CANIS MAJOR

Rigel

ORION

Aldebaran

Procyon

GEMINI

WEST

ANDROMEDA

Mirach

AURIGA

Pollux

EAST

Regulus

Capella

PEGASUS

Enif

CASSIOPEIA

URSA MAJOR

LEO

CEPHEUS

POLARIS
(The North Star)

THE BIG
DIPPER

Deneb

CYGNUS

LYRA   Vega

NORTH

Arcturus

BOÖTES

HERCULES

Signpost Map Selector						
Local Sidereal Time	Evening (PM)			Morning (AM)		
	7	9	11	1	3	5
January		2		3		4
February	2		3		4	
March		3		4		5
April	3		4		5	
May		4		5		6
June	4		5		6	
July		5		6		1
August	5		6		1	
September		6		1		2
October	6		1		2	
November		1		2		3
December	1		2		3	

Magnitudes

-1 0 1 2 3 4

Signpost Map 3

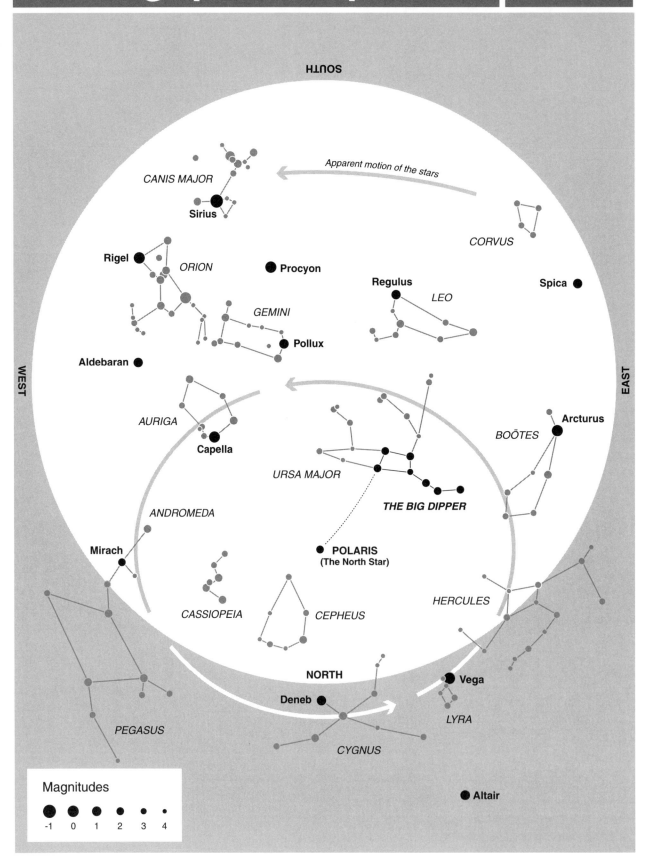

SOUTH

Apparent motion of the stars

CANIS MAJOR

Sirius

CORVUS

Rigel

ORION

● **Procyon**

Regulus

LEO

Spica ●

GEMINI

WEST

● **Pollux**

Aldebaran ●

EAST

AURIGA

Arcturus

Capella

BOÖTES

URSA MAJOR

ANDROMEDA

THE BIG DIPPER

Mirach

● **POLARIS**
(The North Star)

HERCULES

CASSIOPEIA

CEPHEUS

NORTH

● **Vega**

Deneb ●

LYRA

PEGASUS

CYGNUS

Magnitudes

● ● ● ● · ·
-1 0 1 2 3 4

● **Altair**

Signpost Map 4

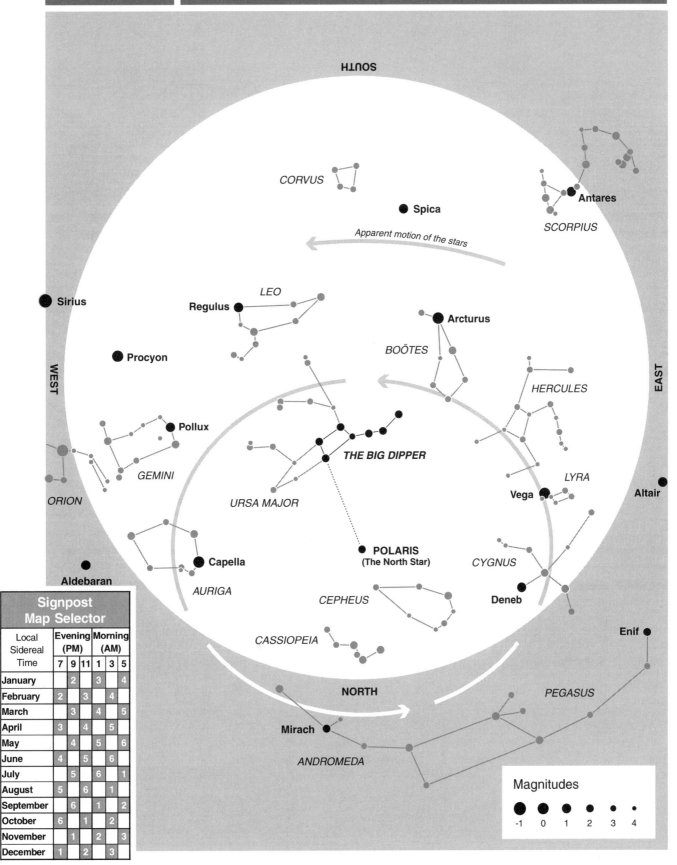

SOUTH

CORVUS

● Spica

Antares ●
SCORPIUS

Apparent motion of the stars

● Sirius

LEO

Regulus ●

● Arcturus

BOÖTES

HERCULES

WEST

● Procyon

EAST

● Pollux

THE BIG DIPPER

LYRA

GEMINI

URSA MAJOR

Vega ●

Altair ●

ORION

● Capella

POLARIS
(The North Star)

CYGNUS

● Aldebaran

AURIGA

CEPHEUS

Deneb ●

Enif ●

CASSIOPEIA

PEGASUS

NORTH

Mirach ●

ANDROMEDA

Magnitudes

● ● ● ● ● ·
-1   0   1   2   3   4

Signpost Map Selector						
Local Sidereal Time	Evening (PM)			Morning (AM)		
	7	9	11	1	3	5
January		2		3		4
February	2		3		4	
March		3		4		5
April	3		4		5	
May		4		5		6
June	4		5		6	
July		5		6		1
August	5		6		1	
September		6		1		2
October	6		1		2	
November		1		2		3
December	1		2		3	

Signpost Map 5

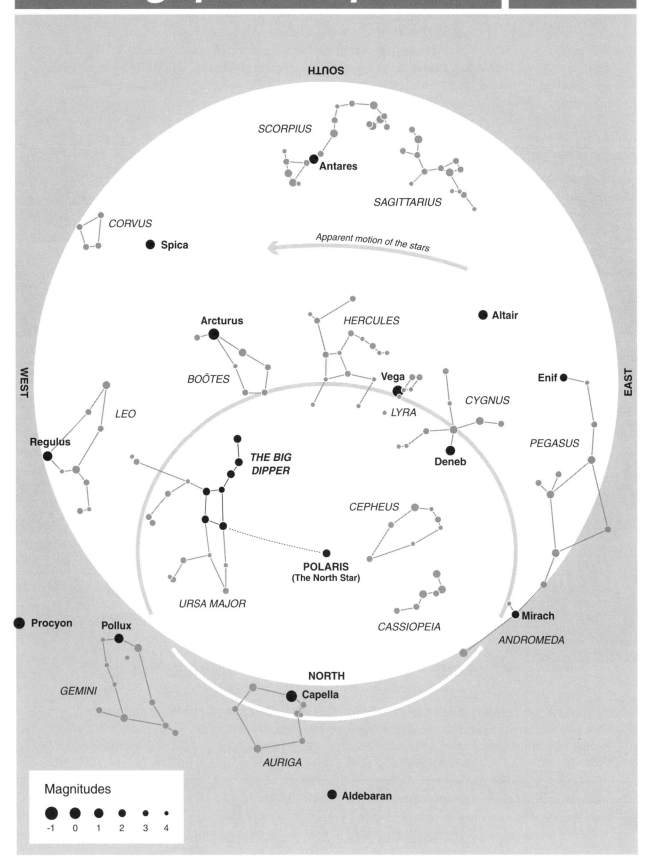

SOUTH

SCORPIUS

● Antares

SAGITTARIUS

CORVUS

● Spica

Apparent motion of the stars

Arcturus

HERCULES

● Altair

BOÖTES

Vega

Enif ●

CYGNUS

LYRA

LEO

PEGASUS

Regulus

THE BIG DIPPER

Deneb

CEPHEUS

POLARIS
(The North Star)

URSA MAJOR

CASSIOPEIA

Procyon

Pollux

● Mirach

ANDROMEDA

NORTH

GEMINI

Capella

AURIGA

Magnitudes

● ● ● ● • ·
-1 0 1 2 3 4

● Aldebaran

WEST

EAST

The Year-Round Messier Marathon Field Guide

Signpost Map 6

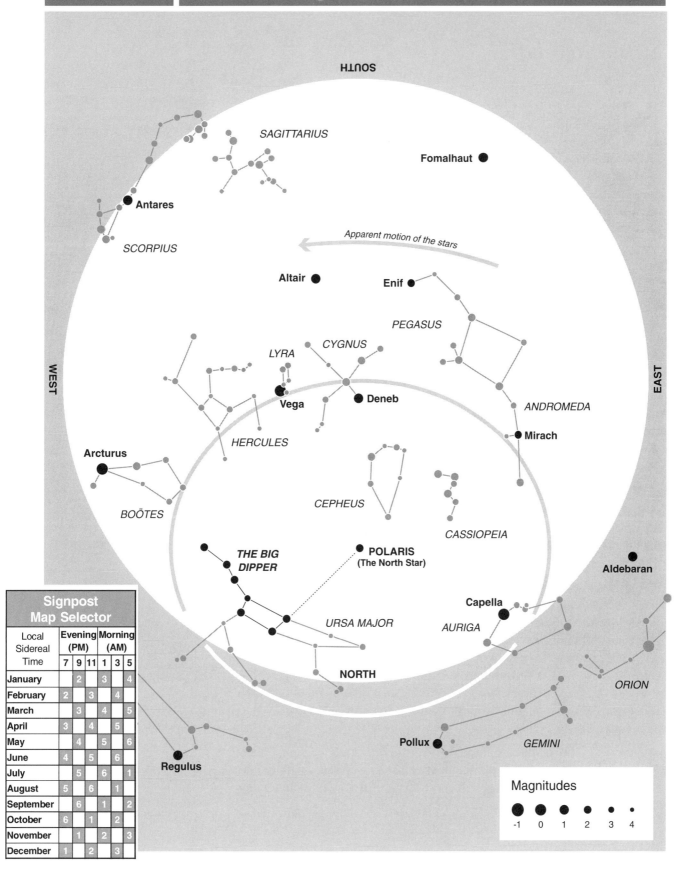

SOUTH

SAGITTARIUS

Fomalhaut ●

● Antares

Apparent motion of the stars

SCORPIUS

Altair ●

Enif ●

PEGASUS

WEST

LYRA   CYGNUS

Vega ●   ● Deneb

EAST

ANDROMEDA

● Mirach

Arcturus ●

HERCULES

CEPHEUS

CASSIOPEIA

BOÖTES

THE BIG DIPPER   ● POLARIS (The North Star)

Aldebaran ●

Capella ●

URSA MAJOR   AURIGA

NORTH

ORION

Regulus

Pollux ●   GEMINI

Signpost Map Selector

Local Sidereal Time	Evening (PM)			Morning (AM)		
	7	9	11	1	3	5
January		2		3		4
February	2		3		4	
March		3		4		5
April	3		4		5	
May		4		5		6
June	4		5		6	
July		5		6		1
August	5		6		1	
September		6		1		2
October	6		1		2	
November		1		2		3
December	1		2		3	

Magnitudes

● ● ● ● · ·
-1 0 1 2 3 4

On the next clear night, go outside and look for the signpost stars. Refer to the Signpost Maps to identify the signpost stars and constellations. Even though you might feel as lost as I did at first, the stars are waiting for you. Whatever the time of year, start now.

Summing Up

Now you have a number of jumping-off places that include stars *and* constellations — only 82 more to go. Actually, you don't have to learn all 88 constellations, since a fair number are in the southern hemisphere, and you can't see them anyway. Of the northern constellations, there are only thirty that you have to be able to *find* in order to successfully complete the Messier Marathon and get all 110 objects. Of the thirty that you have to find, you only have to actually know about 17 — from these 17 you can find the others. Now isn't that easier than 88?

Let's get back to the task at hand — learning the night sky quickly. Above I explained the concept of finding *signposts* in the sky. First find and identify the brightest stars. Using these stars as references — *signposts* — identify the constellations associated with them. Then, use those constellations to find the ones in between. Use the charts and the Signpost Maps in this book and in no time you will know enough to find your way easily.

Oh yes — one important point I almost forgot — you don't have to learn the stars alone. If you know a few signpost stars and some of your friends know a few different stars, you can help each other learn them all. At first you will simply pool your collective ignorance, but it won't be long before Arcturus, Spica, Polaris, and the Big Dipper seem like old buddies.

At this point I can see a question forming in your mind: "Why not just learn the constellations and skip the individual stars? Wouldn't that make things even simpler?" Yes, it would make things simpler and would work if you could always see all of the constellations at once, but what do you do when you have to identify a constellation when it is setting or rising and not entirely visible? You locate and identify a prominent star, of course. After you know the sky like the back of your hand, you will know many more stars and constellations than a mere fifteen or twenty.

If you would like to supplement your learning library, I can recommend *The Star Guide* by Steven L. Beyer (Little, Brown and Company). This is an excellent book on sky lore with a unique method of learning the 100 brightest stars. Beyer's method is to teach you the location of one new star every few days. Although the method is programmed to take an entire year, you can use it to accelerate your learning as it is well laid out, easy to use, and loaded with very clear illustrations.

Don't forget your friends — you may know someone who really knows the sky. Also, check out the local astronomy club or visit a planetarium during a "sky show" program. After a couple of hours with the local guru, your knowledge level will surge ahead. After a few hours under dark skies, you'll absolutely amaze yourself.

6 | Calibrating Your Telescope
Take the Guesswork Out of Locating Objects

Any telescope with an aperture of 60 mm or larger is suitable for doing the Messier Marathon. My personal philosophy is that anything is better than nothing. A telescope smaller than 60 mm or binoculars are just fine, but you will not be able to see the fainter objects. If you have a telescope with an aperture of 6, 8, or 10 inches, you are in heaven. If you use low magnification, you will find the Messier objects just waiting for you. Any type of mount is just fine too, as long as it is steady. In fact a steady mount is more important than a large aperture, especially for novices.

It is important to know the telescope that you already own. As much as you might be tempted to get a telescope that takes a pickup truck to carry or one of the fancy ones that take enough batteries to light up the whole San Fernando Valley and then some, you don't need a new telescope to find the Messier objects. What you need is a telescope that you know inside and out, backwards and forwards. That's why you need to calibrate your telescope.

The secrets to calibration are, first, knowing that the finders have been lined up with the telescope; and, second, knowing how much sky your finder shows. Next you need to know how much sky your eyepiece shows.

Aligning the Finder

Before you can even begin to calibrate your optics, you must first align them so that what you see in the center of your finder is also in the center of the eyepiece. Originally I wasn't going to include this step in the book. But one night I saw a fellow who was packing up to leave a star party early. When I asked him why he was packing up, he said that his telescope was in desperate need of repair because the finder couldn't be aligned with the eyepiece.

He had a 6-inch commercial telescope. Wanting to be helpful, I volunteered to take a look at it. I found that the finder was solidly mounted, and optically it seemed fine. The telescope was also well collimated and the mount was solid. Since there wasn't any obvious problem, I asked the fellow to demonstrate the difficulty.

I was not prepared for what followed. He pointed the telescope at a star near the eastern horizon. Then he proceeded to look through the finder — not the eyepiece, but the finder. Now I was definitely puzzled. *What in the world is he doing?* I thought. After moving the telescope around for a while, presumably to center the star in the finder, he then proceeded to look in the eyepiece and move the telescope again. I watched for a few minutes then said, "What are you doing?" "Trying to get that *@!!star in the eyepiece," he replied with considerable agitation. It was obvious that the finder scope was simply not aligned. Mind you, this fellow was not inept, but this "optical thing" simply had him buffaloed.

After I aligned his finder and showed him how to do it (for which he thanked me for the rest of the night), I decided to take a little survey and find out how many people actually know how to align their finders. Was I surprised! It is so amazingly simple to do and yet so many people don't know how to do it. What is more amazing is that because everyone who knows how to do it knows it is so simple that they assume everyone knows how to do it. Moreover, most telescope manuals give aligning the finder pretty short shrift.

The "trick" is to use an alignment target that does not move and to *align the finder to the telescope*, not the other way around. So with that long and windy preamble, I will now tell you how to align your finder with your telescope's primary optics. It takes about three minutes.

1. Start during daylight by selecting an alignment target. A telephone pole or power-line insulator is a good daytime choice. Anything at a distance of at least a half-mile or more will do. Center the target in the *telescope* eyepiece.

2. Look in the finder and locate the target. *Do not move the telescope.* Notice that your finder has at least three adjusting screws. Some finders have three screws in the front and some have six — three in the front and three in the back. We will use the screws in the front only (unless you run out of "screw travel" using the front screws only). In order to orient the finder, one screw must always be loosened (backed out) and two must be tightened (screwed in).

   The figures on the right show how the screws are adjusted to move the finder in various directions. Make all adjustments in small increments — movements no larger than one-half turn at one time. First loosen the screw that is closest to the direction in which you want to move. Tighten the other two in proportion to the direction you want to move.

3. Adjust the screws so that the target is centered under the crosshairs of the finder scope. To make very fine adjustments without loosening any screws, tighten one screw at a time until the target is centered and the finder scope is firmly held by the screws.

4. Check the telescope eyepiece image. If the target has gotten bumped slightly off center, re-center it and repeat step 3 above.

5. Now that the finder is roughly aligned, you can use a star for the final alignment. The reason for going through this rough alignment is that putting a star into the eyepiece without benefit of a finder is not as easy as you might think. Polaris will be the star

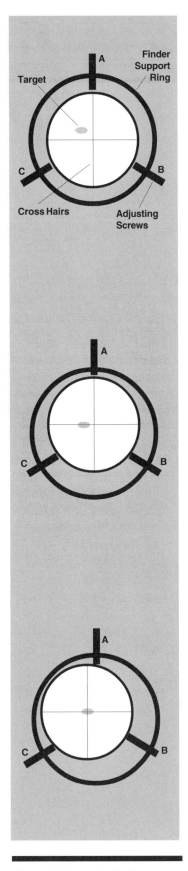

Figure 6-1 Steps in aligning an optical finder. Note that when the finder is aligned, it might be off-center in its mounting rings.

used to make the final alignment if your local latitude is greater than 10°; otherwise pick a star and work fast.

The reason for using Polaris is that it does not move while you are making your adjustments. (Actually, it does move a little — it describes a circle a little less than one degree in 24 hours, but this motion is so minor that it can be ignored.)

6. Regardless of your telescope's mount, point the telescope at Polaris. If your telescope is equatorially mounted, it does not need to be polar aligned. If you have a clock drive, turn it off. You are simply going to align the two optical systems so that whatever is in the center of the finder scope is also in the center of the eyepiece.

Since the finder is roughly aligned, center Polaris in the finder, then look in the eyepiece. It should be close. Center Polaris in the telescope's eyepiece. If you can, lock the telescope so that it cannot move. If you cannot lock it, be careful not to move it when you make adjustments to the finder.

7. Using the same procedures described in steps 3 and 4, center Polaris in the finder scope by adjusting the alignment screws. Don't forget to double check the telescope eyepiece, and recenter and readjust the finder until both images are dead center.

If you have a Telrad or other one power finder, the principle is identical: Center a stationary target in the telescope eyepiece, then center the finder on the target without moving the telescope. The Telrad has three adjusting nuts with the same purpose as the three alignment screws on the finder.

Aligning a Telrad Finder

The most useful finder — the one I use most — is the Telrad. It is one power (no magnification), relatively inexpensive, incredibly simple, easy to use, and virtually foolproof. It is actually a "reflex gunsight finder" — it is like the gunsights used on World War II and Korean era fighter aircraft. It has illuminated rings that are "projected" onto the sky. The reflex gunsight finder is unique in that it does not have any parallax problems, and it is accurate. Whatever the finder rings are on appears in your eyepiece; and if you move your head, the rings do not move because there is no aligning of front and rear sight elements. What you see is what you get. The Telrad has three adjusting nuts to align the finder rings with the telescope's eyepiece view.

The Telrad uses two AA batteries that last about a year. The brightness of the projected target rings can be adjusted from "barely perceptible" to "blast your socks off." Calibration is unnecessary — the outer ring is 4 degrees, the middle ring is 2 degrees, and the innermost ring is ½ degree. All that is necessary is that it be aligned with the telescope. Other open sight finders can use any of the methods described below.

Figure 6-2 The Telrad® is an illuminated "gunsight" finder of one Power. The Telrad makes pointing a telescope quick and easy.

Figure 6-3 The Telrad sight rings are "projected" onto the sky. Unlike the traditional gunsight there is no parallax. Alignment is unaffected by how close the eye is placed to the Telrad. It's used with both eyes open.

Calibrating a Finder

Depending on the size of the finder's objective and eyepiece, it will cover between four and eight degrees of sky — the "true" or "actual" field of view.

Unlike the Telrad or other open type finders, you do not have the luxury of seeing the entire sky while aligning the telescope with an object. The usual method of using a finder scope is to sight along the scope tube and adjust the telescope until it is pointed in the general direction of the object. Then look into the *telescope* and scan until you have some reference object or star in the field. From there, center the target in the finder cross hairs. Even when locating objects with the finder, I usually start by pointing the telescope in the general direction I want by using a Telrad. I then use the finder scope to zero-in on the quarry, although most of the time the finder is unnecessary because the Telrad is accurate to the degree that the object is already in the main eyepiece. There are three methods that you can use to find out exactly how much sky your finder actually covers, regardless of the type.

Method one: Locate a couple of fairly bright stars whose distance (in degrees) from each other is known. (You can determine the distances between stars by measuring the distance in an atlas.) Then try to put both stars in the finder. If they easily fit inside the eyepiece, then pick two more stars which are farther apart. When you find two stars that you can just barely fit inside the eyepiece, the distance between them is the true field of your finder. The stars that make up the Big Dipper are very good for this purpose. See Figures 6-4 and 6-5.

Method two: This method requires a watch with a second hand. Pick a bright star near the celestial equator and almost due south. Turn off your clock drive if you have one and position the finder so that the star will drift across the

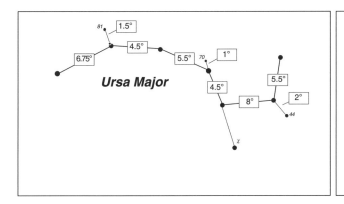

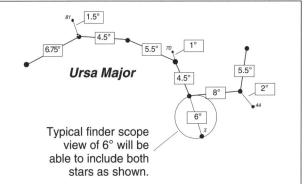

Figure 6-4 (Left) The angular separation of the stars in the Big Dipper is featured in this illustration.

Figure 6-5 (Right) This illustration shows how stars are "fitted" into an eyepiece to determine the true field.

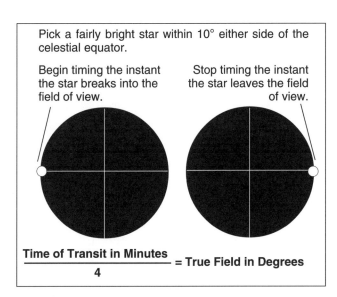

Pick a fairly bright star within 10° either side of the celestial equator.

Begin timing the instant the star breaks into the field of view.

Stop timing the instant the star leaves the field of view.

$$\frac{\text{Time of Transit in Minutes}}{4} = \text{True Field in Degrees}$$

Figure 6-6 To determine the true field of view, a star is timed as it crosses from edge to edge of the major diameter of the field of view. If you pick a star that is 10° off the equator your results will be within about 1½% (2 decimal places). As you move closer to the equator the error is reduced.

center of the finder eyepiece (see Figure 6-6). Time how long it takes to go from one edge to the other. Divide the number of minutes by four. The answer is your finder's true field of view in degrees.

Method three: Don't laugh! Check the advertising literature for your finder. The information might be there in black-and-white, ready to read—but run your own test to make sure it is accurate. If all else fails, you might try contacting the manufacturer or distributor and pry the information from them. Don't be disappointed if they don't seem to know much.

Calibrating an Eyepiece

You can use the first two methods described above, or you can use this one — this method requires some simple arithmetic. If you know the apparent field of view of an eyepiece, you can calculate the actual field of view by dividing the apparent field by the magnification. Since the magnification is calculated by dividing the focal length of the telescope by the focal length of the eyepiece, you can readily determine everything you need to know in under a minute. For instance, suppose your telescope has a focal length of 1000 mm and your favorite eyepiece is a 26 mm Plössl with a 55-degree apparent field. First calculate the magnification:

$$\frac{\text{Telescope Focal Length}}{\text{Eyepiece Focal Length}} = \text{Magnification} \qquad \frac{1000\text{mm}}{26\text{mm}} = 38.46$$

Now you know the magnification. Next divide the apparent field by the magnification:

$$\frac{\text{Apparent Field}}{\text{Magnification}} = \text{True Field} \qquad \frac{55}{38.46} = 1.43 \text{ Degrees}$$

In this case, the actual field of view is close enough to 1½ degrees that you might as well call it 1½ degrees. You can find the apparent field of view of most eyepieces by checking the advertising literature or specifications of the manufacturer of the eyepiece.

For the Messier Marathon, an eyepiece providing a field of one degree is ideal. Why one degree? For one thing, most of the Messier objects are of a size that fits nicely into a one degree field (roughly one-half degree more or less), which will make them easier to recognize. Second, a wider field of view makes objects much easier to find. And third, when scanning through areas such as the Virgo cluster, a one degree field makes the objects easier to find and simpler to identify because you can move in one degree "jumps" from one object to another, using the eyepiece view to gauge your moves. For example, to move "up" one degree and "left" three degrees, you would move the stars in the eyepiece field from edge-to-edge in the appropriate directions.

My favorite eyepiece is a 32 mm Erfle on either my Celestron C8 or Coulter 17½-inch. Both telescopes have a focal length of 2000 mm, so the magnification as well as the actual field of view are the same on both telescopes. This particular eyepiece has an apparent 65-degree field of view. Using the arithmetic shown above, this eyepiece's actual field of view is about one degree, and it is the one I use the most.

Which Way is "Up"

I have to assume that you have a reasonable star atlas such as *SkyAtlas 2000.0, Bright Star Atlas 2000.0* or the atlas in *Peterson's Field Guide to the Stars and Planets*. You have probably already noticed that you can see many more stars in the finder telescope and eyepiece than are noted on *any* atlas chart. In fact, you might have concluded that using the atlas is hopeless because you couldn't make heads or tails out of the finder image and what is in the atlas.

Another complication (as if you needed more) is that a "Newtonian" view is reversed left-to-right and top-to-bottom, and a straight-through refractor's view is the same. A refractor with a right angle diagonal is reversed left-to-right, in relation to the atlas chart, which is presented just as you will see things in the sky.

These are the same problems, more or less, that you have with the finder scopes. It's funny, but most folks get a little confused with directions when they are applied to the celestial sphere. We think of any movement that is parallel to the ground as left and right, and any movement perpendicular to the horizon as up and down.

Altazimuth telescope mounts (especially Dobsonian types) are suited to thinking of the tube movements as left/right and up/down since they move horizontal to the ground (azimuth) and perpendicular to the horizon (altitude). When guiding an altazimuth telescope tube by hand as you observe an object in the eyepiece, you might have experienced some trouble keeping the object in view, especially at high powers. In fact, you have probably lost an object more than once and have had to start over to find it. The following story might have a familiar ring to it.

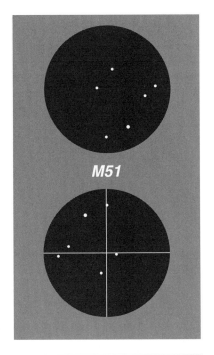

Figure 6-7 A comparison of a naked-eye view (top) and the view as seen in an eyepiece (bottom). The view shown here is what would be seen in a refractor optical system without a diagonal which is the way most finder scopes work. Note that the view is reversed vertically and is what you will see in the 8 x 50 "straight through" finder charts.

With your eye firmly glued to the eyepiece and your right hand on the scope tube, ready to move it as necessary to keep the object centered, you notice that the object is moving to your "left" and "down." The usual procedure is to mentally review the image orientation and the direction of movement. As an intellectual exercise, you decide that left is right and down is down. While you are making the mental calculations, the object drifts out of view, but you are confident of your calculations and move the scope to the imagined position — WHAT THE...! It's not there. You frantically move the scope back to the place where you think you were and rethink your moves. You conclude that left is right and down is up and make the move. No luck. Drat! Back again, and this time you decide left is left, but down is still up. Nope. After a few fruitless minutes you start from scratch, only this time you decide to pay more attention so that the object won't get out of the field of view.

The following tip works for all Newtonian optical systems, regardless of the type of mount you're using. If you follow this tip, you will never have the problem I have just described. I call this the "Trapp Method" after its "discoverer," Charles Trapp. Fundamentally, all you have to do is change your perception of what is happening. Instead of thinking of having your hand on the telescope tube, imagine that you have hold of the sky. When the object drifts, move the "sky," as you naturally would, to keep the object centered. If the object moves down, then pull the "sky" up. If the object moves left, pull the "sky" right, and so on. Don't get intellectual about it— just do it and you can track anything.

Figure 6-8 "Moving the sky" instead of the telescope to keep an object centered in the eyepiece. This technique works with a Newtonian optical system.

With the Dobsonian mounts, we tend to think in terms of left/right and up/down. With equatorially mounted telescopes it is much more convenient to think in terms of *north, south, east* and *west*. The reason for this is that the equatorially mounted telescope does not move parallel and horizontally to the ground — it moves on a polar axis.

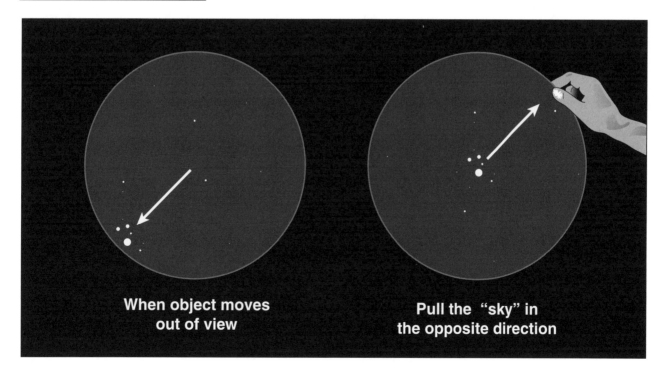

When object moves
out of view

Pull the "sky" in
the opposite direction

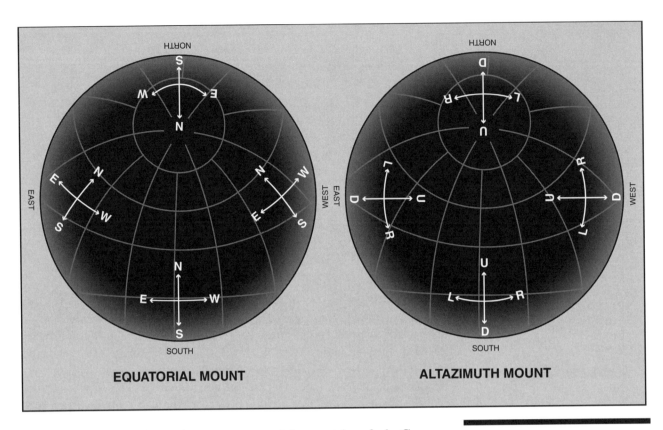

| EQUATORIAL MOUNT | ALTAZIMUTH MOUNT |

Regardless of whether your equatorial mount is a fork, German equatorial mount, ring, horseshoe, or yoke, it is an equatorial mount and moves over the celestial sphere with the same geometry to the ground (unless you are at the north or south pole!). The reason you cannot think of moving the telescope in terms of up/down and right/left is that the orientation of the scope tube changes depending on which direction the tube is pointed.

For instance, if you are looking at something on the meridian, right ascension movements are "left and right" and the declination axis is "up and down." On the other hand, if you are looking at something near the western horizon, the right ascension is "up and down" (relative to the horizon), and declination moves are "right and left."

The simple and obvious solution is to quit thinking in terms of left/right and up/down. Instead, think of moving the telescope north/south in declination and east/west in right ascension.

To get a better picture of moving north/south and east/west, set up your telescope in an area that can be lighted — you are not going to be doing any serious observing. Set up the telescope so that it is roughly polar aligned. Find a bright star — any star will do. Center it in the eyepiece and turn the declination slow-motion knob so that the telescope tube moves toward Polaris a couple of degrees — toward the +90-degree mark on the declination setting circle if you have one. That direction is north regardless of what you perceive "north" to be. This is true no matter what direction the telescope tube is pointed.

Next, unlock the right ascension and turn the telescope a few degrees toward the next highest hour number on the right ascension setting circle. If you do not have setting circles, move the scope tube so that it moves clock-

Figure 6-9 The illustration on the left shows the path of an equatorially mounted telescope on the celestial sphere when moved in right ascension and declination. The "right angle" path of a telescope on an altazimuth mount as it moves on the celestial sphere is shown on the right. Notice that the equatorial mount moves in circular arcs that correspond to the sweep of right ascension and declination while the equatorial mount's movements are always at right angles. This is most obvious at the pole.

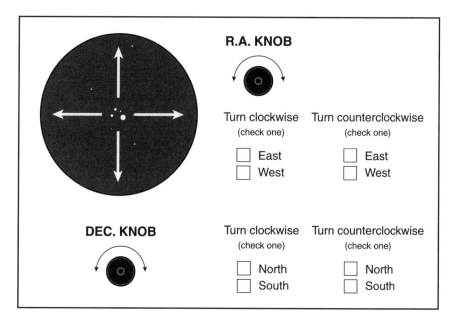

R.A. KNOB

Turn clockwise
(check one)

☐ East
☐ West

Turn counterclockwise
(check one)

☐ East
☐ West

DEC. KNOB

Turn clockwise
(check one)

☐ North
☐ South

Turn counterclockwise
(check one)

☐ North
☐ South

Figure 6-10 Make a sketch, similar to the one here, of how the slow-motion knobs move your telescope.

wise when facing Polaris. This direction is east — when you are swinging the telescope in any direction that causes the hour number to be higher than it was, you have moved east. While you are making all of these moves, also note which way the images move in the eyepiece. This information will come in handy later.

Directions in the sky are not always obviously related to those on land. Turn the book around so that you can read "North" correctly on the equatorial mount diagram in Fig. 6-9. You are facing north. Notice that the directions seem backwards to locations beneath the pole.

You might make a rough sketch of the movements in the front of your notebook so that you can refresh your memory later on. Now you know which way is "up."

7 | Locating The Messier Objects
The Geometric Method

The best method for finding the Messier objects is so simple that no one ever talks about it. Well, that's partially true. The human eye is an excellent judge of geometry—you walk into a room and instantly spot a picture that is hanging ever-so-slightly crooked. You can read about star hopping and setting circles and offsetting, but I want you to try the "geometric eyeball" method for finding Messier objects because it's fast and it's easy.

Starhopping works well with moderately dark skies, and thousands upon thousands of amateurs swear by it. But it doesn't work from my backyard at all — I am in the middle of the Los Angeles smog basin. There is a constant pall of haze, light, and atmospheric pollution hanging over the "Pennington Backyard Observatory." After magnitude 4, the stars and background sky are equally bright most of the time. The only way I can see anything is to use a Light Pollution Rejection (LPR) filter, and that only works when I am looking through the eyepiece — the LPR filter doesn't do any good at all when trying to find something.

The "geometric eyeball" method uses a Telrad as the primary finder. This is the same as the starhopper's method up to the point of locating the constellation from which to locate the object. The constellation might not be the actual constellation that the object is in — it could be a constellation which is simply an easier reference point, hence, a "finder constellation." From there I place the Telrad's 4-degree outer circle in a *geometric relationship* to the reference star or stars of the finder constellation.

I had wanted to see the Owl Nebula (M97) and the Whirlpool Galaxy (M51) in my own telescope ever since I had seen them in a 13-inch Coulter at the Riverside Telescope Maker's Conference at Big Bear, California. I looked and looked and searched and searched. I tried starhopping, scanning, and using setting circles —all to no avail. I simply chalked up my failure to inexperience and decided to try again after I was better at finding things in general. Then I hit on the idea of using geometry. Actually, I was "reinventing the wheel." It turns out that a large number of people use this method, but it hasn't been written about very much.

I drew a circle which represented the 4 degree outer circle of my

Telrad finder on a *SkyAtlas 2000.0* chart. Then, noting the relationship between the circle and the nearby stars in the atlas, I set the 4-degree circle of my Telrad in the same geometric relationship to the reference stars in the sky.

I was prepared for another failure, but I thought, "What the heck, I'll just look through the eyepiece first — I might get lucky." Luck indeed! There was the Halloween specter of M97 floating against the artificially dark sky created by the LPR filter, almost dead-center in the eyepiece.

I was glued to the eyepiece for twenty minutes or so; then I decided to try for M51, since I didn't know whether I had just gotten lucky or whether the new method was that much better. M51 is located off the handle of the Big Dipper. It is quite a bit further from a reference star than M97. I estimated the angles, and placed the finder ring of the Telrad in the appropriate spot. Again, I went directly to the eyepiece. Not there. With some apprehension, I then took a look through the finder. Nothing. I started to get that sinking feeling — maybe finding M97 so quickly was just a fluke. I decided to scan the area and moved the scope tube ever so slightly. Suddenly, those big knotty spirals swam into view — bigger than life. It had worked again. Once more I stood at the eyepiece for more than half an hour, admiring creation's work.

To test my newly found method, I tried again for M97. I swung the scope back to the pan of the Dipper and positioned the finder ring. With confidence I looked into the eyepiece again. It wasn't there, but with a couple of jiggles to scan the area for one or two degrees, I had it again. Then back to M51, and it was even easier this time — not that it was all that hard in the first place.

In the next few hours, I found three more objects that I had not found before, and I spent at least 20 minutes looking at each one. This method really worked. All I needed to do now was really learn the sky, make some "geometric finder charts," and I could probably put anything in the eyepiece in a few seconds. Needless to say, my newfound ability was powerful motivation to learn the constellations.

Estimating angles and distances is something for which we all have a talent. We do it all the time; we are just not aware of it. For instance, when you pitch a wad of paper at the wastebasket, you are estimating distance, velocity, and angle; when you are driving a car, you are constantly estimating distance, angle, time, and velocity — if you didn't, you would constantly have your car in the body shop. The "geometric method" is nothing more than noting the relationships between a few references and placing the Telrad or other finder rings in the proper relationship to them.

Geometric Finding Without a Telrad

Using a finder scope requires combining the geometric method and the starhopper method. The cross hairs are your "geometric" reference. Start with some prominent star that is easy to see in the finder. Do this by sighting along the telescope or the finder tube to get within the neigh-

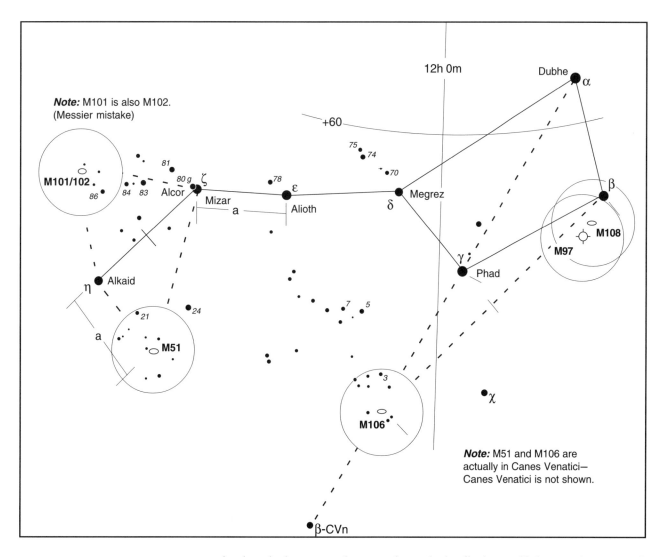

Note: M101 is also M102. (Messier mistake)

Note: M51 and M106 are actually in Canes Venatici— Canes Venatici is not shown.

Figure 7-1 This chart of Ursa Major shows the elements of the *geometric* method. The dashed lines show the geometric relationships; the "tick" marks show distances in halves, thirds or quarters of relative distance. The large circle represents a Telrad's outer target ring.

borhood, then scan the area through the finder until the star is centered. From here, starhop to a recognizable asterism close to the object and then place the crosshairs in the correct geometric relationship to the asterism. Finally go to the eyepiece and scan until you find the object.

If you don't have any success after a few minutes, recheck your finder image to see how far off you have wandered. Reset the telescope and begin again. Don't, under any circumstances, give up. Persistence will get you farther than talent. When you are absolutely sure that you have searched every square degree of the area and still haven't found the object, recheck your charts — you may have gotten turned around and simply be looking in the wrong spot. After you have a little experience, you won't have this problem at all. The main thing is to keep at it!

Now, we have to discuss the two types of finders — the straight through type and the type with a right angle prism or mirror.

The straight-through type is a simple, small, low power refractor. The right-angle type is a small low power refractor with a prism or mirror star-diagonal between the eyepiece and objective lens. The right-angle prism makes using the finder a little easier since you can "bend" the image around to some convenient place for viewing. With the straight-through variety, you always have to get your eye in line with the telescope. Sometimes, this is difficult to do, espe-

cially when the telescope is pointed straight up.

The other finder scope problem is image orientation. In the straight-through finder, left and right are reversed, and up and down are backwards. In the right angle variety the image is right side up, but left and right are reversed. At first, moving the telescope toward the desired spot while looking through the finder is confusing. There is only one solution: do it a lot and it will become second nature to you. (See *Calibrating a Finder Scope* and *Which Way is Up*, Chapter 6.)

The Geometric Method With Alternative Finders

There are a couple of other finders that you can make that work fine when using the geometric method. First is the traditional ring-gunsight finder like those you see in pictures of World War II antiaircraft guns. They are easy to make as they only require a bit of patience and minimum skill with an X-ACTO® knife, some glue, wire and a soldering iron. The other type of finder is even easier to make since it is made with a toilet tissue or paper towel tube. The "plans" for these finders are shown in Figures 7-4 and 7-5.

To make the ring gunsight finder you will need a wire coat hanger, 60/40 solder, a couple of small washers, white sewing thread, a can of flat black spray paint, epoxy glue and half an hour. The tools you need are a soldering iron, a pair of heavy side-cutters, a pair of pliers and a place to work. When the gunsight is complete, it can be mounted on the telescope with nylon straps like those used by backpackers.

The second type of finder is made from a cardboard tube from a roll of gift wrap and some masking or duct tape.

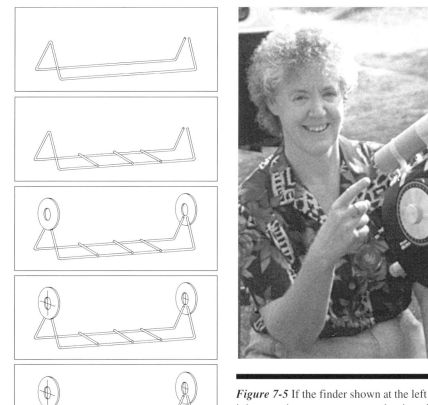

Figure 7-5 If the finder shown at the left is too difficult to make or you could really do it but you just never got around to it and tonight is the club marathon you can still be competitive—that is if you can scare up some masking or duct tape and a cardboard tube. Dorothy Woodside bagged 97 objects with this set-up.

Figure 7-4 A simple one power finder can be assembled from a wire coathanger, large diameter washers and some thread for crosshairs.

As you can see, even the mounting of these two finders is easy. Neither requires drilling, tapping, or cutting of the telescope tube, and both are mounted with Velcro or nylon straps.

You might think that something as simple and low-tech as the tube finder would be a big handicap. It is not. Dorothy Woodside, using the charts I provided, the geometric method, and a cardboard tube from a roll of gift wrapping paper taped to the regular finder of her 8-inch Meade, survived her first Messier Marathon with a 97! What is more amazing is that Dorothy had located fewer than 25 of the Messier objects in the year she had owned her telescope previous to doing a Marathon.

Believe me, you can do it.

8 | Messier Objects
An Overview

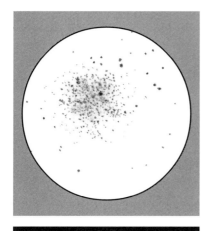

Figure 8-1 M11, in Scutum, is an open cluster which has a definite globular appearance in the eyepiece of a small telescope. Field of view is 45'.

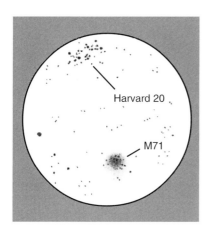

Figure 8-2 M71 located in Sagitta, is a globular cluster which is so sparse that it can be mistaken for an open cluster. In this view the open cluster Harvard 20 is also shown. Field of view is 45'.

There are **fourteen types** of Messier objects:

38	Galaxies
1	Double Galaxy (M51)
1	Galaxy Nucleus (M54)
28	Globular Clusters
25	Open Clusters
6	Nebulous Open Clusters
1	Milky Way Bright Patch (M24)
1	Possible Asterism (73)
1	Double Star (M40)
4	Planetary Nebulae
1	Emission Nebula (M43)
1	Reflection Nebula (M78)
1	Super-Nova Remnant (M1)
1	Duplication (M102)
110	Total Messier Objects

Each classification has a unique appearance. That fact would lead you to believe one cannot be mistaken for another — almost true. M11, in Scutum, can be mistaken for a globular cluster, especially in smaller telescopes. It is, in fact, a compact open cluster. A close study with a telescope of moderate aperture will reveal over 600 bright points of light. On the other hand, M71, a globular cluster in Sagitta, almost has the appearance of an open cluster — unless you are aware of these visual anomalies, you might think, just from a reading of the object's type, that you are looking at the wrong object, when in fact you are looking at the right one.

In the descriptive material on the page facing each chart in this book, I have provided a number of aids, which include drawings and descriptive information to eliminate any confusion on objects that might cause you a problem, regardless of the size of your telescope or familiarity with the Messier objects.

I have also provided supplementary charts where needed. In all cases, the charts and the information are contiguous. The charts are arranged for the March Maxi Marathon when time is of the essence—but of course you can use them any time of year. I have provided tables that direct you from chart to chart with a minimum of inconvenience.

Galaxies

Galaxies are incredibly huge collections of stars, gas and dust, like our own galaxy, the Milky Way. Galaxies come in many shapes and sizes and are very distant objects. They could have a spiral, spindle or elliptical shape, and could be face-on, edge-on or somewhere in between. Because of the incredible distances, they cannot be resolved into individual stars except in very large telescopes, and then only photographically.

There are only two hard-to-see Messier galaxies. Paradoxically, one is one of the largest and closest galaxies to our own: M33, the Pinwheel Galaxy. It can be seen easily in binoculars with moderately good seeing conditions. However, in a telescope, because it is so large and spread out, it is hard-to-find until you have developed your observing skills.

The other toughie is M74, a galaxy in Pisces. This is one of the fainter Messier objects (magnitude 9.5). Although there are some that are fainter, this one is especially difficult during the March Maxi Marathon since it must be found in the twilight — a task of some difficulty if you have never done it before.

Once you know *where* to look and *what* to look for, and are intimately familiar with methods of finding them, none of the Messier objects are all that difficult.

With the exception of these two galaxies, the rest are relatively easy to see *and* identify. You will not confuse a galaxy with another type of object.

Figure 8-3 A typical photograph of M33, the Pinwheel Galaxy. Compare this photo with the figure below. Photo by Martin C. Germano

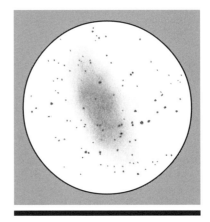

Figure 8-4 A drawing showing the eyepiece representation of M33. Field of view is 45'.

Globular Clusters

A globular cluster is a spherically shaped group of stars of common proper motion. Each star that is a member of a globular cluster orbits the gravitational center of the group. In a photograph, a globular cluster appears as a dazzling ball of light with only the outer edges of the ball resolved into stars. Radiating from the ball is a halo of individual points which become less dense with increasing distance from the center.

In a telescope of moderate size (8 inches and up), a globular cluster appears to be a thousand individual points of light arranged into chains or random "spokes" that stream into the globular center of the cluster, increasing in density until they combine to become a dancing swirl of uncountable thousands of dazzling points that populate the center of the dancing sphere.

Visually, you will see "chains" of stars at the outer edges. Each increase of magnification reveals layer upon layer of tiny dazzling points of light and allows you to go deeper and deeper into the globular's central core. The photograph is a disappointment compared to the sight you will see in the eyepiece.

In telescopes under 8 inches aperture, the thousands of faint stars within the globular cluster will not be resolved except possibly at the outer edges; the globular will appear more like a diffuse ball of dim light with the

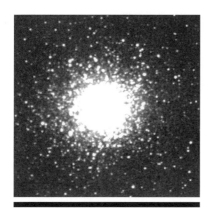

Figure 8-5 A typical photo of M13. Note the "burned in" core. Photo by Martin C. Germano

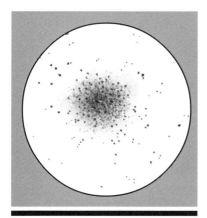

Figure 8-6 This drawing more accurately represents the image of M13 as seen in the telescope eyepiece. Field of view is 45'.

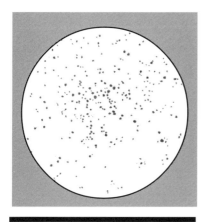

Figure 8-7 M38 in the constellation Auriga. Can you find the cross asterism noted by Reverend T.W. Webb? Hint, it is just above and to the right of center and somewhat "flattened." Field of view is 45'.

outer stars forming a faint "texture" against the blackness of the night sky—still a magnificent sight to behold with your own eyes.

Globular clusters will take all the magnification that the telescope and conditions will permit.

Open Clusters

Open clusters are irregular groupings of stars which have a common origin and common proper motion. Open clusters might contain fewer than a dozen stars or a few thousand. An open cluster often has an irregular shape.

The main difference between the photographic and visual appearance of these objects is that on photographs the bright stars appear to be larger rather than brighter. Visually you will notice that all the stars are *points* of light, but some are brighter than others. On the whole, however, open clusters visually resemble their photographs more often than not. Many times the "details" you can see in the eyepiece are not at all evident on photographs.

You can see "chains," loops, swirls and asterisms within the clusters that might not be apparent on photographs. M38 in Auriga is a case in point.

The first time I saw this open cluster, I noticed a cross-like asterism within it and commented about it to a friend. Although he had observed the cluster a few minutes beforehand, he had not noticed the cross that I had seen. After my description, he was able to make it out and later researched it in *Burnham's Celestial Handbook*. To my delight, Burnham cited Webb's description of the cluster (made in the 1850's) as, "...an oblique cross with a pair of stars in each arm." (After this experience, I decided it was okay to believe my own eyes!)

Open clusters do not generally require high power. Indeed, they often appear more cluster-like at minimum power. Small sparse clusters, especially those within the Milky Way, can be seen and identified more easily when low powers are used.

Nebulae

Nebulae defy any kind of general description except to say that all are cloud-like. Each one is remarkably different in shape, size, color, and content; each the result of different circumstances of creation. In all cases, nebulae appear as unique hazy masses. Probably the most famous of the nebulae are M42 and its companion, M43 — the Great Orion Nebula.

There are only six Messier objects classed as nebulae. Of the six, three are located in Orion: M42, M43 and M78. The other three are located in Sagittarius: the Lagoon Nebula, M8; the Trifid Nebula, M20 and the Omega Nebula, M17.

Once again, photographs are misleading — in an effort to show the extent of the faint outer regions of a nebula (M42), the delicate folds, the tracery of the filaments and the swirls of gas in the central body are obliterated in photographs. Nebulae have an unmistakable appearance in the eyepiece as well as in a photograph.

Nebulae — Planetary

Planetary nebulae are the shells of gas that have been ejected by dying stars. In smaller telescopes or at low powers in large telescopes, they show visible disks like faint planets, which is how they got their name, "planetary" nebulae.

There is considerable diversity in the appearance of planetary nebulae. Only one of the four planetary nebulae in Messier's list, M97, the Owl Nebula, actually has the disk appearance of a planet. The Ring Nebula (M57), the Dumbbell (M27) and the Little Dumbbell (M76), as their names imply, have a decidedly different appearance. However, all four planetary nebulae have some symmetry to their shape, unlike other types of nebulae.

Supernova Remnants

The Crab Nebula is the expanding cloud of gas left over when a star blew up in 1054 A.D. Chinese astronomers saw and recorded the explosion. In photographs it appears as a stunning array of tentacle-like filaments swathed in a roiling nebulous cloud. Visually, in small telescopes, it has been described as a small, colorless oblong patch of haze. In any case, regardless of the aperture of your telescope, you will know when you have captured the Crab because it is the only object near the southern horn of Taurus the bull.

The Messier Mistakes

Each Messier Mistake is an error of a different nature. Although this classification has only four objects in it, there are actually seven "mistakes" in the Messier Catalog: M24, M40, M47, M48, M73, M91 and M102. Three of the mistakes have been rectified to virtually everyone's satisfaction, and a deep-sky object has been assigned to each number except M102, which is the same object as M101.

M24, a star cloud within the Milky Way, is easily identified. It is part of an interior spiral arm of our Galaxy.

M40 is a double star in Ursa Major. It is not difficult to find or identify. It is a "mistake" because it is not a true deep-sky object. Messier actually knew that M40 was a double star, but thought he could detect some faint nebulosity surrounding it as had been described by an earlier astronomer.

M47 and M48 were "lost objects" for many years, but both numbers are now assigned to open clusters. Messier's original positions for these ob-

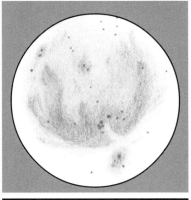

Figure 8-8 The Great Orion Nebula, M42/M43. It is probably the most famous of all deep-sky objects. Sketch field of view is 120'. Photo by Lee C. Coombs

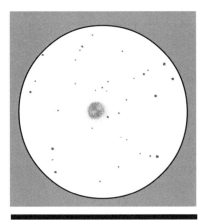

Figure 8-9 The Owl Nebula has a planet-like appearance. Messier cataloged only four planetary nebulae. Field of view is 45'.

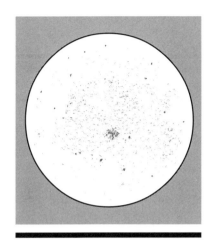

Figure 8-10 M24 is a star cloud in the Milky Way. In spite of its appearance, it is not an open cluster. Field of view is 2°.

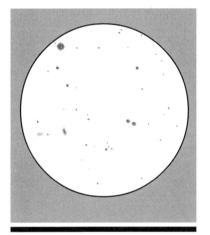

Figure 8-11 M40 is a double star in the constellation Ursa Major. It is one of the more unspectacular members of Messier's catalog. Field of view is 45'.

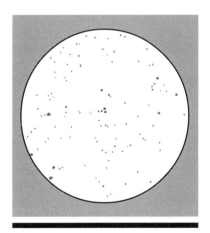

Figure 8-12 M73 is an asterism of four stars slightly southeast of M72. Field of view is 45'.

jects were recorded incorrectly by Messier himself. NGC 2422 is so close to M46 as to make it probable that this was the next object seen by Messier. It is also in the general region of Messier's coordinates for M47. Therefore it has been assigned number M47 in the Messier catalogue. NGC 2548 has been assigned the designation as M48 since this cluster is also in the vicinity of Messier's original coordinates. Both are bright enough to be seen in the equipment he had at the time.

M73 is an asterism of four stars. There is serious speculation that they might actually be a "little cluster" of four stars. Paul Murdin and David Allen, authors of *Catalogue of the Universe*, conclude that the chances are one in four that four stars brighter than magnitude 12 which are so closely associated in such a small area of sky might in fact be a little cluster with common proper motion (page 75).

M91 was another "missing object" that is now assigned to NGC 4548, a magnitude 9.5 galaxy in the general area of Messier's original co-ordinates. Some claim that M91 is a duplicate listing of M58.

M102 is a duplication of M101 — a genuine mistake, all other arguments to the contrary. Méchain, Messier's close associate and co-worker, acknowledged this mistake in a letter which was published in 1786. For that reason, another object has never been assigned convincingly to this M-number.

Now you know the types of objects you are looking for, a little bit about them and some facts concerning the "Messier Mistakes." The next order of business is to find out how easy or how hard these objects will be to find and see.

Difficulty in Finding

There are only a few "hard-to-find" Messier Objects. Three of them (M74, M77 and M30) are "hard" only because they have to be found in the twilight of evening and dawn of the March Maxi Marathon. In January, they are easy to find. M33, M31, M32 and M110 are slightly difficult to find (see "Galaxies," above) if you wait until March to learn where they are and what they will look like in your telescope. If you learn where to look, they are pretty easy to locate.

The rest of the so called "hard-to-find" objects are difficult to find only because there are no nearby reference stars or asterisms, the constellations in which they are found are faint or only partially visible or they are in a dense portion of the Milky Way.

There are 19 of these objects: M2, M11, M15, M26, M27, M29, M39, M40, M48, M51, M55, M56, M71, M72, M73, M75, M81, M82, and M83.

As you run the Marathon, you wonder why none of the Virgo cluster objects are mentioned here. That is because the Virgo galaxies are not hard to find — they are only difficult to identify (because there are so many) and that problem is also discussed below.

Difficulty in Seeing

There are only four "hard to see" objects: M74, M77, M33 and M30. Three of the four, M74, M77 and M33, are the first three objects of the March Maxi Marathon, and all three must be found in the twilight. M30 is hard to see because it is the very last object in the March Maxi Marathon, and it is viewed in the morning twilight.

M74 is actually "difficult" to see and is usually considered difficult even under good conditions because it has a low surface brightness — smaller telescopes will find it more easily than large ones. M77 and M33 are only "slightly" difficult. These objects are harder if you have never seen or found them before. M76 is tiny and faint. In small telescopes it is hard to find because you can go past it so easily.

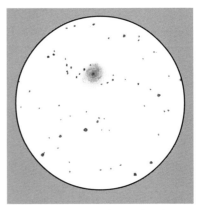

M74 Field of view is 45'.

Difficulty in Identification

The Virgo cluster galaxies are not actually difficult if you have some method of locating them in a predefined order, and if you have a clue about their appearance. These objects are only considered difficult by those who have never worked out a plan to handle the problem. There are only 13 galaxies and each one has a unique appearance. All are bright enough that they will not to be confused with the hundreds and hundreds of other faint galaxies in the Virgo-Coma cluster. A special series of charts is included in this book to help you work your way through the Virgo cluster problems.

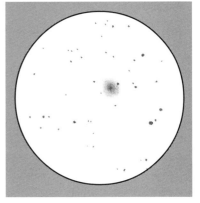

M77 Field of view is 45'.

Solutions

I will now tell you how you are going to accomplish the "impossible" in the March Messier Marathon; then you are going to practice on the tough ones.

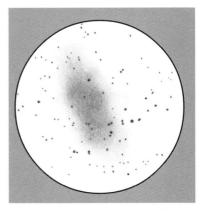

M33 Field of view is 45'.

1. Learn how to find and identify these five Messier objects in your sleep: M74, M77, M33, M76 and M30. The first three and the last one have to be found in twilight on March Maxi Marathon night. Learn what they look like under good conditions first. Practice finding these five "twilight" objects every time you set up your telescope.

   When you go for all 110 objects in the March Messier Marathon, you will have four of these objects "in the bag" before the sky is really dark because you will know where they are and what they look like.

M Number	Finder Constellation	Marathon Chart
M74	Pisces	1
M77	Cetus	2
M33	Andromeda	4
M76	Andromeda	5
M30	Capricornus	48

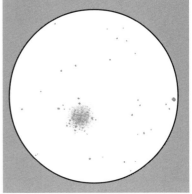

M30 Field of view is 45'.

2. Again, practice is the key. Find these 19 objects at least once and you will know that you can find them again. For the most part, they are a bit difficult because there are no reference stars close by. Confidence, persistence and perseverance will lead you to them.

M Number	Finder Constellation	Marathon Chart
M48	Canis Minor	14
M51	Ursa Major	20
M40	Ursa Major	21
M81, M82	Ursa Major	22
M83	Corvus	26
M56	Lyra	30
M27, M71	Cygnus	31
M29, M39	Cygnus	32
M11, M26	Scutum	36
M55	Sagittarius	44
M75	Sagittarius	45
M15	Pegasus	46
M2, M72, M73	Aquarius	47

3. The Virgo cluster is sometimes called "hard" — it is not. There are 13 objects in the Virgo cluster, all of them galaxies. Go through the Virgo "clutter" at least once before Marathon night. With this book and one practice session you will be able to find and identify each galaxy as easily as you can find any other object—more easily in fact because you hardly have to move the telescope as you go from one to the next! Marathon Charts 28a through 28d present a "programmed" method for finding and identifying these objects.

The rest of your Marathon is all downhill.

What are you waiting for? Get out there and *do it!*

A Second Chance?

In virtually every discussion and article on the Messier Marathon, there is much made of those objects which never set. These articles would lead you to believe that there are a substantial number of objects at which you will have a second chance if you should miss them the first time around. Lots of smoke, little fire.

Following the hoopla about the non-setting objects is usually a discussion of those objects which will rise again. In the March Messier Marathon, only M52 and M103 in Cassiopeia "set" then rise again before twilight. Even then they will be fairly close to the horizon where atmospheric transparency is not good. Fortunately, they are open clusters, so you should be able to make them out even when they are near the horizon.

The non-setting objects constitute a moot point anyway. There are a total of 37 objects which will not set for most U.S. observers. If you get behind, you could skip any of the "non-setting" objects listed below and go back to them when you get ahead at some later time. But if you follow the instructions in this book, you will probably not have this problem.

"Non-setting" Messier Objects for Most U.S. Locations

M Number	Chart
M65	16
M66	16
M95	17
M96	17
M105	17
M3	18
M53	18
M64	19
M85	19
M51	20
M101	20
M102	24
M106	21
M58	28a
M59	28a
M60	28a
M84	28b
M86	28b
M87	28b
M102 (M101 again)	24
M40	21
M81	22
M82	22
M97	22
M108	23
M109	23
M63	25
M94	25
M49	28
M61	27
M104	27
M81	22
M88	28b
M89	28c
M90	28c
M91	28c
M98	28d
M99	28d
M100	28d

9 | How to Use the Charts
Your Guide to Running an Efficient Marathon

Everything up to now has been moving toward this point—you are ready to get out under the stars with your telescope to start hunting the Messier objects. You have done your homework and you can locate signpost stars and constellations. The next step in the process is to "zero" you in on the 110 Messier objects. That is exactly what the last section of this book will do for you. It gathers together the pictures, maps and facts in the correct order to successfully run an Ordinary, Maxi, or March Messier Marathon. All of the information you need to locate and identify each Messier object is on one or two contiguous chart pages. You will not have to resort to using three or four atlases or to flipping from one page to another and then back again. The only thing extra you'll have to do is to turn the chart until it matches the sky at the time you want to conduct the Marathon. In fact, you do not even need a list of the objects — the charts themselves are in March Marathon order, and each chart has a table to cycle you though a Marathon at other times. To accomplish this I have structured this section around five different page designs which are as follows:

1. **One-Power Finder Chart Pages.** These show one or more Messier Objects in relation to a finder constellation and star fields. A 4° circle, representing the outer target ring of a Telrad (and most other one-power finders) shows how to aim your telescope so that the Messier Object will be within the field of view of a eyepiece that shows a 30-arc minute (one-half degree) field. Most of the charts provided here are One-Power Finder Charts.

2. **Supplemental Data Pages.** Opposite each One-Power Finder Chart is a page containing supplemental data describing the objects, field of views in finder scopes and a sketch of how the object will look to you through the eyepiece.

3. **Twilight Charts.** At the beginning and ending of the March Marathon, you will begin observing at the first possible moment and while the sky is not completely dark. These are difficult conditions. I have created large scale maps to assist you. In some instances these charts are further supplemented by Eyepiece Starhopper Charts.

4. **Eyepiece Starhopper Charts.** For certain objects that may be difficult to locate, special charts with "hopper paths" guide you to the object.

5. **Virgo Cluster Charts.** These are a series of charts that logically guide you through the "Virgo Clutter" of galaxies.

Supplemental Data Pages

These pages are opposite the one power finder charts and contain useful information to aid you in locating and identifying each Messier object. An example is shown in Figure 9-1. The information is arranged as follows:

Descriptive text for each Messier object shown on the facing chart. The descriptions include the popular name, if it has one, visual magnitude, visual index and angular size of each object in minutes ('). The visual index is from Fred Klein's *Visibility of Deep Sky Objects*. It generally represents the ease (0 = easiest, 6 = hardest), with which an object may be seen since the "integrated visual magnitude" may be misleading, especially in the case of galaxies.

Conflicts, tips, notes and tricks are also noted. Usually a picture or illustration will also accompany descriptions of conflicts.

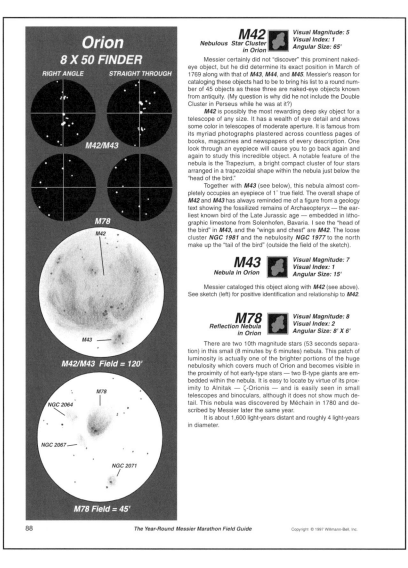

Finder Constellation Name: The finder constellation is not necessarily the actual constellation in which an object is located, but is the constellation used to locate the object when using this book.

8 x 50 Finder View: When an object is noted as *Shows weakly in finder*, or *No show in finder* (see below), a representation of the finder view is shown opposite the chart. This view does not include all of the stars visible in the finder — only one or two prominent asterisms which are instantly recognizable are shown. Fields are shown for a finder with a diagonal (reversed image) and a straight through finder (reversed and inverted image). The crosshairs shown are aligned with the lines of right ascension and declination.

Eyepiece View: These are sketches that show what you will see through the eyepiece. Each sketch has the object's name immediately below it along with the field scale. Most of these drawings were done with a field scale of 45 minutes of arc ('), but when an object is extraordinarily large, like M42/M43 shown above, the scale is expanded. Elsewhere in this book (pp. 44–46) instructions are given on how to determine the scale of your telescope/eyepiece combination.

Figure 9-1 This is a Supplemental Data Page for M42, 43 and 78. In the Finder Chart section of this book it is a left hand page that is opposite Marathon Chart 7.

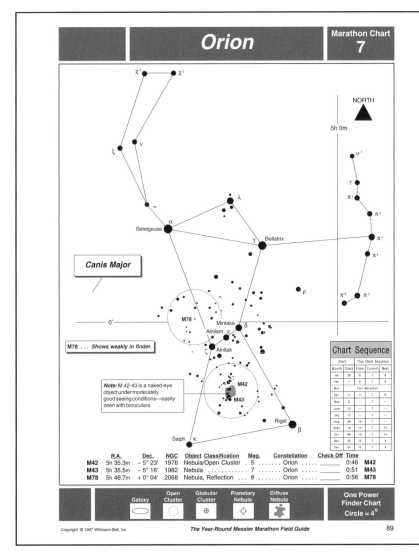

The Year-Round Messier Marathon Field Guide   89

One Power Finder Chart Pages

These pages are opposite the Supplemental Data pages. An example is shown in Figure 9-2. The information is arranged as follows:

Marathon Chart Number. In the information boxes and in the text opposite each chart, the Marathon chart numbers are always noted as "Marathon Chart *nn*," where *nn* represents the chart number.

Information Box. A box with the name of the next finder constellation to proceed to when engaged in a Messier Marathon is on the Marathon Chart. There is a line pointing in the direction of the named constellation relative to the one shown on the chart.

Orientation Arrow. Most charts are oriented with north at the top of the chart.

Supplemental Chart References: If supplemental charts exist, or might be required, they are noted in a box. Supplemental Charts are always numbered with the same number as the main chart and an alphabetic dash number, i.e., 1, 1-a, 1-b, etc.

Notes: Various informational notes appear on the charts.

Messier Catalog List. In the lower portion of each chart is a list, in numerical order, of the Messier objects. This list contains right ascension; declination (epoch 2000.0); NGC or other reference number; the object classification; visual magnitude, the actual constellation in which the object is located; a space to check off the item (to note the date if not using the charts for a Messier Marathon); and the elapsed time, to maintain a schedule if doing a March Messier Marathon.

Legend. At the bottom of the page is a summary of the symbols used to denote the various Messier object types. The symbols are those used in *SkyAtlas 2000.0* and *Uranometria 2000.0*. The size of a symbol (galaxy, globular cluster, nebula, etc.) does not indicate an object's magnitude or size except in a general sense.

Figure 9-2 This is Marathon Chart 7 for M42, 43, and 78. In the Finder Chart section of this book it is a right hand page which appears opposite the Supplemental Data page for M42, 43, and 78.

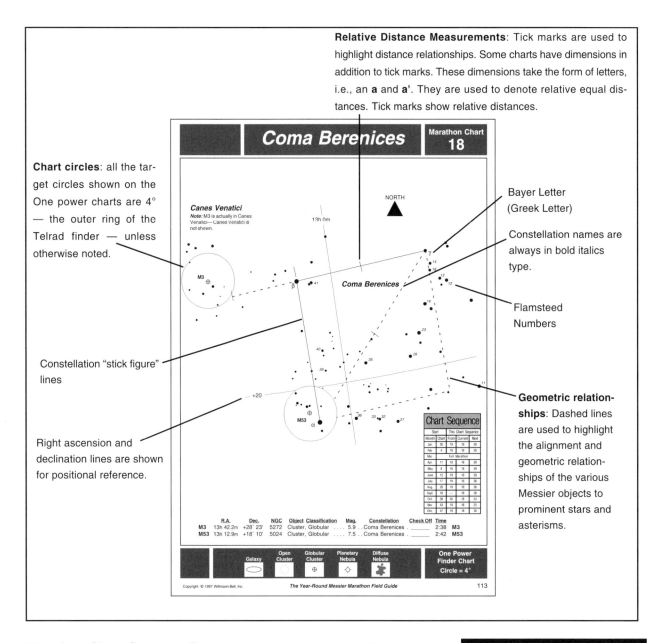

Chart circles: all the target circles shown on the One power charts are 4° — the outer ring of the Telrad finder — unless otherwise noted.

Bayer Letter (Greek Letter)

Constellation names are always in bold italics type.

Flamsteed Numbers

Constellation "stick figure" lines

Geometric relationships: Dashed lines are used to highlight the alignment and geometric relationships of the various Messier objects to prominent stars and asterisms.

Right ascension and declination lines are shown for positional reference.

Marathon Chart Sequence Tables The charts are in order for the March Marathon, but why limit yourself? Even the worst month for a Marathon can yield numbers in the high eighties. To run a Marathon for any time of year just follow the chart numbers opposite the month shown in the Chart Sequence Table usually displayed in the lower right hand corner of the page.

Scale: The charts are drawn at arbitrary scales. Each chart is as large as practical or possible. Making them all to the same scale served no practical purpose in view of their intended use.

Double and variable stars: These are generally not noted by special symbols since they do not serve any purpose on these charts.

Magnitudes: Although the magnitudes are indicated by the size of the stars, there is no magnitude scale for each chart. Brighter stars are larger; dimmer stars are smaller. Since the charts are drawn to arbitrary scales, the relative sizes of the stars indicate the magnitudes in proportion to the scale.

Figure 9-3. There is extensive data on each of the Messier Marathon charts but it is arranged to be easily understandable. Take a few minutes and study these charts. In no time you will have all the information you need to locate and identify the objects on each map.

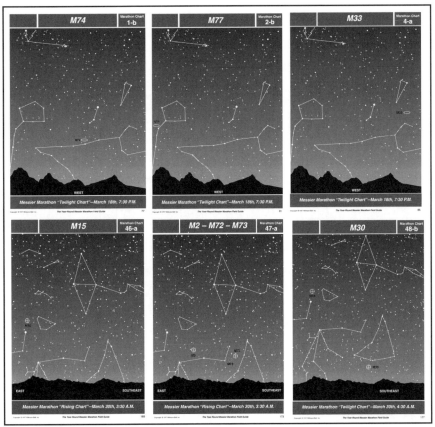

*Figure 9-4.*Twilight, Rising, and Setting Charts. Marathon Charts 1-b, 2-b, 4-a, 46-a, 47-a, and 48-b show the positions of the constellations relative to the horizon in twilight conditions in March. These are especially helpful when it is not possible to see the entire finder constellation as it is setting or rising. They show a crude representation of the sky at 35°–40° latitude during the evening and dawn twilight at the time and date noted at the bottom of the chart. The target object is shown with its corresponding symbol and its Messier Catalog number.

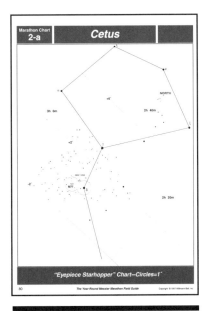

Figure 9-5. **Eyepiece Starhopper Charts.** Marathon Charts 1-a, 2-a, and 48-a are to assist you in finding objects in bright sky conditions by starhopping, using the eyepiece instead of the finder. They are especially useful for the objects that will be located in evening or dawn twilight on March Marathon night.

The stars on "twilight" and "rising" supplemental charts are shown to magnitude 6. The stars on the "Eyepiece Starhopper" charts are shown to about magnitude 9.

Chart accuracy: No doubt there are many minor inaccuracies in the plotting of the stars on the charts since they are hand drawn. However, each chart has been checked for gross plotting errors many times. If you detect errors, please communicate them to the publisher, and they will be corrected in future editions.

Right ascension and declination lines: On each chart, a line of right ascension and declination is shown for reference. The purpose of these lines is for general orientation when the charts are used with an atlas or other charts.

Star names: Many sources were consulted to determine the "correct" names of the stars. The final determination was made somewhat arbitrarily by consulting the more popular atlases and star guides, as many of the star names have several popular name variations as well as some unpopular ones.

Tirion's *SkyAtlas 2000.0* was used to determine the Bayer (Greek) letter or Flamsteed number. Flamsteed numbers are not used on the main stars of a constellation unless there is no Bayer letter.

Star selection: Deciding which stars to plot on a given chart presented a problem — should all the stars within the chart area be plotted or just those necessary? Since these charts provide the basis for the starhopper charts and the setting circle charts, they contain more star information than is necessary

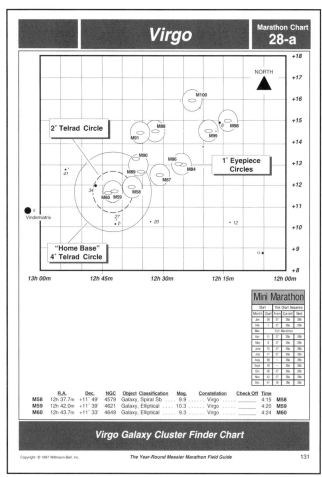

Virgo Galaxy Cluster Finder Chart

Copyright © 1997 Willmann-Bell, Inc.   *The Year-Round Messier Marathon Field Guide*   131

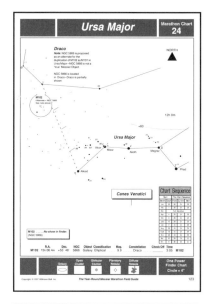

Figure 9-6. **Virgo Detail Charts.** Marathon Charts 28-a through 28-d are detailed Eyepiece Starhopper Charts. The order and starhopping path are clearly shown on these charts. These charts will help you to identify and move through the cluster using the eyepiece starhopper method. The order as well as the location of each object is noted on the charts.

Figure 9-7. Alternate M102 Chart. Marathon Chart 24 is provided as an alternate object to replace M102 for those non-purists who wish to make an observation of an object instead of making a duplicate observation of M101. The alternate object is a galaxy in Draco (NGC 5866) which is reputed to have been observed by Messier but was not included in the catalog. There are many who argue that Messier actually intended to catalog this object as M102. All arguments to the contrary, the fact is that the matter was settled by no less than Pierre Méchain, Messier's associate and close friend, in a letter published in 1786. In the letter he specifically states that the listing of M102 is a duplication of M101. End of argument. However, the author bows to the clamor of those not convinced and provides the suitable charts to locate NGC 5866.

for use with a Telrad or one power finder. In many cases prominent stars are included because they help to identify the general area. In other cases stars are included because this author just didn't know when to stop — a definite problem. In any case, the star fields shown could prove useful to those wishing to make a starhopper route other than the one shown or to plot other objects using the star fields to calibrate the plot position.

You have had a quick tour of how the charts are designed. Now dive in and get started. Remember you do not have to wait until March to run a Messier Marathon. Any clear, moonless night will do.

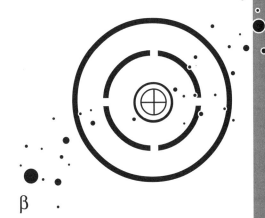

The Year-Round Messier Marathon Field Guide

Finder Charts

For "One Power" Finders

Pisces

8 X 50 FINDER

RIGHT ANGLE   **STRAIGHT THROUGH**

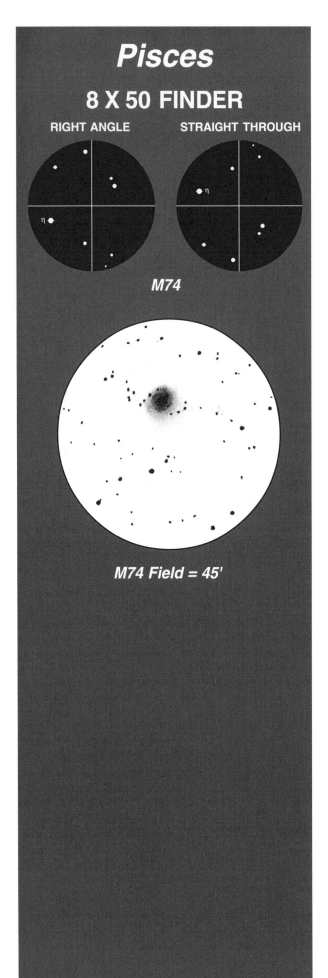

M74

M74 Field = 45'

 M74
Spiral Galaxy in Pisces

Visual Magnitude: 9.4
Visual Index: 6
Angular Size: 9'

Although there are 21 Messier objects which are fainter, this is one that is particularly difficult on March marathon nights because of its low surface brightness and the twilight conditions in which it must be found. Its appearance in the eyepiece on marathon night is similar to that of a small globular cluster. This galaxy was first observed by Méchain in September of 1780, and confirmed by Messier one month later.

This object is best seen by large aperture telescopes using low power. Small telescopes should also use low power for this, the most elusive and hardest to see of the Messier list on marathon night. However, under clear dark skies, **M74** is not particularly difficult to see or hard to find.

Its distance is close to 40 million light-years. Its calculated diameter is about 100,000 light-years. It shines with the light output of about 5 billion suns.

 Note: It should not escape your attention that **M74** also has the highest visual index (6) of any object in the list. In fact, it is the *only* object with a visual index of 6! Aperture is helpful under these conditions. Fortunately it is located only 1.5° east-northeast of η-Piscium (magnitude 3.72) which helps to make it easier to locate than it would be otherwise.

 Tip: Use the *Eyepiece Starhopper Chart* (**Marathon Chart 1-a**) to locate this object in twilight conditions. Start with **Marathon Chart 1-b** to locate Aries as soon as you can see stars in the twilight. Using the Pleiades which is higher and in a darker portion of the sky, constellation-hop down to Aries. Use α and β-Arietis as pointers to η-Piscium. Once you have η-Piscium centered in the eyepiece, you can hop to **M74** with one and one-half eyepiece moves.

If you are attempting to locate this object in April — later than the optimal time — η-Piscium will be very low in the atmospheric muck and haze at twilight and very close to the sun. You may have to "eyepiece starhop" from α or β-Arietis to η-Piscium — definitely hard work, but not impossible. *The Eyepiece Starhopper Chart* clearly shows the route to follow.

 Tip: To see faint objects is to make them move — your eye has the peculiar ability to detect objects in low contrast conditions when they are in motion. You can accomplish this by very slightly bumping or "jiggling" the telescope so that the eyepiece image is disturbed. Normally, you would avoid such antics, but under extreme low contrast conditions an unsteady image may be helpful. Once your eye locates the moving image, it is easier to see the faint object when it is finally still.

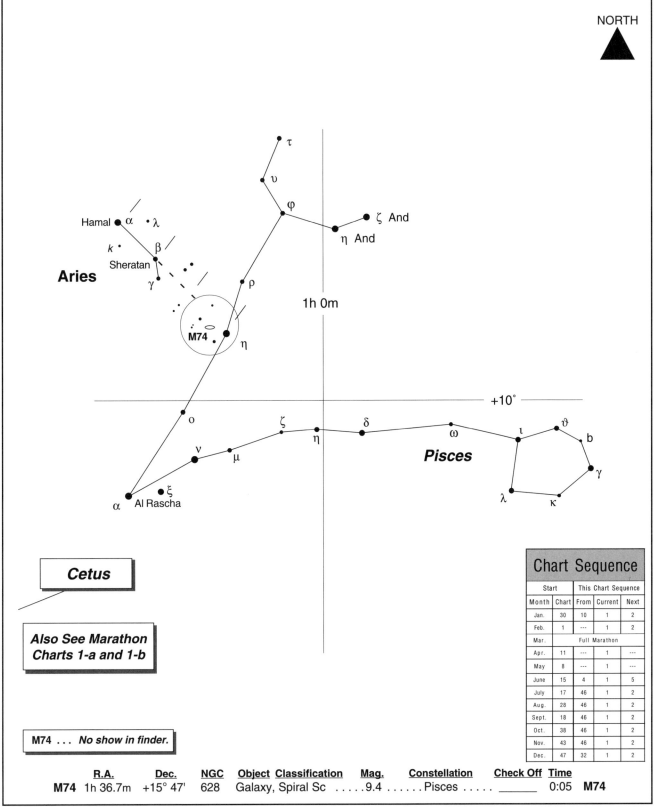

NORTH

Aries

Hamal ● α • λ

k •

Sheratan β

γ

ρ

M74

η

τ

υ

φ

ζ And

η And

1h 0m

+10°

o

ζ

δ

η

ω

ι

ϑ

b

γ

κ

λ

ν

μ

Pisces

α

Al Rascha ξ

Cetus

Also See Marathon Charts 1-a and 1-b

M74 ... *No show in finder.*

Chart Sequence

Start		This Chart Sequence		
Month	Chart	From	Current	Next
Jan.	30	10	1	2
Feb.	1	---	1	2
Mar.	Full Marathon			
Apr.	11	---	1	---
May	8	---	1	---
June	15	4	1	5
July	17	46	1	2
Aug.	28	46	1	2
Sept.	18	46	1	2
Oct.	38	46	1	2
Nov.	43	46	1	2
Dec.	47	32	1	2

	R.A.	Dec.	NGC	Object Classification	Mag.	Constellation	Check Off	Time	
M74	1h 36.7m	+15° 47'	628	Galaxy, Spiral Sc	....9.4	......Pisces	_____	0:05	**M74**

 Galaxy

 **Open Cluster**

 Globular Cluster

 Planetary Nebula

 Diffuse Nebula

One Power Finder Chart
Circle = 4°

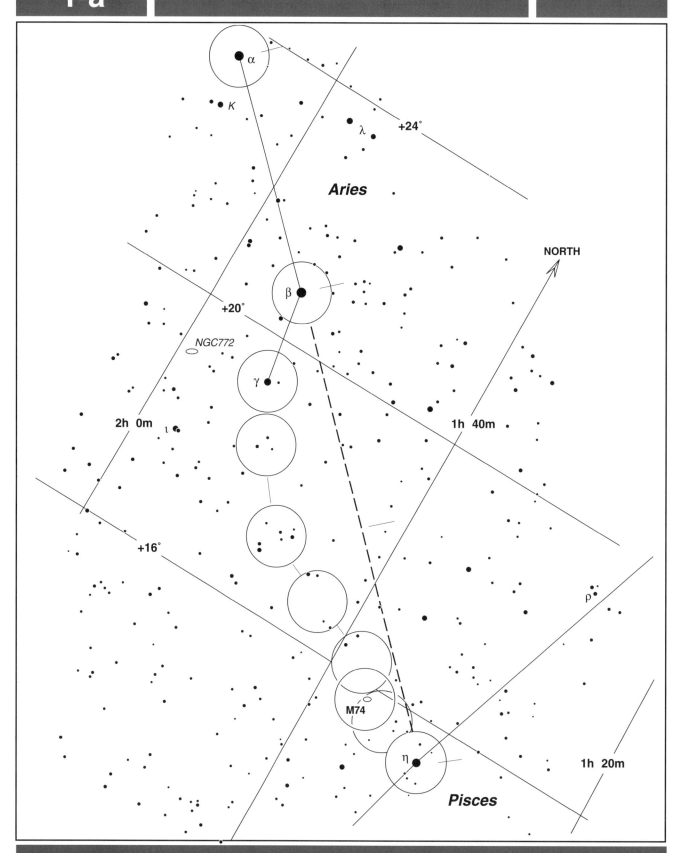

"Eyepiece Starhopper" Chart—Circles=1°

M74

α

WEST

Messier Marathon "Twilight Chart"–March 18th, 7:30 P.M.

The Year-Round Messier Marathon Field Guide

Cetus

8 X 50 FINDER

RIGHT ANGLE **STRAIGHT THROUGH**

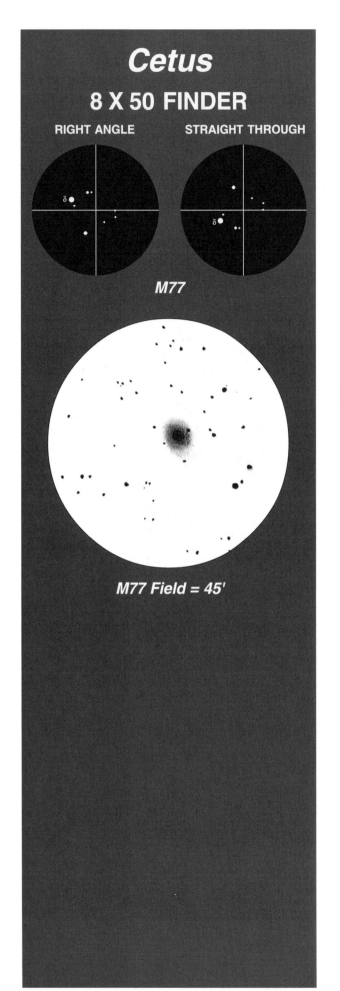

M77

M77 Field = 45'

M77

Spiral Galaxy in Cetus

Visual Magnitude: 8.9
Visual Index: 3
Angular Size: 3' X 2'

M77 is another of Méchain's discoveries (October, 1780) which Messier later confirmed. This object is located in a region otherwise devoid of any Messier objects. It is an unusual system in that it is the brightest member of a select group of peculiar "Seyfert galaxies." This type of galaxy shows a very small bright central nucleus whose spectrum reveals strong emission lines, and it is a fairly strong radio source. This object is best seen in large aperture instruments with high power. **M77** has very high surface brightness and shows spiral structure at 200+x. Small telescopes will have some difficulty with this object, although not nearly as much as with **M74**. In telescopes as small as 4 inches, some mottling and knots might be glimpsed on nights of good seeing.

The probable distance of **M77** is over 60 million light-years. The diameter of its main mass is calculated at 40,000 light-years while the full extent of the galaxy is placed at 100,000 light-years. The mass is about 100 billion suns while its total luminosity lies in the range of 20 to 40 billion suns.

 Note: This, the second Messier Marathon object, is also located in twilight conditions on March Marathon night. It is slightly brighter (visual magnitude 8.9) than **M74** (visual magnitude 9.4) is easier to locate since the sky will be slightly darker and **M77** will be slightly higher in the sky. It also has a lower visual index: 3. Only the central core of the galaxy is discernible on marathon night, which makes this object even more difficult to detect — it will have an appearance similar to a small, faint globular cluster rather than that of a galaxy.

 Tip: It is located about 1° southeast of d-Ceti. Use the *Eyepiece Starhopper Chart* (**Marathon Chart 2-a**) to locate this object. Also see **Marathon Chart 2-b** to help locate Cetus on marathon night.

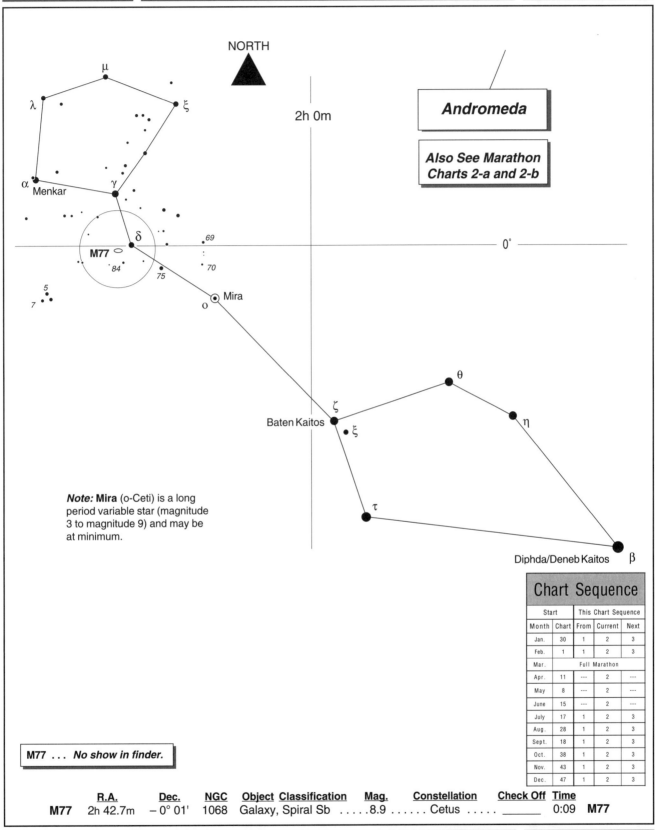

NORTH

μ

λ

ξ

α
Menkar

γ

δ

M77

2h 0m

Andromeda

Also See Marathon Charts 2-a and 2-b

0°

69

84

70

75

5

7

o
Mira

θ

ζ

ξ

η

Baten Kaitos

τ

Diphda/Deneb Kaitos   β

Note: Mira (o-Ceti) is a long period variable star (magnitude 3 to magnitude 9) and may be at minimum.

Chart Sequence

Start		This Chart Sequence		
Month	Chart	From	Current	Next
Jan.	30	1	2	3
Feb.	1	1	2	3
Mar.	Full Marathon			
Apr.	11	---	2	---
May	8	---	2	---
June	15	---	2	---
July	17	1	2	3
Aug.	28	1	2	3
Sept.	18	1	2	3
Oct.	38	1	2	3
Nov.	43	1	2	3
Dec.	47	1	2	3

M77 . . . No show in finder.

	R.A.	Dec.	NGC	Object Classification	Mag.	Constellation	Check Off	Time	
M77	2h 42.7m	– 0° 01'	1068	Galaxy, Spiral Sb	.....8.9	...... Cetus	_____	0:09	**M77**

Galaxy	Open Cluster	Globular Cluster	Planetary Nebula	Diffuse Nebula

One Power Finder Chart Circle = 4°

Cetus

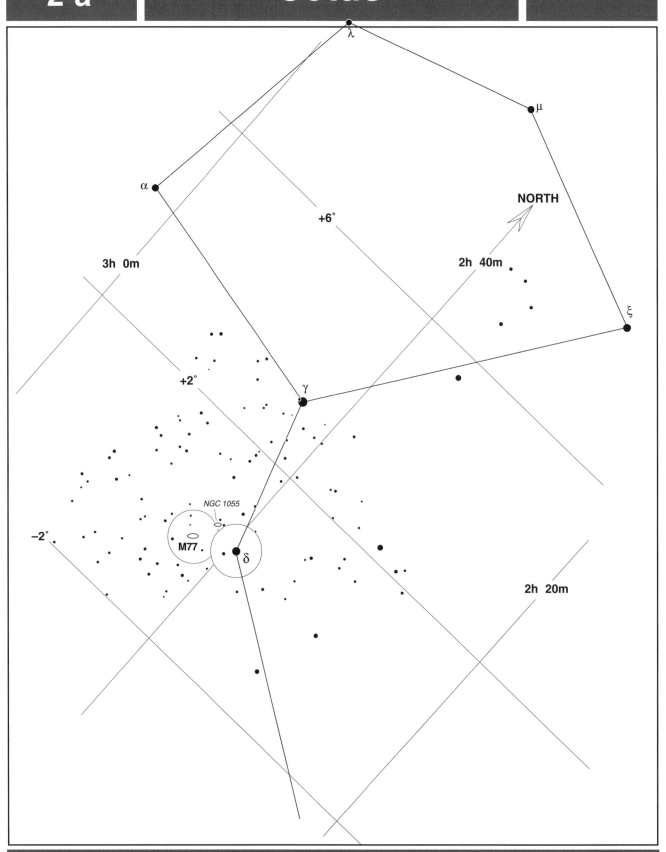

λ

μ

α

NORTH

+6°

3h 0m

2h 40m

ξ

+2°

γ

NGC 1055

M77

−2°

δ

2h 20m

"Eyepiece Starhopper" Chart—Circles=1°

The Year-Round Messier Marathon Field Guide

M77

WEST

Messier Marathon "Twilight Chart"—March 18th, 7:30 P.M.

The Year-Round Messier Marathon Field Guide

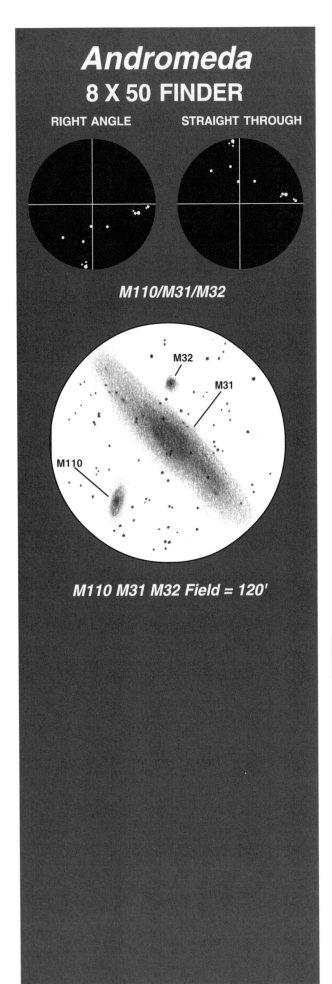

Andromeda
8 X 50 FINDER

RIGHT ANGLE   **STRAIGHT THROUGH**

M110/M31/M32

M110 M31 M32 Field = 120'

M31
The Great Andromeda Galaxy

Visual Magnitude: 4.4
Visual Index: 0
Angular Size: 160' X 40'

This is the main object of interest in the constellation Andromeda. It is a naked eye object first noted in the 10th century by the Persian astronomer Al Sûfi. **M31** is over 4° in diameter, and therefore only the central portion will be visible in an eyepiece with a true field of 1°. To call this object "immense" is an understatement. It is huge beyond words. Although its visual magnitude is placed at 4.4, this number represents the object's luminosity if it were condensed to a single point — not spread over several square degrees of sky. This is an easy object for small telescopes and binoculars. Users of large telescopes should use as low a power as possible when locating this giant. **M31** is one of Messier's many discoveries in the year 1764.

M31 is estimated to be 2.2 million light-years distant and 110,000 light-years across. Its total mass is calculated to be about 400 billion suns, and it has a luminosity equal to 68 billion suns.

M110
Elliptical Galaxy in Andromeda

Visual Magnitude: 8.8
Visual Index: 5
Angular Size: 8' X 3'

A companion galaxy to **M31**, **M110** is located 35 minutes northwest of the central mass of **M31**. Its shape is distinctly oval. **M110** will appear as a small spot of light near **M31** in small telescopes; it is not visible in binoculars.

Messier never included **M110** in his last supplement to the original catalog. He stopped at number 103 — but he did observe this object in 1773 as evidenced by a label, in his own hand, on a drawing a full 10 years before Caroline Herschel, who is generally credited with the discovery. This object was "added to the Messier List" sometime after 1967 when it was proposed by K. Glyn Jones. Owen Gingerich has much to say about the additions to the Messier catalog in Mallas and Kreimer's *Messier Album*. It is entertaining and enlightening reading.

The distance to **M110** is approximately the same as **M31**: 2.2 million light-years. Its diameter is estimated at 5,400 light-years.

 Note: M32 and **M110** (**NGC 205**), the Great Andromeda Galaxy's companions, are easily located by moving the telescope slightly south (**M32**) and northwest (**M110**) less than 1°. See **M32** and **M110**.

M32
Elliptical Galaxy in Andromeda

Visual Magnitude: 9.0
Visual Index: 3
Angular Size: 3'

A companion galaxy of **M31**, **M32** is located just 24 minutes south of the central mass of **M31**. Its shape is distinctly circular. Messier discovered **M32** along with **M31** in 1764. **M32** will appear as a small blob of light on the outer edge of **M31** in small telescopes. In large telescopes, this small galaxy's major extent is quite visible.

The distance to **M32** is approximately the same as **M31**: 2.2 million light-years. Its diameter is probably about 2,400 light-years. Its luminosity is roughly that of 2.5 billion suns.

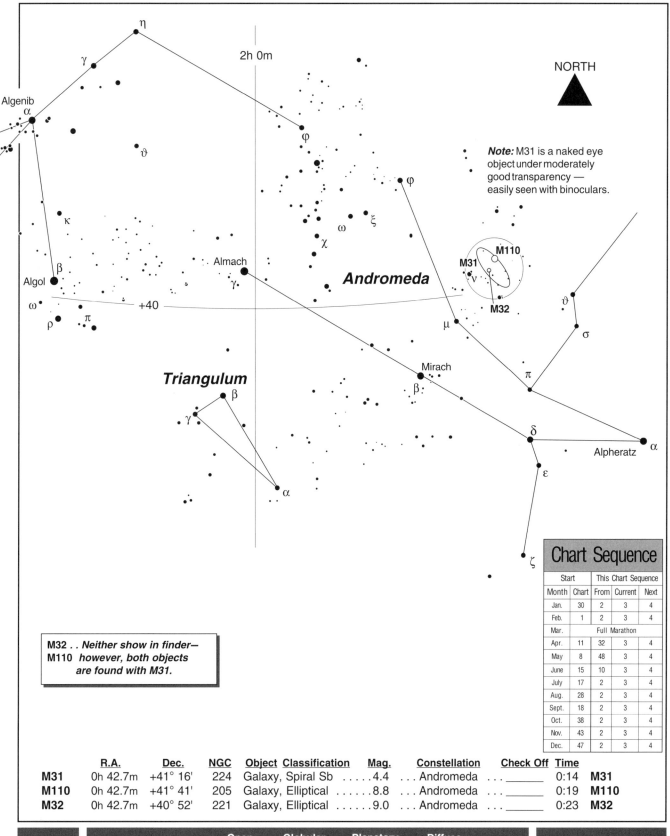

2h 0m

NORTH

η
γ
Algenib
α
ϑ
φ
φ

Note: M31 is a naked eye object under moderately good transparency — easily seen with binoculars.

κ
β
Algol
ω
ρ
π

Almach
γ

ω ξ
χ

Andromeda

M110
M31
ν
M32

μ

ϑ
σ

π

Triangulum
β
γ
α

Mirach
β

δ

ε

ζ

α

Alpheratz
Alangle
α

M32 . . *Neither show in finder—*
M110 *however, both objects are found with M31.*

Chart Sequence			
Start		This Chart Sequence	
Month	Chart	From	Current	Next
Jan.	30	2	3	4
Feb.	1	2	3	4
Mar.	Full Marathon			
Apr.	11	32	3	4
May	8	48	3	4
June	15	10	3	4
July	17	2	3	4
Aug.	28	2	3	4
Sept.	18	2	3	4
Oct.	38	2	3	4
Nov.	43	2	3	4
Dec.	47	2	3	4

	R.A.	Dec.	NGC	Object Classification	Mag.	Constellation	Check Off	Time	
M31	0h 42.7m	+41° 16'	224	Galaxy, Spiral Sb 4.4		. . . Andromeda . . .	_____	0:14	**M31**
M110	0h 42.7m	+41° 41'	205	Galaxy, Elliptical 8.8		. . . Andromeda . . .	_____	0:19	**M110**
M32	0h 42.7m	+40° 52'	221	Galaxy, Elliptical 9.0		. . . Andromeda . . .	_____	0:23	**M32**

Galaxy

Open Cluster

Globular Cluster

Planetary Nebula

Diffuse Nebula

One Power Finder Chart
Circle = 4°

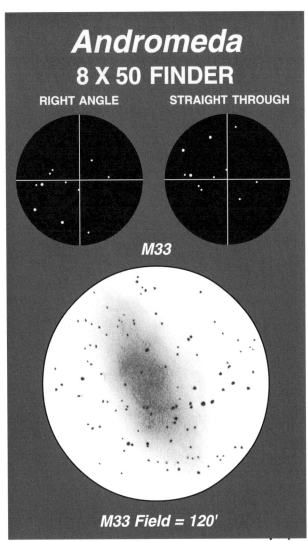

Andromeda
8 X 50 FINDER

RIGHT ANGLE **STRAIGHT THROUGH**

M33

M33 Field = 120'

M33
The Pinwheel Galaxy

Visual Magnitude: 6.3
Visual Index: 2
Angular Size: 60' X 40'

This huge galaxy was discovered in August, 1764 by Messier. However, its true nature was not revealed until the invention of photography, although early observers noted "knots" and mottled patches of luminosity.

This object is large but very faint as its light is spread over a large extent. It is actually easier to see in smaller telescopes or binoculars than with larger telescopes at moderate powers. With this object, the lower the power used, the better it is seen as a galaxy. Under very dark and clear conditions it may be seen with the naked eye using averted vision.

M33's distance is about 2.3 to 2.4 million light-years while its diameter is estimated at 60,000 light-years. The galaxy's total mass is about 8 billion suns. Total light output is about 6.7 billion suns.

Tip: It is a good idea to view this object under various light conditions in order to familiarize yourself with it well before March Marathon night. It is easy to miss this object, not because you can't find it, but because you can't see it! It should be noted that the visual index is not representative of an object's visibility under twilight conditions. This is especially true of **M33**. Until you have seen this object in your own telescope, it is hard to recognize.

M33

Marathon Chart
4

M33 . . . *Shows weakly in finder.*

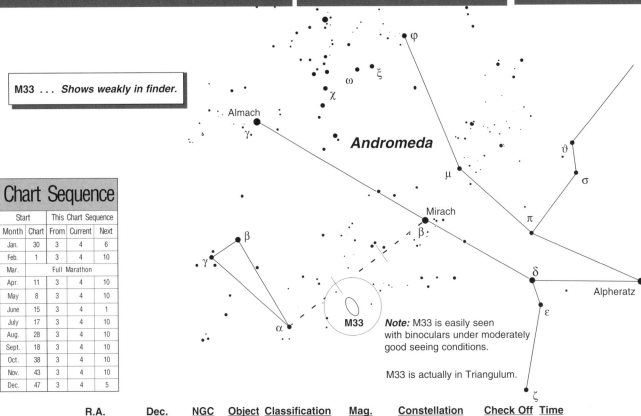

Andromeda

Almach
γ

φ
ξ
ω
χ

μ

ϑ
σ
π

Mirach
β

β

γ

δ

Alpheratz

ε

α

M33

Note: M33 is easily seen with binoculars under moderately good seeing conditions.

M33 is actually in Triangulum.

ζ

Chart Sequence			
Start	This Chart Sequence		
Month	Chart	From	Current	Next
Jan.	30	3	4	6
Feb.	1	3	4	10
Mar.	Full Marathon			
Apr.	11	3	4	10
May	8	3	4	10
June	15	3	4	1
July	17	3	4	10
Aug.	28	3	4	10
Sept.	18	3	4	10
Oct.	38	3	4	10
Nov.	43	3	4	10
Dec.	47	3	4	5

	R.A.	Dec.	NGC	Object Classification	Mag.	Constellation	Check Off	Time	
M33	1h 33.8m	+30° 39'	598	Galaxy, Spiral Sc	. . . . . 6.3	. . . Triangulum	. . . _____	0:25	M33

M33

WEST

Messier Marathon "Twilight Chart"—March 18th, 7:30 P.M.

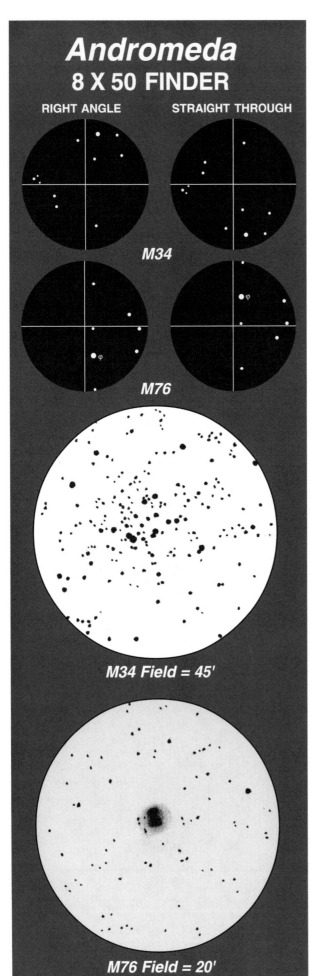

Andromeda
8 X 50 FINDER

RIGHT ANGLE   **STRAIGHT THROUGH**

M34

M76

M34 Field = 45'

M76 Field = 20'

M34
Open Cluster in Perseus

Visual Magnitude: 5.2
Visual Index: 4
Angular Size: 35'

A bright open cluster easily seen in small telescopes and binoculars, **M34** was discovered by Messier in 1764. It is a naked eye object under very good conditions. It is a "low power" object with about 80 stars recognized as true members. This is an easy object for small telescopes and binoculars.

Estimates place its distance between 1,430 and 1,500 light-years with a true diameter about 4 light-years for the main body of easily visible members.

M76
The Little Dumbbell
Planetary Nebulae

Visual Magnitude: 10.1
Visual Index: 3
Angular Size: 2' X 1'

This is a small but distinct object. Its appearance will be like a tiny peanut in telescopes of large aperture (12 inches and up, with moderate magnification) and like a small rectangle in smaller telescopes. Méchain discovered this object in September of 1780, and Messier confirmed it six weeks later. This object is the faintest of all the Messier objects at visual magnitude 10.1, but — and that is a big *but* — its visual index is rated at only 3. It is tiny (2 by 1-minutes of arc), and it is faint, but it is very compact and is in a relatively dark patch of sky with only a scattering of background stars. Telescopes of large aperture using high power will reveal a great deal of detail. Small telescopes will have to settle for a "squarish" patch of light.

Distance estimates place the Little Dumbbell at 3,400 light-years and the extent of the object at 1 light-year.

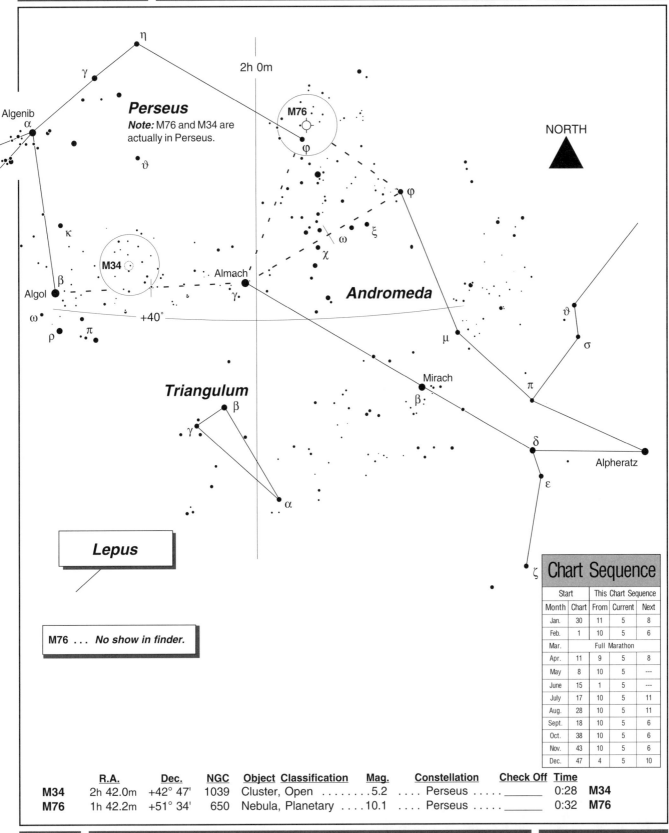

Andromeda

Perseus

Note: M76 and M34 are actually in Perseus.

M76

NORTH

Algenib
α

γ

η

2h 0m

φ

φ

ξ

ω

χ

M34

Almach

γ

Andromeda

ϑ

σ

κ

β

Algol

ω

ρ

π

+40°

μ

π

Triangulum

Mirach

β

γ

β

α

δ

Alpheratz

ε

ζ

Lepus

M76 ... *No show in finder.*

		Start		This Chart Sequence	
Chart Sequence					
Month	Chart	From	Current	Next	
Jan.	30	11	5	8	
Feb.	1	10	5	6	
Mar.	Full Marathon				
Apr.	11	9	5	8	
May	8	10	5	---	
June	15	1	5	---	
July	17	10	5	11	
Aug.	28	10	5	11	
Sept.	18	10	5	6	
Oct.	38	10	5	6	
Nov.	43	10	5	6	
Dec.	47	4	5	10	

	R.A.	Dec.	NGC	Object Classification	Mag.	Constellation	Check Off	Time	
M34	2h 42.0m	+42° 47'	1039	Cluster, Open 5.2		.... Perseus	_____	0:28	**M34**
M76	1h 42.2m	+51° 34'	650	Nebula, Planetary 10.1		.... Perseus	_____	0:32	**M76**

Galaxy

Open Cluster

Globular Cluster

Planetary Nebula

Diffuse Nebula

One Power Finder Chart

Circle = 4°

The Year-Round Messier Marathon Field Guide

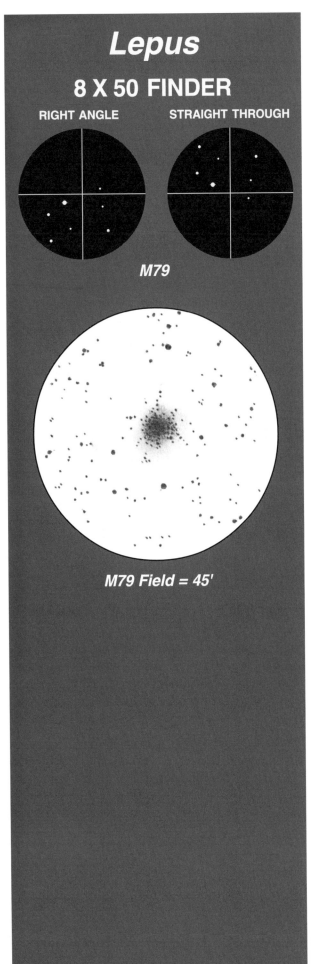

Lepus

8 X 50 FINDER

RIGHT ANGLE   **STRAIGHT THROUGH**

M79

M79 Field = 45'

M79
Globular Cluster
in Lepus

Visual Magnitude: 7.8
Visual Index: 4
Angular Size: 8'

Another of Méchain's 1780 discoveries, **M78** is not one of the more impressive examples of a globular cluster. It is, however, somewhat condensed, and telescopes of large aperture will resolve the outer regions easily. It is seen in small telescopes as a fuzzy patch and in binoculars as a hazy star. Notable eyepiece features are several arcs of stars outside of the central concentration of the cluster. The bellies of these arcs are oriented towards the center of the cluster and arranged in equal thirds around the periphery. They appear to be quite symmetrical.

The distance to this object is estimated at 41,000 light-years. Its true diameter is calculated at 110 light-years, and its light output is equivalent to about 90,000 suns.

Lepus

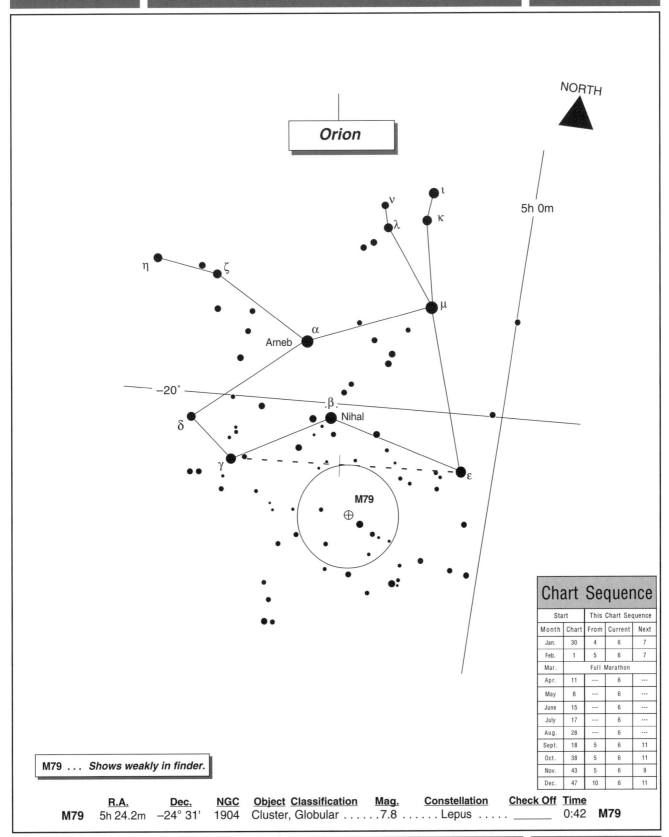

Orion

NORTH

5h 0m

ι

ν

λ

κ

η

ζ

μ

α

Arneb

−20°

.β.

Nihal

δ

γ

ε

M79

Chart Sequence

Start		This Chart Sequence		
Month	Chart	From	Current	Next
Jan.	30	4	6	7
Feb.	1	5	6	7
Mar.		Full Marathon		
Apr.	11	---	6	---
May	8	---	6	---
June	15	---	6	---
July	17	---	6	---
Aug.	28	---	6	---
Sept.	18	5	6	11
Oct.	38	5	6	11
Nov.	43	5	6	9
Dec.	47	10	6	11

M79 . . . *Shows weakly in finder.*

	R.A.	Dec.	NGC	Object Classification	Mag.	Constellation	Check Off	Time	
M79	5h 24.2m	−24° 31'	1904	Cluster, Globular	7.8	. . . . . . Lepus	_____	0:42	M79

 Galaxy  Open Cluster Globular Cluster Planetary Nebula Diffuse Nebula

One Power Finder Chart
Circle = 4°

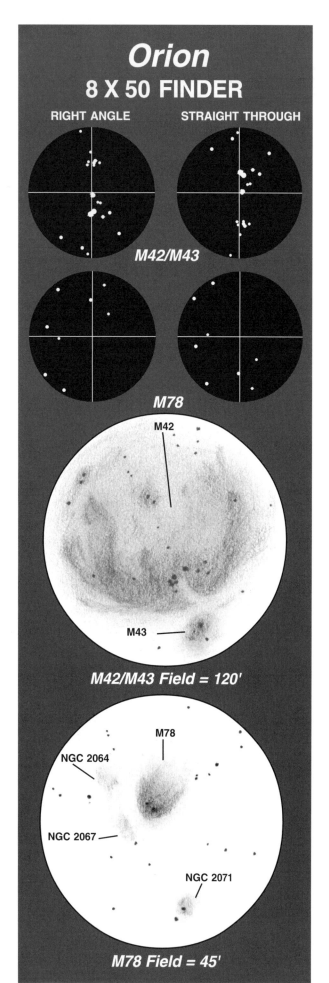

Orion
8 X 50 FINDER

RIGHT ANGLE   **STRAIGHT THROUGH**

M42/M43

M78

M42

M43

M42/M43 Field = 120'

M78

NGC 2064

NGC 2067

NGC 2071

M78 Field = 45'

M42
Nebulous Star Cluster in Orion

Visual Magnitude: 5
Visual Index: 1
Angular Size: 65'

Messier certainly did not "discover" this prominent naked-eye object, but he did determine its exact position in March of 1769 along with that of **M43**, **M44**, and **M45**. Messier's reason for cataloging these objects had to be to bring his list to a round number of 45 objects as these three are naked-eye objects known from antiquity. (My question is why did he not include the Double Cluster in Perseus while he was at it?)

M42 is possibly the most rewarding deep sky object for a telescope of any size. It has a wealth of eye detail and shows some color in telescopes of moderate aperture. It is famous from its myriad photographs plastered across countless pages of books, magazines and newspapers of every description. One look through an eyepiece will cause you to go back again and again to study this incredible object. A notable feature of the nebula is the Trapezium, a bright compact cluster of four stars arranged in a trapezoidal shape within the nebula just below the "head of the bird."

Together with **M43** (see below), this nebula almost completely occupies an eyepiece of 1° true field. The overall shape of **M42** and **M43** has always reminded me of a figure from a geology text showing the fossilized remains of Archaeopteryx — the earliest known bird of the Late Jurassic age — embedded in lithographic limestone from Solenhofen, Bavaria. I see the "head of the bird" in **M43**, and the "wings and chest" are **M42**. The loose cluster **NGC 1981** and the nebulosity **NGC 1977** to the north make up the "tail of the bird" (outside the field of the sketch).

M43
Nebula in Orion

Visual Magnitude: 7
Visual Index: 1
Angular Size: 15'

Messier cataloged this object along with **M42** (see above). See sketch (left) for positive identification and relationship to **M42**.

M78
Reflection Nebula in Orion

Visual Magnitude: 8
Visual Index: 2
Angular Size: 8' X 6'

There are two 10th magnitude stars (53 seconds separation) in this small (8 minutes by 6 minutes) nebula. This patch of luminosity is actually one of the brighter portions of the huge nebulosity which covers much of Orion and becomes visible in the proximity of hot early-type stars — two B-type giants are embedded within the nebula. It is easy to locate by virtue of its proximity to Alnitak — ζ-Orionis — and is easily seen in small telescopes and binoculars, although it does not show much detail. This nebula was discovered by Méchain in 1780 and described by Messier later the same year.

It is about 1,600 light-years distant and roughly 4 light-years in diameter.

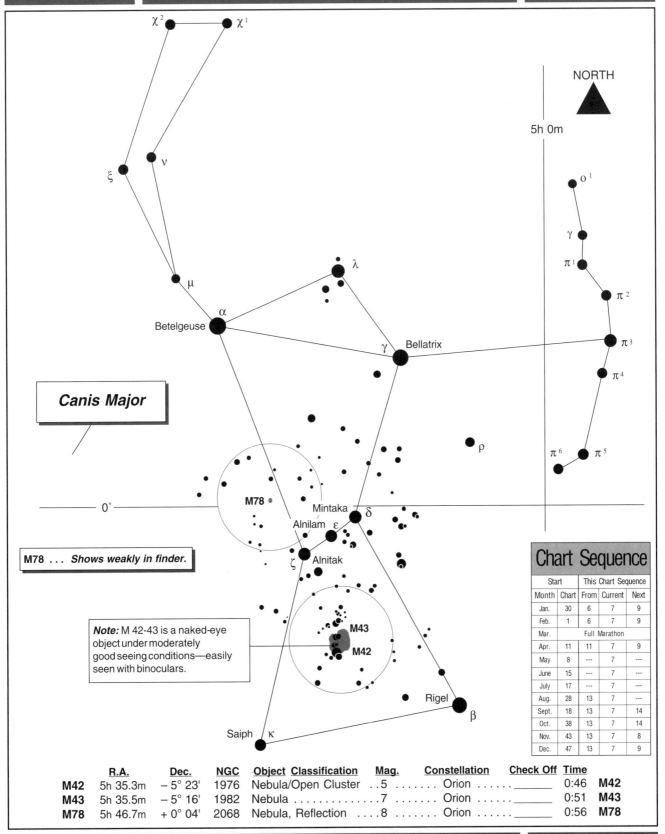

NORTH

5h 0m

χ²   χ¹

ν

ξ

μ

α
Betelgeuse

λ

γ   Bellatrix

o¹

γ

π¹

π²

π³

π⁴

π⁶   π⁵

ρ

Canis Major

0°

M78

Mintaka
Alnilam   ε   δ

M78 ... Shows weakly in finder.

ζ   Alnitak

Note: M 42-43 is a naked-eye
object under moderately
good seeing conditions—easily
seen with binoculars.

M43
M42

Rigel

Saiph   κ   β

Chart Sequence

Start		This Chart Sequence		
Month	Chart	From	Current	Next
Jan.	30	6	7	9
Feb.	1	6	7	9
Mar.		Full Marathon		
Apr.	11	11	7	9
May	8	---	7	---
June	15	---	7	---
July	17	---	7	---
Aug.	28	13	7	---
Sept.	18	13	7	14
Oct.	38	13	7	14
Nov.	43	13	7	8
Dec.	47	13	7	9

	R.A.	Dec.	NGC	Object Classification	Mag.	Constellation	Check Off	Time	
M42	5h 35.3m	− 5° 23'	1976	Nebula/Open Cluster	..5	Orion	_____	0:46	**M42**
M43	5h 35.5m	− 5° 16'	1982	Nebula	7	Orion	_____	0:51	**M43**
M78	5h 46.7m	+ 0° 04'	2068	Nebula, Reflection	8	Orion	_____	0:56	**M78**

Galaxy

**Open
Cluster**

**Globular
Cluster**

**Planetary
Nebula**

**Diffuse
Nebula**

**One Power
Finder Chart
Circle = 4°**

The Year-Round Messier Marathon Field Guide

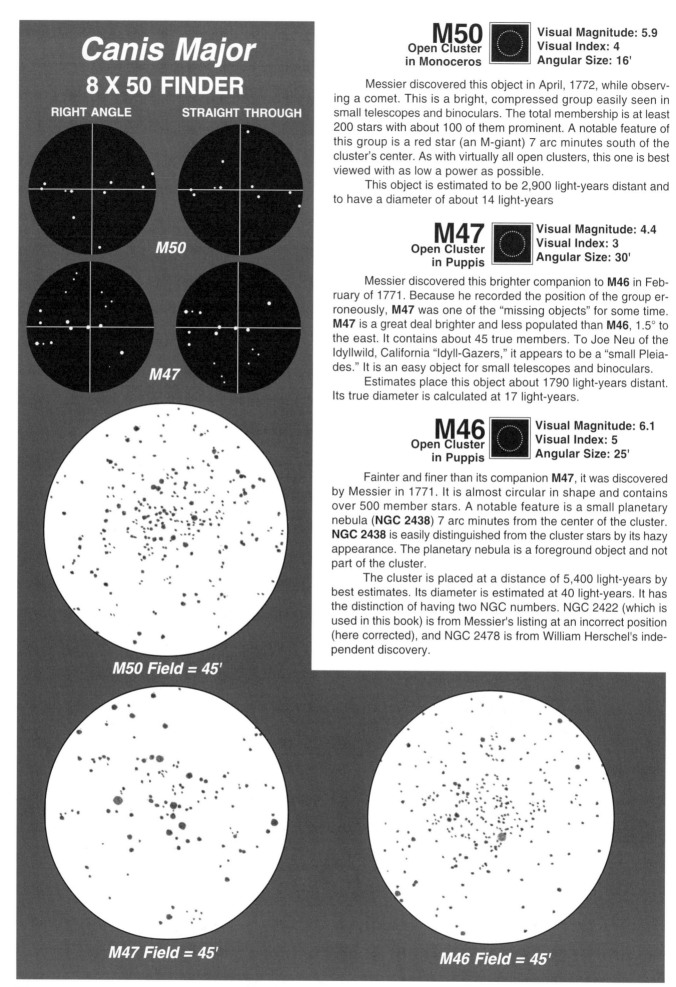

Canis Major
8 X 50 FINDER

RIGHT ANGLE   STRAIGHT THROUGH

M50

M47

M50 Field = 45'

M47 Field = 45'

M46 Field = 45'

M50
Open Cluster in Monoceros

Visual Magnitude: 5.9
Visual Index: 4
Angular Size: 16'

Messier discovered this object in April, 1772, while observing a comet. This is a bright, compressed group easily seen in small telescopes and binoculars. The total membership is at least 200 stars with about 100 of them prominent. A notable feature of this group is a red star (an M-giant) 7 arc minutes south of the cluster's center. As with virtually all open clusters, this one is best viewed with as low a power as possible.

This object is estimated to be 2,900 light-years distant and to have a diameter of about 14 light-years

M47
Open Cluster in Puppis

Visual Magnitude: 4.4
Visual Index: 3
Angular Size: 30'

Messier discovered this brighter companion to **M46** in February of 1771. Because he recorded the position of the group erroneously, **M47** was one of the "missing objects" for some time. **M47** is a great deal brighter and less populated than **M46**, 1.5° to the east. It contains about 45 true members. To Joe Neu of the Idyllwild, California "Idyll-Gazers," it appears to be a "small Pleiades." It is an easy object for small telescopes and binoculars.

Estimates place this object about 1790 light-years distant. Its true diameter is calculated at 17 light-years.

M46
Open Cluster in Puppis

Visual Magnitude: 6.1
Visual Index: 5
Angular Size: 25'

Fainter and finer than its companion **M47**, it was discovered by Messier in 1771. It is almost circular in shape and contains over 500 member stars. A notable feature is a small planetary nebula (**NGC 2438**) 7 arc minutes from the center of the cluster. **NGC 2438** is easily distinguished from the cluster stars by its hazy appearance. The planetary nebula is a foreground object and not part of the cluster.

The cluster is placed at a distance of 5,400 light-years by best estimates. Its diameter is estimated at 40 light-years. It has the distinction of having two NGC numbers. NGC 2422 (which is used in this book) is from Messier's listing at an incorrect position (here corrected), and NGC 2478 is from William Herschel's independent discovery.

The Year-Round Messier Marathon Field Guide

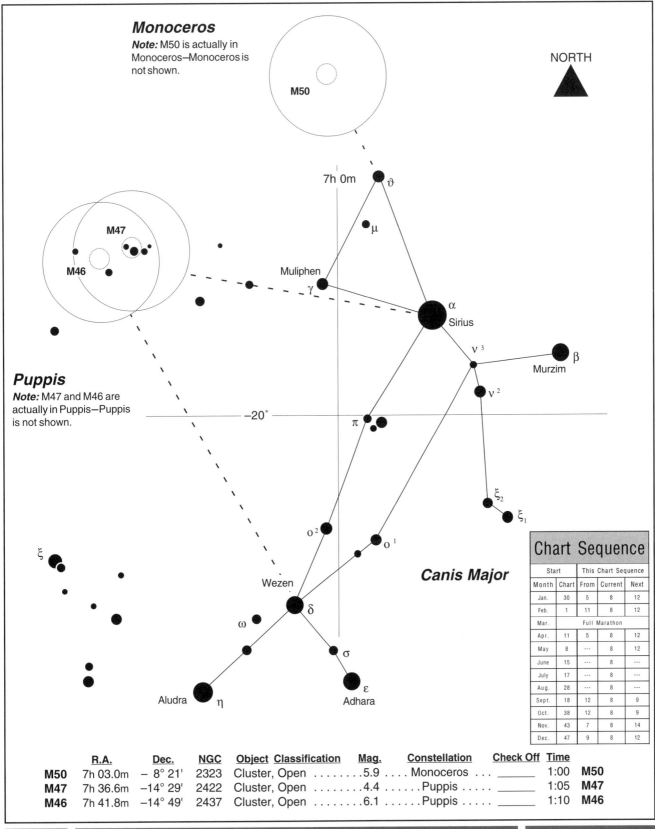

Monoceros
Note: M50 is actually in Monoceros—Monoceros is not shown.

M50

NORTH

7h 0m

ϑ

μ

Muliphen
γ

α
Sirius

ν³

β
Murzim

M47

M46

Puppis
Note: M47 and M46 are actually in Puppis—Puppis is not shown.

−20°

π

ν²

ξ₂

ξ₁

o²

o¹

Canis Major

ξ

Wezen

ω

δ

σ

Aludra   η

ε
Adhara

Chart Sequence				
Start		This Chart Sequence		
Month	Chart	From	Current	Next
Jan.	30	5	8	12
Feb.	1	11	8	12
Mar.	Full Marathon			
Apr.	11	5	8	12
May	8	---	8	12
June	15	---	8	---
July	17	---	8	---
Aug.	28	---	8	---
Sept.	18	12	8	9
Oct.	38	12	8	9
Nov.	43	7	8	14
Dec.	47	9	8	12

	R.A.	Dec.	NGC	Object Classification	Mag.	Constellation	Check Off	Time	
M50	7h 03.0m	− 8° 21'	2323	Cluster, Open	5.9	Monoceros	_____	1:00	**M50**
M47	7h 36.6m	−14° 29'	2422	Cluster, Open	4.4	Puppis	_____	1:05	**M47**
M46	7h 41.8m	−14° 49'	2437	Cluster, Open	6.1	Puppis	_____	1:10	**M46**

Galaxy

Open Cluster

Globular Cluster

Planetary Nebula

Diffuse Nebula

One Power Finder Chart
Circle = 4°

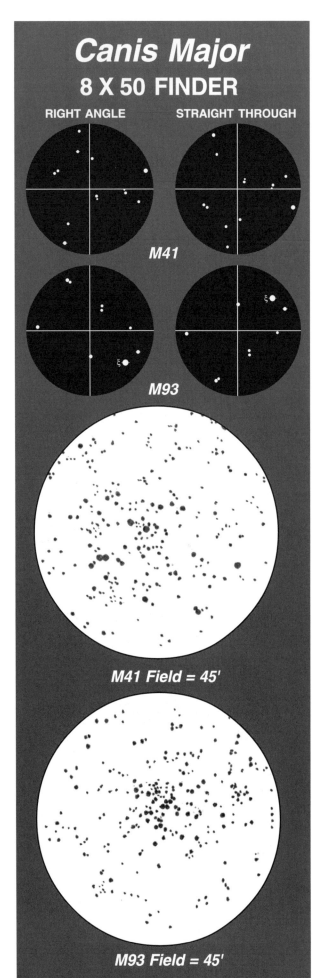

Canis Major
8 X 50 FINDER

RIGHT ANGLE **STRAIGHT THROUGH**

M41

M93

M41 Field = 45'

M93 Field = 45'

M41
Open Cluster
in Canis Major

Visual Magnitude: 4.5
Visual Index: 4
Angular Size: 38'

Visible to the naked eye under moderately good seeing conditions and easily visible in small telescopes and binoculars, this object has about 100 member stars from 7th to 13th magnitudes. Messier discovered this cluster in January of 1765. It is a naked-eye object under moderate seeing conditions and about the same diameter as the moon.

M41 is about 2,350 light-years distant. It has an estimated diameter of about 24 light-years.

M93
Open Cluster
in Puppis

Visual Magnitude: 6.2
Visual Index: 4
Angular Size: 22'

Messier added this group to his catalog in March of 1781. It is smaller and brighter than **M46**, but not as bright as **M47**. This group is distinctly fan or wedge-shaped. The group has over 60 true members. My impression is that it appears to be a more populous, scattered, brighter and enlarged version of **M103** in Cassiopeia. It is an easy object for small telescopes and binoculars. Under moderately good transparency, this is a naked-eye object.

Estimates place it at a distance of 3,400 light-years. Its diameter is estimated to be about 22 light-years.

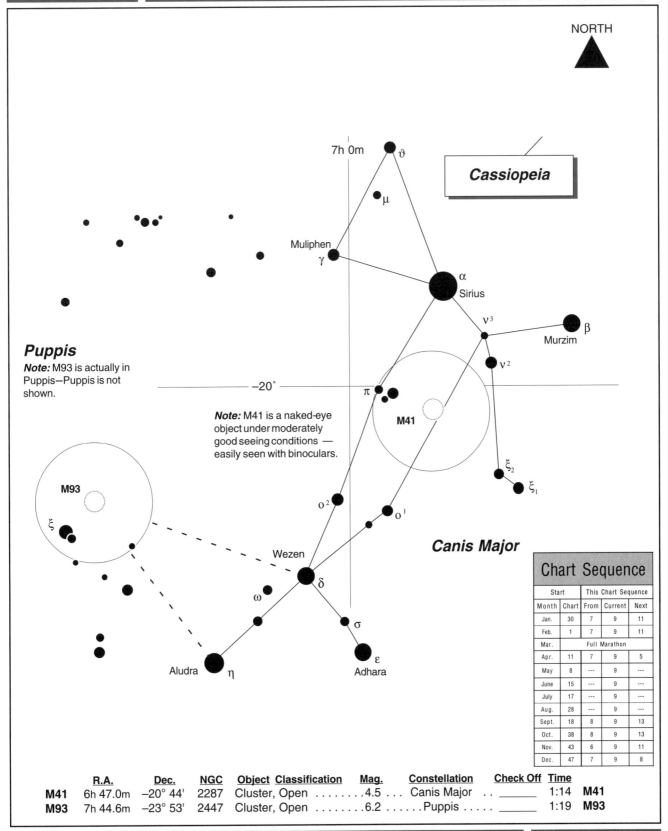

NORTH

7h 0m

Cassiopeia

ϑ

μ

Muliphen
γ

α
Sirius

ν³

β
Murzim

ν²

Puppis

Note: M93 is actually in
Puppis—Puppis is not
shown.

−20°

π

M41

Note: M41 is a naked-eye
object under moderately
good seeing conditions —
easily seen with binoculars.

ξ₂

ξ₁

M93

ξ

o²

o¹

Canis Major

Wezen

ω

δ

σ

ε
Adhara

Aludra
η

Chart Sequence

Start		This Chart Sequence		
Month	Chart	From	Current	Next
Jan.	30	7	9	11
Feb.	1	7	9	11
Mar.		Full Marathon			
Apr.	11	7	9	5
May	8	---	9	---
June	15	---	9	---
July	17	---	9	---
Aug.	28	---	9	---
Sept.	18	8	9	13
Oct.	38	8	9	13
Nov.	43	6	9	11
Dec.	47	7	9	8

	R.A.	Dec.	NGC	Object Classification	Mag.	Constellation	Check Off	Time	
M41	6h 47.0m	−20° 44'	2287	Cluster, Open	4.5	. . . Canis Major	. . _____	1:14	M41
M93	7h 44.6m	−23° 53'	2447	Cluster, Open	6.2	. . . . . . Puppis	. . . . . _____	1:19	M93

Galaxy

Open Cluster

Globular Cluster

Planetary Nebula

Diffuse Nebula

One Power Finder Chart

Circle = 4°

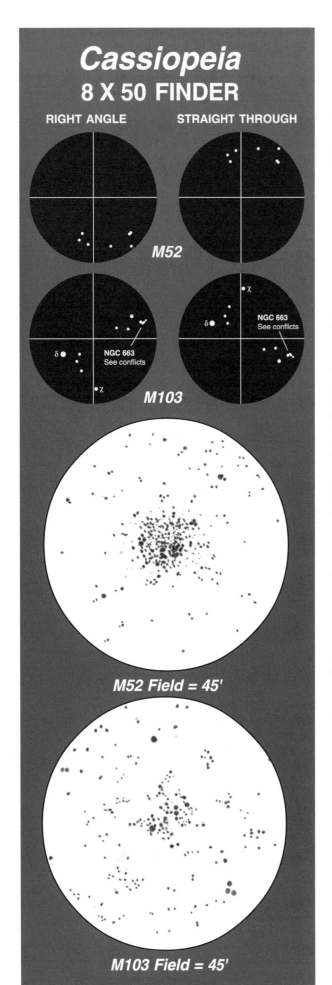

Cassiopeia
8 X 50 FINDER

RIGHT ANGLE   **STRAIGHT THROUGH**

M52

δ ●   NGC 663
See conflicts

● χ   δ ●   NGC 663
See conflicts

M103

M52 Field = 45'

M103 Field = 45'

 M52
Open Cluster
in Cassiopeia

Visual Magnitude: 6.9
Visual Index: 5
Angular Size: 12'

Messier discovered this object on September 7, 1774. It is larger and brighter than **M103**. **M52** also has a definite fan shape, although coarser and not as well defined as the fan shape exhibited by **M103** or **NGC 663** (see **M103** and *Conflicts* below). It is also a richer group and shows well in an 8 X 50 finder scope, an easy object for small telescopes and binoculars.

Its distance is estimated at 3,900 light-years with a diameter in the range of 10 to 15 light-years.

 M103
Open Cluster
in Cassiopeia

Visual Magnitude: 7.0
Visual Index: 5
Angular Size: 6'

Recorded by Méchain in 1781 and later confirmed by Messier, **M103** is one of the less notable of the open clusters in Messier's catalog. It has a definite fan shape, as does two other objects in Cassiopeia — **M52** and **NGC 663**. In the case of **M103**, the nearby NGC object presents a small problem — it shows well in a finder scope while **M103** does not. It is a common mistake for beginners to aim the scope in the general area of **M103**, look in the finder, spot the obvious cluster (**NGC 663**) and then make the small alignment adjustments which put the wrong object in the eyepiece. **M103** does not show in the finder — it is next to three small stars (see **8 X 50 FINDER**, left, and *Conflicts*, below). This object shows well in a small telescope once located. It is not a good object for binoculars, but can be discerned against the Milky Way background as a hazy patch.

This is the last object in Messier's original catalog of 103 objects. Numbers 104 through 110 have been added in recent years on the basis that Messier did observe them and probably would have included them had another supplement been published.

M103 is estimated to have a couple hundred true members. Estimates of its distance are somewhat over 9,000 light-years with a true diameter of about 15 light-years.

 Conflict: A conflict exists as the nearby **NGC 663** has a fan appearance similar to **M103**. **NGC 663** also shows well in the finder scope while **M103** does not show at all. Instead, **M103** appears to be three small stars. (See **8 X 50 FINDER**, left.) **NGC 663** is mistaken for **M103** more often than not. The appearance of the two clusters is similar, but with major differences. **M103** is more compact, smaller and has a more regular outline to its fan shape. Both objects are shown in the 8x50 Finder View in the adjacent panel.

The Year-Round Messier Marathon Field Guide

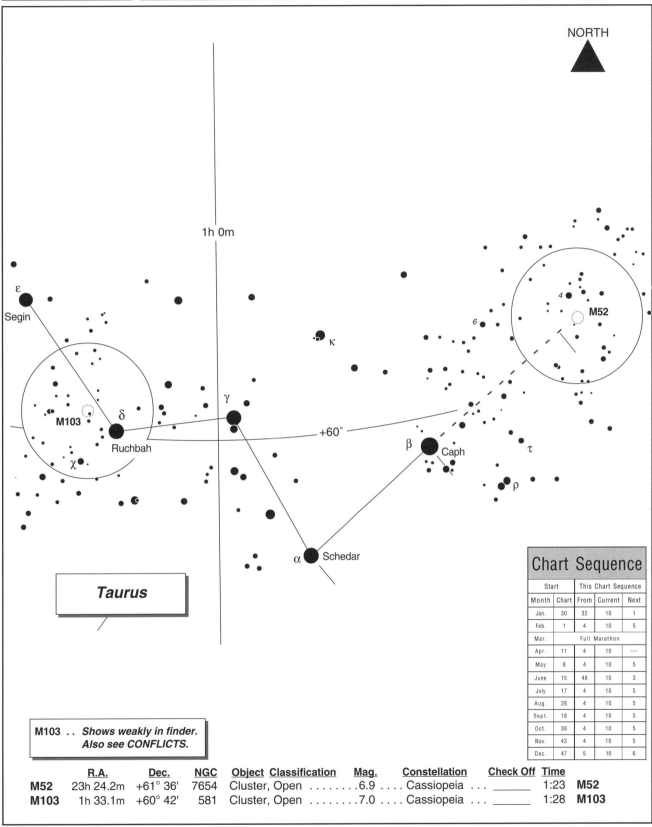

NORTH

1h 0m

ε
Segin

κ

M103

δ
Ruchbah

χ

γ

+60°

β
Caph

τ

ρ

α Schedar

4 M52

6

Taurus

Chart Sequence

Start		This Chart Sequence		
Month	Chart	From	Current	Next
Jan.	30	32	10	1
Feb.	1	4	10	5
Mar.		Full Marathon		
Apr.	11	4	10	---
May	8	4	10	5
June	15	48	10	3
July	17	4	10	5
Aug.	28	4	10	5
Sept.	18	4	10	5
Oct.	38	4	10	5
Nov.	43	4	10	5
Dec.	47	5	10	6

M103 .. *Shows weakly in finder.
Also see CONFLICTS.*

	R.A.	Dec.	NGC	Object Classification	Mag.	Constellation	Check Off	Time	
M52	23h 24.2m	+61° 36'	7654	Cluster, Open	6.9	.... Cassiopeia ...	_____	1:23	**M52**
M103	1h 33.1m	+60° 42'	581	Cluster, Open	7.0	.... Cassiopeia ...	_____	1:28	**M103**

Galaxy	Open Cluster	Globular Cluster	Planetary Nebula	Diffuse Nebula

**One Power
Finder Chart
Circle = 4°**

Taurus

8 X 50 FINDER

RIGHT ANGLE **STRAIGHT THROUGH**

M1

M1 Field = 20'

M45 Field = 120'

The Year-Round Messier Marathon Field Guide

M1
The Crab Nebula

Visual Magnitude: 8.0
Visual Index: 3
Angular Size: 6' X 4'

Famous from striking photographs depicting tenuous tendrils against a background of nebulosity, the Crab Nebula is not quite so striking a sight in the telescope. The tendrils are "photographic" details not seen in a telescope, although the main body of the nebula can be observed clearly. In smaller telescopes it is an easy object with an irregular oval outline. Some detail is notable in instruments 10 inches or larger. In very large telescopes, a great deal of the filamentary structure detail can be seen.

The Crab was formed in July, 1054, when its progenitor, a star, blasted away most of its mass in a supernova explosion. The event was recorded at several places around the globe, but there are no known European references to the explosion. It is still rapidly expanding at the rate of over 600 miles per second — almost 50 million miles per day! Although created by an event similar, but much more violent than that which creates a planetary nebula, the Crab does not have a typical planetary nebula's form. It is classed instead as a supernova remnant.

This is the first object of the Messier Catalog. About the famous list Messier wrote, "What caused me to undertake the catalog was the nebula I discovered above the southern horn of Taurus on September 12, 1758, while observing the comet of that year... This nebula had such a resemblance to a comet, in its form and brightness, that I endeavored to find others, so that astronomers would not confuse these same nebulae with comets just beginning to shine. I observed further with the proper refractors for the search of comets, and this is the purpose I had in forming the catalog. ..."

The irony is that he is remembered for this list and not for any of the 21 comets he claimed to have discovered in his lifetime. Owen Gingerich notes that "...modern astronomers with their more discriminating standards of what constitutes a discovery would reduce this number to perhaps fifteen" which is still a prodigious number of discoveries.

Estimates put **M1** about 6,300 light-years distant, over 7 light-years in diameter, and growing fast.

M45
The Pleiades

Visual Magnitude: 1.2
Visual Index: 1
Angular Size: 100'

Messier's reason for cataloging this object in March of 1769, along with **M42**, **M43** and **M44,** had to be to bring his list to a round number of 45 objects as these three are naked eye objects, well known since antiquity. The major members of this cluster can be seen in a slight haze of nebulosity in larger telescopes. They will appear like distant street lights in a very slight, almost invisible, ground fog. Photographs reveal broad brush-stroke-like swatches of nebulosity.

Estimates of the distance to **M45** place it at 380 light-years. The diameter of its bright central group is 7 light-years while some cluster members extend to 20 light-years.

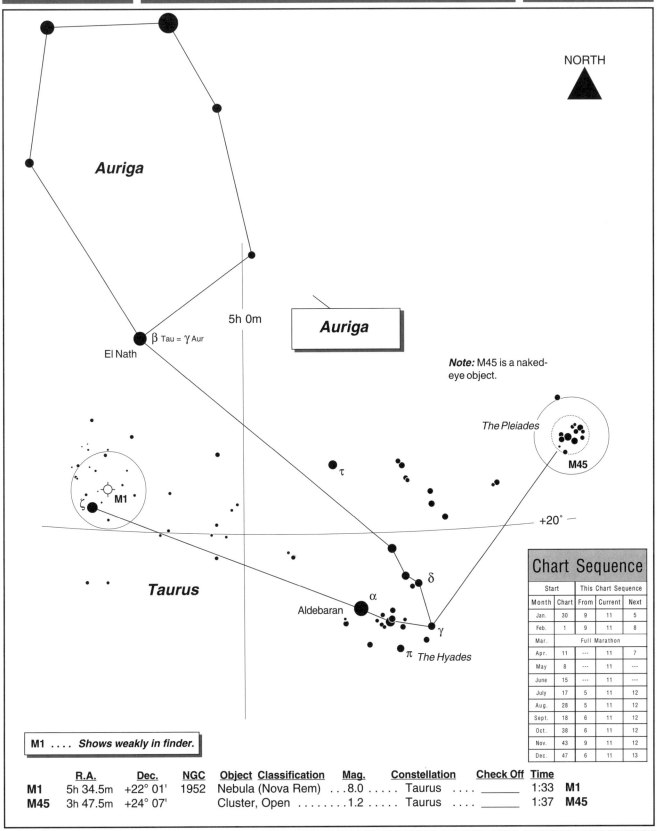

NORTH

Auriga

5h 0m

Auriga

β Tau = γ Aur

El Nath

Note: M45 is a naked-eye object.

The Pleiades

M45

● τ

ζ   ○ **M1**

+20°

Taurus

● α
Aldebaran

δ

γ

π *The Hyades*

Chart Sequence

Start		This Chart Sequence		
Month	Chart	From	Current	Next
Jan.	30	9	11	5
Feb.	1	9	11	8
Mar.		Full Marathon		
Apr.	11	---	11	7
May	8	---	11	---
June	15	---	11	---
July	17	5	11	12
Aug.	28	5	11	12
Sept.	18	6	11	12
Oct.	38	6	11	12
Nov.	43	9	11	12
Dec.	47	6	11	13

M1 .... *Shows weakly in finder.*

	R.A.	Dec.	NGC	Object Classification	Mag.	Constellation	Check Off	Time	
M1	5h 34.5m	+22° 01'	1952	Nebula (Nova Rem)	...8.0	Taurus	_____	1:33	**M1**
M45	3h 47.5m	+24° 07'		Cluster, Open	...1.2	Taurus	_____	1:37	**M45**

Galaxy

Open Cluster

Globular Cluster

Planetary Nebula

Diffuse Nebula

One Power Finder Chart
Circle = 4°

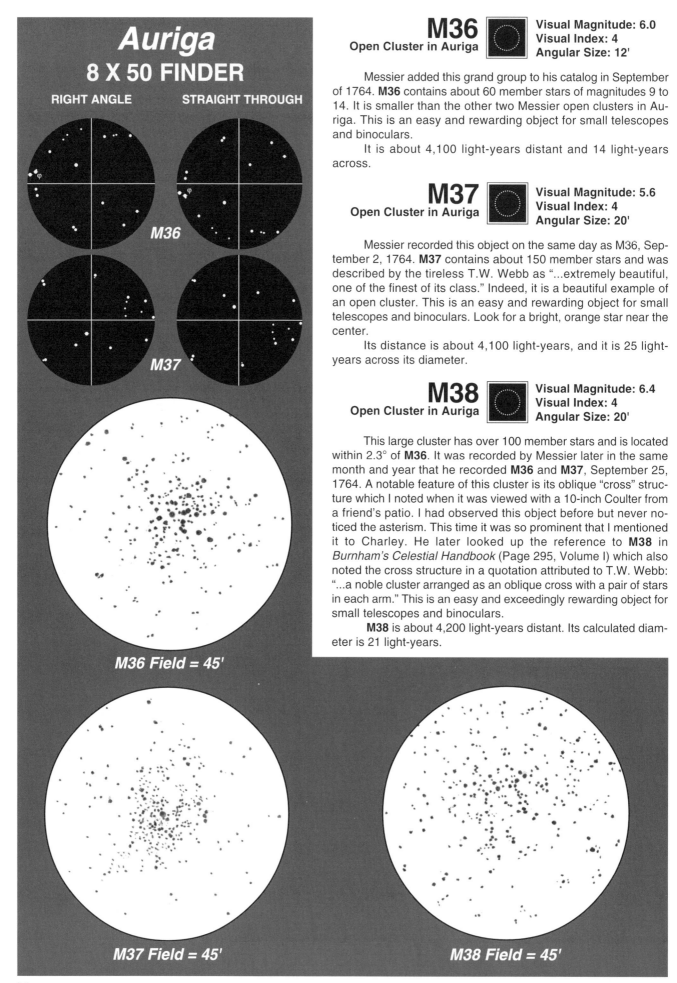

Auriga
8 X 50 FINDER

RIGHT ANGLE   **STRAIGHT THROUGH**

M36

M37

M36 Field = 45'

M37 Field = 45'

M36
Open Cluster in Auriga

Visual Magnitude: 6.0
Visual Index: 4
Angular Size: 12'

Messier added this grand group to his catalog in September of 1764. **M36** contains about 60 member stars of magnitudes 9 to 14. It is smaller than the other two Messier open clusters in Auriga. This is an easy and rewarding object for small telescopes and binoculars.

It is about 4,100 light-years distant and 14 light-years across.

M37
Open Cluster in Auriga

Visual Magnitude: 5.6
Visual Index: 4
Angular Size: 20'

Messier recorded this object on the same day as M36, September 2, 1764. **M37** contains about 150 member stars and was described by the tireless T.W. Webb as "...extremely beautiful, one of the finest of its class." Indeed, it is a beautiful example of an open cluster. This is an easy and rewarding object for small telescopes and binoculars. Look for a bright, orange star near the center.

Its distance is about 4,100 light-years, and it is 25 light-years across its diameter.

M38
Open Cluster in Auriga

Visual Magnitude: 6.4
Visual Index: 4
Angular Size: 20'

This large cluster has over 100 member stars and is located within 2.3° of **M36**. It was recorded by Messier later in the same month and year that he recorded **M36** and **M37**, September 25, 1764. A notable feature of this cluster is its oblique "cross" structure which I noted when it was viewed with a 10-inch Coulter from a friend's patio. I had observed this object before but never noticed the asterism. This time it was so prominent that I mentioned it to Charley. He later looked up the reference to **M38** in *Burnham's Celestial Handbook* (Page 295, Volume I) which also noted the cross structure in a quotation attributed to T.W. Webb: "...a noble cluster arranged as an oblique cross with a pair of stars in each arm." This is an easy and exceedingly rewarding object for small telescopes and binoculars.

M38 is about 4,200 light-years distant. Its calculated diameter is 21 light-years.

M38 Field = 45'

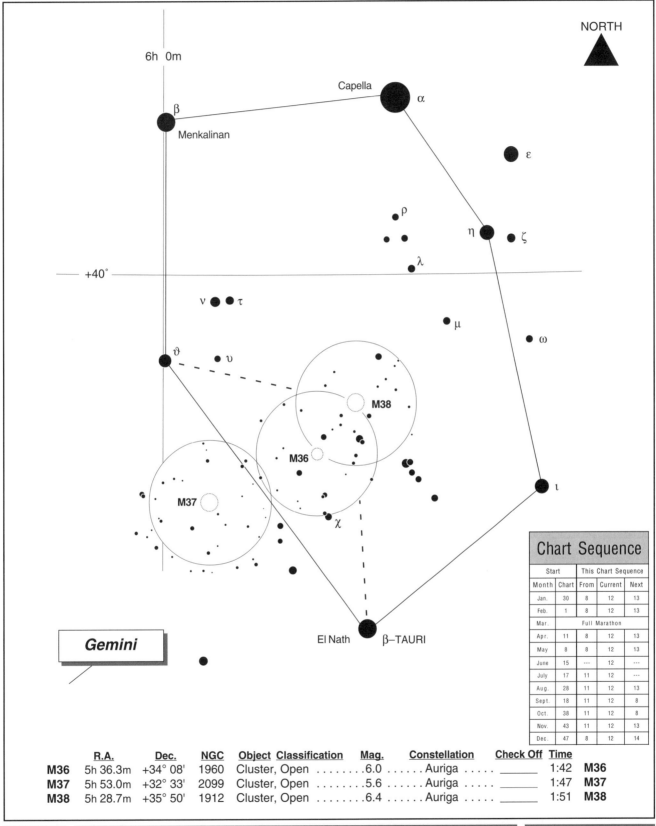

NORTH

6h 0m

Capella

α

β

Menkalinan

ε

ρ

η

ζ

λ

+40°

ν τ

μ

ω

ϑ

υ

M38

M36

ι

M37

χ

Chart Sequence

Start		This Chart Sequence		
Month	Chart	From	Current	Next
Jan.	30	8	12	13
Feb.	1	8	12	13
Mar.	Full Marathon			
Apr.	11	8	12	13
May	8	8	12	13
June	15	---	12	---
July	17	11	12	---
Aug.	28	11	12	13
Sept.	18	11	12	8
Oct.	38	11	12	8
Nov.	43	11	12	13
Dec.	47	8	12	14

Gemini

El Nath   β–TAURI

	R.A.	Dec.	NGC	Object Classification	Mag.	Constellation	Check Off	Time	
M36	5h 36.3m	+34° 08'	1960	Cluster, Open	6.0	..... Auriga	_____	1:42	**M36**
M37	5h 53.0m	+32° 33'	2099	Cluster, Open	5.6	..... Auriga	_____	1:47	**M37**
M38	5h 28.7m	+35° 50'	1912	Cluster, Open	6.4	..... Auriga	_____	1:51	**M38**

Galaxy

Open Cluster

Globular Cluster

Planetary Nebula

Diffuse Nebula

One Power Finder Chart
Circle = 4°

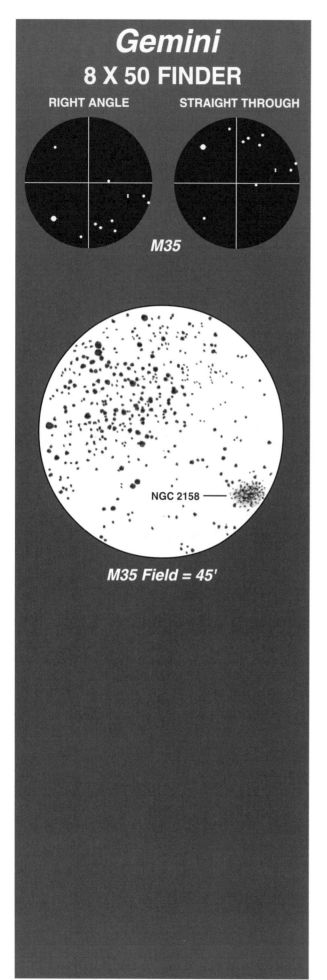

Gemini

8 X 50 FINDER

RIGHT ANGLE   **STRAIGHT THROUGH**

M35

M35 Field = 45'

NGC 2158

M35
Open Cluster in Gemini

Visual Magnitude: 5.1
Visual Index: 4
Angular Size: 30'

Another of Messier's discoveries of 1764, **M35** is easily visible in small telescopes and binoculars. It has about 120 member stars brighter than 13th magnitude. A wide angle view of **M35** with an aperture of 10 inches provides a most rewarding view. On very clear dark nights, **M35** can be detected with the naked eye. Just outside the Southwest edge of **M35** is the open cluster **NGC 2158** which looks like a faint patch of nebulosity in 6-inch telescopes and is about six times more distant than the big cluster. In large telescopes it is resolved with high power. Another notable feature of **M35**, and one much noted by many observers, is remarked upon by Burnham: "...the curving rows of bright stars which give an impression of rows of glittering lamps on a chain; fainter stars form a sparkling background with an orange star near the center."

Estimates place this object about 2,200 light-years distant and give it a true diameter estimated at 18 light-years.

The Year-Round Messier Marathon Field Guide

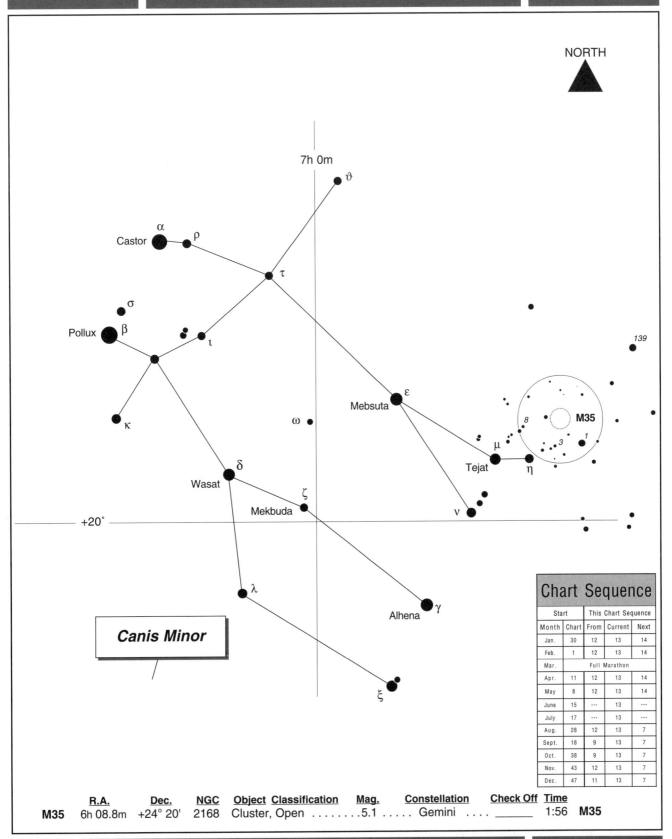

NORTH

7h 0m

α
Castor
ρ
τ
ϑ

σ

Pollux β
ι

κ

Mebsuta ε

139

8
M35
3
1

μ
Tejat
η

ω

δ
Wasat
ζ
Mekbuda
ν

+20°

λ

Alhena γ

Canis Minor

ξ

Chart Sequence

Start		This Chart Sequence		
Month	Chart	From	Current	Next
Jan.	30	12	13	14
Feb.	1	12	13	14
Mar.	Full Marathon			
Apr.	11	12	13	14
May	8	12	13	14
June	15	---	13	---
July	17	---	13	---
Aug.	28	12	13	7
Sept.	18	9	13	7
Oct.	38	9	13	7
Nov.	43	12	13	7
Dec.	47	11	13	7

	R.A.	Dec.	NGC	Object Classification	Mag.	Constellation	Check Off	Time	
M35	6h 08.8m	+24° 20'	2168	Cluster, Open 5.1		Gemini	_____	1:56	**M35**

  Galaxy Open Cluster Globular Cluster Planetary Nebula  Diffuse Nebula

One Power Finder Chart
Circle = 4°

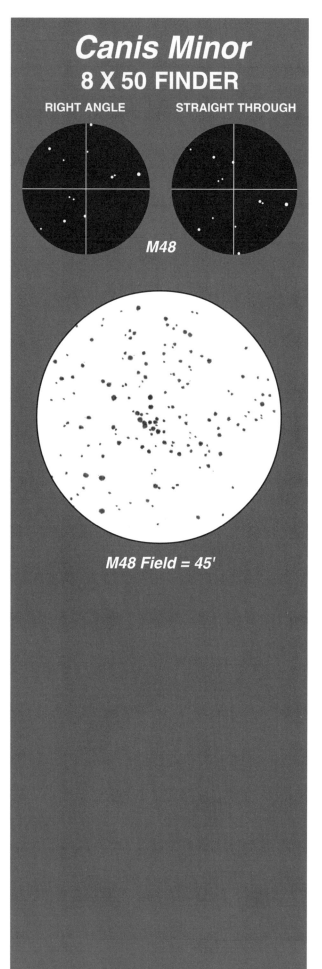

Canis Minor
8 X 50 FINDER

RIGHT ANGLE   **STRAIGHT THROUGH**

M48

M48 Field = 45'

M48
Open Cluster in Hydra

Visual Magnitude: 5.8
Visual Index: 3
Angular Size: 54'

Messier recorded this object on February 19, 1771. And that was the last anyone saw of it as a member of the Messier Catalog for almost 200 years. Messier's original recording of the object's position contained a 4° error in declination. His description of the object and the correction for the error leave no doubt as to **NGC 2548**'s legitimate claim to be included in the famous list as **M48**. This formerly "missing" Messier number is a large cluster that is an easy object for small telescopes and binoculars and is naked-eye from a dark site. It has about 50 member stars with magnitudes down to 13. A central chain of 10th and 11th magnitude stars dominate this magnificent open cluster.

Its distance is placed at 1,530 light-years, and its diameter has been determined to be about 20 light-years.

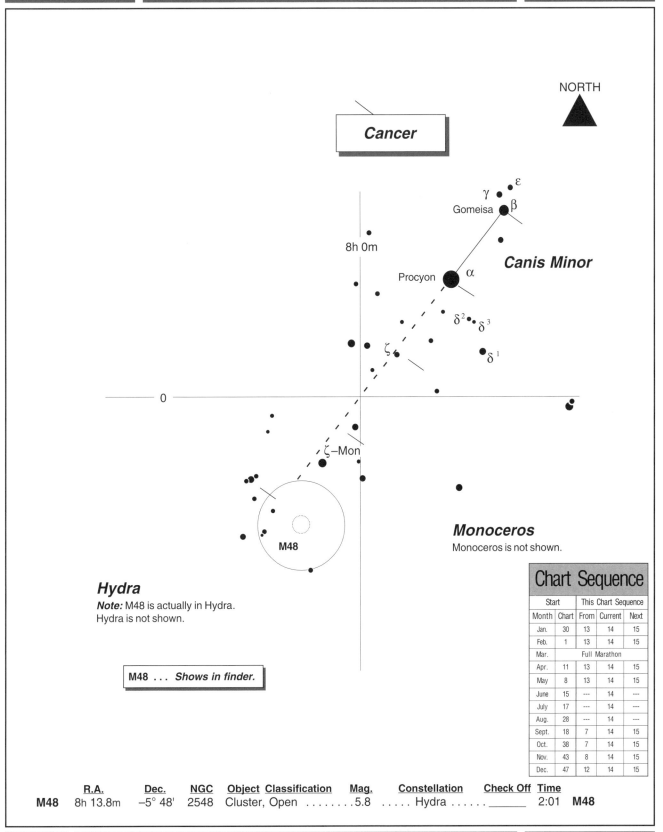

NORTH

Cancer

ε
γ
β
Gomeisa

Canis Minor

8h 0m

Procyon
α

δ² δ³

δ¹

0

ζ

ζ–Mon

Monoceros
Monoceros is not shown.

M48

Hydra
Note: M48 is actually in Hydra.
Hydra is not shown.

M48 . . . *Shows in finder.*

Chart Sequence			
Start		This Chart Sequence	
Month	Chart	From	Current	Next
Jan.	30	13	14	15
Feb.	1	13	14	15
Mar.	Full Marathon			
Apr.	11	13	14	15
May	8	13	14	15
June	15	---	14	---
July	17	---	14	---
Aug.	28	---	14	---
Sept.	18	7	14	15
Oct.	38	7	14	15
Nov.	43	8	14	15
Dec.	47	12	14	15

	R.A.	Dec.	NGC	Object Classification	Mag.	Constellation	Check Off	Time	
M48	8h 13.8m	–5° 48'	2548	Cluster, Open	5.8	. . . . . Hydra . . . . . . ____		2:01	M48

Galaxy

Open Cluster

Globular Cluster

Planetary Nebula

Diffuse Nebula

One Power Finder Chart
Circle = 4°

The Year-Round Messier Marathon Field Guide

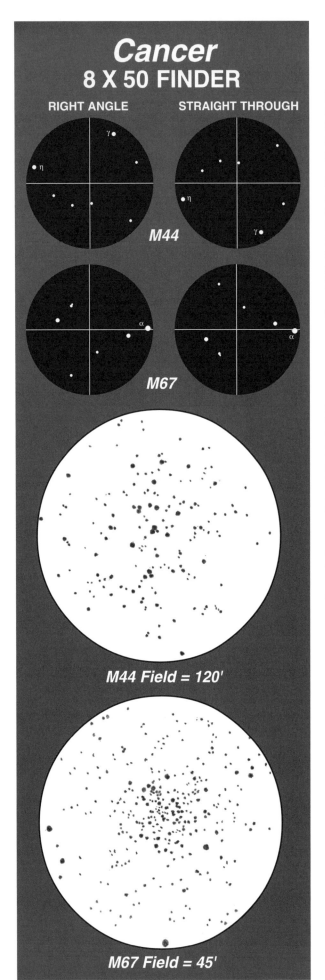

Cancer
8 X 50 FINDER

RIGHT ANGLE   STRAIGHT THROUGH

M44

M67

M44 Field = 120'

M67 Field = 45'

M44
Praesepe/The Beehive
Open Cluster

Visual Magnitude: 3.1
Visual Index: 3
Angular Size: 95'

Praesepe is a naked-eye object over 1° in apparent size. It is composed of over 350 member stars with magnitudes ranging as low as 17. About 200 stars, with magnitudes ranging from 6.3 to 14, are known to be physical members of the group. This is a most gratifying cluster for small telescopes and binoculars. Low powers on telescopes of all apertures are recommended.

Messier's reason for cataloging this object, along with **M42**, **M43** and **M45,** had to be to bring his list to a round number of 45 objects as these are naked eye objects known from antiquity. Indeed, Burnham documents the statements of Aratus and Pliny, two ancient astronomers. They stated that the invisibility of Praesepe in an otherwise clear sky is considered to forecast the approach of a violent storm. I have noticed that when the jet stream is overhead and **M44** is not plainly visible, planetary viewing is very bad, and deep sky viewing is not at all satisfactory.

Its distance is estimated to be 577 light-years, and its diameter about 15 light-years.

M67
Open Cluster in Cancer

Visual Magnitude: 6.9
Visual Index: 5
Angular Size: 15'

M67 is a fair sized — half the diameter of the moon — rich cluster with about 500 members with magnitudes ranging from 10 to 16. Messier added this object to the catalog on April 6, 1780. The group is peculiar in that it is one of the oldest galactic clusters known. It has some of the color-magnitude characteristics of a globular, but is obviously not that type of object. Coupled with that, the evolved stars of **M67** seem to have half the luminosity of similar stars in a globular cluster because of a difference in chemical composition. According to spectroscopic data, the population of **M67** is comparable in age and chemical composition to the sun. It is an easy object for small telescopes and binoculars, and is easily seen in a finder scope. With a very dark site this is a naked-eye object.

Its distance is estimated to be 2,500 light-years, and its diameter is estimated at 12 light-years.

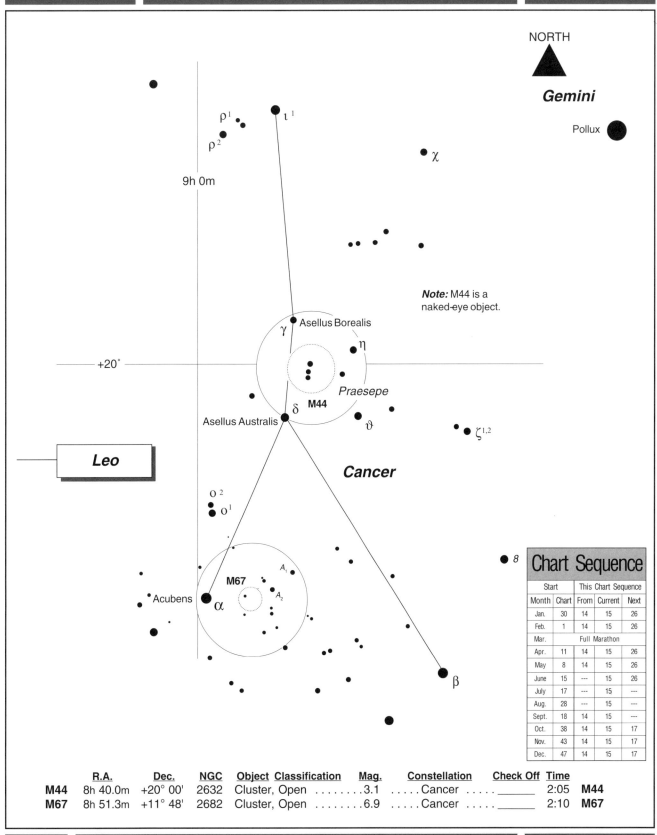

NORTH

Gemini

Pollux

ρ¹
ρ²

ι¹

9h 0m

χ

Note: M44 is a
naked-eye object.

γ Asellus Borealis

η

+20°

Praesepe

δ   **M44**

Asellus Australis

ϑ

ζ¹,²

Leo

Cancer

ο²
ο¹

8

o¹

M67

A₁

Acubens

A₂

α

β

	Start		This Chart Sequence	
Month	Chart	From	Current	Next
Jan.	30	14	15	26
Feb.	1	14	15	26
Mar.		Full Marathon		
Apr.	11	14	15	26
May	8	14	15	26
June	15	---	15	26
July	17	---	15	---
Aug.	28	---	15	---
Sept.	18	14	15	---
Oct.	38	14	15	17
Nov.	43	14	15	17
Dec.	47	14	15	17

Chart Sequence

	R.A.	Dec.	NGC	Object Classification	Mag.	Constellation	Check Off	Time	
M44	8h 40.0m	+20° 00'	2632	Cluster, Open 3.1		.....Cancer	_____	2:05	**M44**
M67	8h 51.3m	+11° 48'	2682	Cluster, Open 6.9		.....Cancer	_____	2:10	**M67**

 **Galaxy**
 Open Cluster
 Globular Cluster
 Planetary Nebula
 Diffuse Nebula

**One Power
Finder Chart**
Circle = 4°

The Year-Round Messier Marathon Field Guide

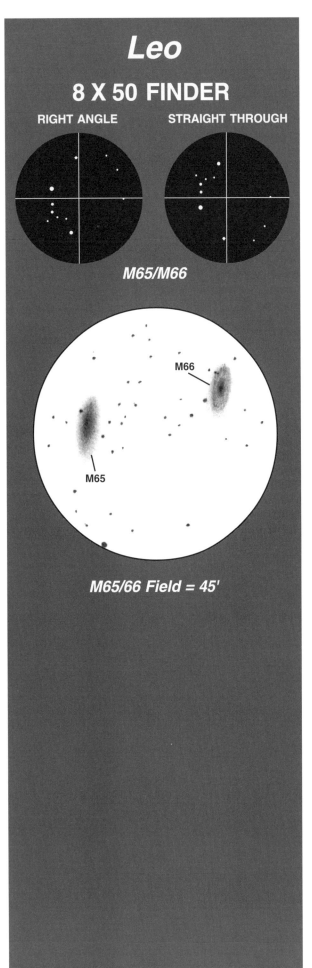

Leo

8 X 50 FINDER

RIGHT ANGLE   **STRAIGHT THROUGH**

M65/M66

M66

M65

M65/66 Field = 45'

M65
Spiral Galaxy in Leo

Visual Magnitude: 9.3
Visual Index: 4
Angular Size: 8' X 2'

This galaxy is one of a pair (**M65** and **M66**) which will come into view at the same time when using an eyepiece of 1° true field — less than half a degree separates **M65** and **M66**. Less than 1° north is **NGC 3628**. **M65** is easily seen in small telescopes and binoculars. **M65** was discovered by Méchain in March 1780. Also see **Conflicts**, below.

Its distance is given at about 29 million light-years. The diameter is calculated at 60,000 light-years.

M66
Spiral Galaxy in Leo

Visual Magnitude: 8.9
Visual Index: 4
Angular Size: 8' X 3'

Discovered at the same time as **M65** by Méchain (March 1780) and confirmed by Messier shortly thereafter, **M66** is brighter than **M65** and is an easy object for small telescopes and binoculars. Also see **Conflicts**, below.

The distance for **M66** is the same as that given for **M65**, about 29 million light-years. Its diameter is placed at 50,000 light-years.

Conflict: M65 and **M66** are easily seen within a 1°-eyepiece view. **M66** is rounder and brighter. **M65** has a definite spindle shape. About ½° north is **NGC 3628**, an edge-on spiral at magnitude 9.5. It could be mistaken for **M65** or **M66** by novice users of larger telescopes.

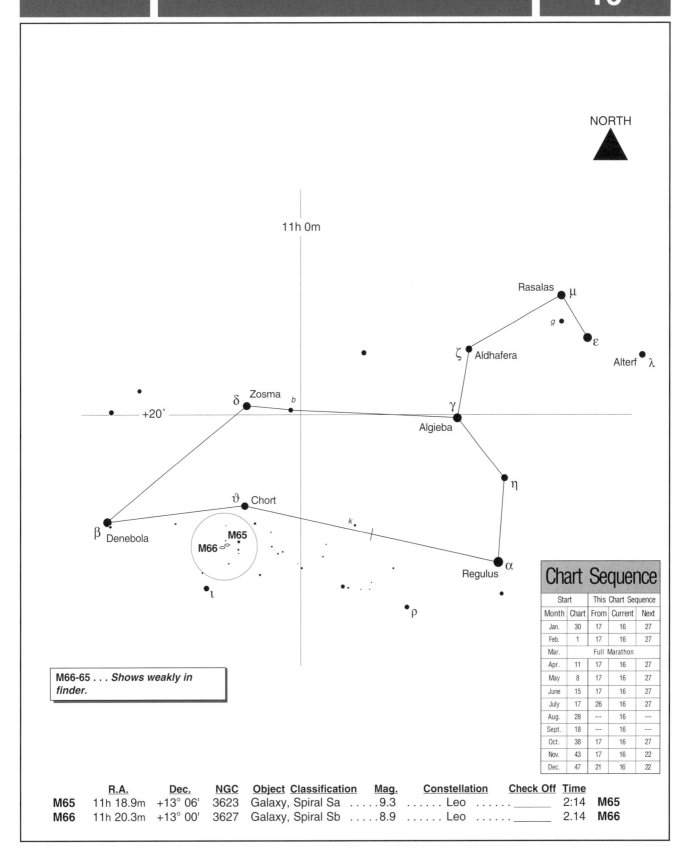

NORTH

11h 0m

Rasalas μ

g

ε

ζ Aldhafera

Alterf λ

δ Zosma *b*

+20°

γ

Algieba

η

ϑ Chort

k

β Denebola

M65

M66

ι

α

Regulus

ρ

M66-65 . . . *Shows weakly in finder.*

Chart Sequence				
Start		This Chart Sequence		
Month	Chart	From	Current	Next
Jan.	30	17	16	27
Feb.	1	17	16	27
Mar.	Full Marathon			
Apr.	11	17	16	27
May	8	17	16	27
June	15	17	16	27
July	17	26	16	27
Aug.	28	---	16	---
Sept.	18	---	16	---
Oct.	38	17	16	27
Nov.	43	17	16	22
Dec.	47	21	16	22

	R.A.	Dec.	NGC	Object Classification	Mag.	Constellation	Check Off	Time	
M65	11h 18.9m	+13° 06'	3623	Galaxy, Spiral Sa	9.3	Leo	_____	2:14	**M65**
M66	11h 20.3m	+13° 00'	3627	Galaxy, Spiral Sb	8.9	Leo	_____	2.14	**M66**

Galaxy **Open Cluster** **Globular Cluster** **Planetary Nebula** **Diffuse Nebula**

One Power Finder Chart

Circle = 4°

The Year-Round Messier Marathon Field Guide

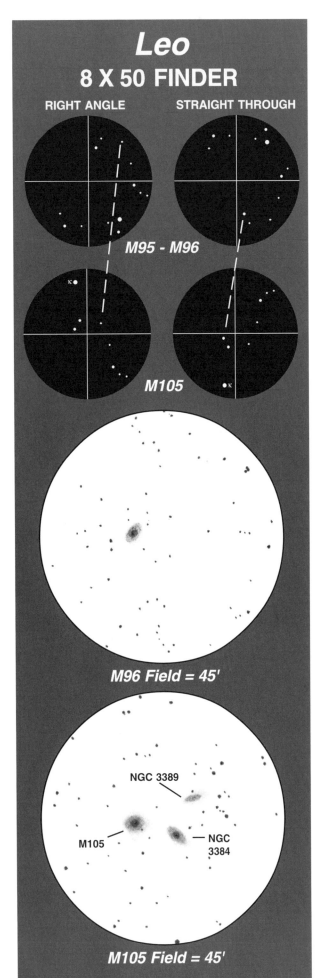

Leo
8 X 50 FINDER

RIGHT ANGLE   **STRAIGHT THROUGH**

M95 - M96

M105

M96 Field = 45'

NGC 3389

M105

NGC 3384

M105 Field = 45'

M95
Spiral Galaxy in Leo

Visual Magnitude: 9.7
Visual Index: 4
Angular Size: 8' X 5'

M96
Spiral Galaxy in Leo

Visual Magnitude: 9.2
Visual Index: 4
Angular Size: 6' X 4'

M96 was discovered by Méchain at the same time as **M95**, March, 1781. It has an elliptical appearance and is brighter than **M95**. Novice observers might confuse **M96** with **M95** — **M95** is fainter and elongated.

The distance to **M96** is similar to **M95**, 29 million light-years.

M105
Elliptical Galaxy in Leo

Visual Magnitude: 9.3
Visual Index: 4
Angular Size: 2' X 2'

One of Méchain's discoveries, this object was not in Messier's original list although he observed it sometime between 1785 and 1786. It is one of the smallest objects in the Messier Catalog. It is very nearly round, and there are two other smaller spindle shaped galaxies within the field of a 1° eyepiece (**NGC 3384** and **NGC 3389**). See *Conflicts*, below.

Its distance is about 29 million light years.

Conflicts: Two nearby galaxies can be seen in the same field as **M105**. However, **M105** is larger and brighter and has a circular shape.

    The Year-Round Messier Marathon Field Guide

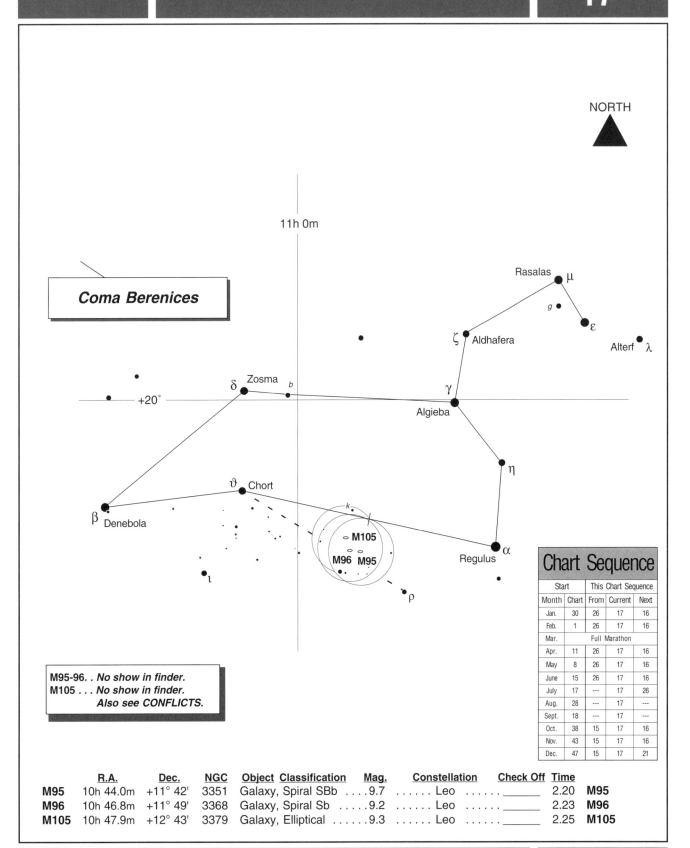

NORTH

11h 0m

Coma Berenices

Rasalas
μ
g
ε
ζ Aldhafera
Alterf λ

δ Zosma b
+20°
γ
Algieba

η

ϑ Chort

β Denebola

k
M105
M96 M95

α
Regulus

ι

ρ

M95-96. . No show in finder.
M105 . . . No show in finder.
          Also see CONFLICTS.

Chart Sequence

Start		This Chart Sequence		
Month	Chart	From	Current	Next
Jan.	30	26	17	16
Feb.	1	26	17	16
Mar.		Full Marathon		
Apr.	11	26	17	16
May	8	26	17	16
June	15	26	17	16
July	17	---	17	26
Aug.	28	---	17	---
Sept.	18	---	17	---
Oct.	38	15	17	16
Nov.	43	15	17	16
Dec.	47	15	17	21

	R.A.	Dec.	NGC	Object Classification	Mag.	Constellation	Check Off	Time	
M95	10h 44.0m	+11° 42'	3351	Galaxy, Spiral SBb	. . . .9.7	. . . . . . Leo	. . . . . . _____	2.20	M95
M96	10h 46.8m	+11° 49'	3368	Galaxy, Spiral Sb	. . . . .9.2	. . . . . . Leo	. . . . . . _____	2.23	M96
M105	10h 47.9m	+12° 43'	3379	Galaxy, Elliptical	. . . . . .9.3	. . . . . . Leo	. . . . . . _____	2.25	M105

 Galaxy

 Open Cluster

 Globular Cluster

 Planetary Nebula

 Diffuse Nebula

**One Power
Finder Chart**
Circle = 4°

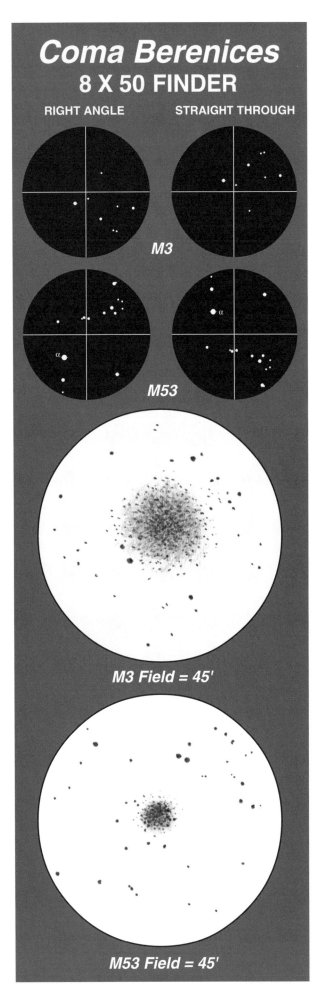

Coma Berenices
8 X 50 FINDER

RIGHT ANGLE   STRAIGHT THROUGH

M3

M53

M3 Field = 45'

M53 Field = 45'

 **M3**
Globular Cluster
in Canes Venatici

Visual Magnitude: 5.9
Visual Index: 3
Angular Size: 9.8'

M3 is one of the three brightest globular clusters in the northern sky; **M13** and **M5** are the other two. It contains many thousands of stars ranging in magnitude from 11 to the limit of detectability. **M3** is easily seen in small telescopes and binoculars.

M3 is estimated to be 35 to 40,000 light-years distant with a diameter of about 90 light-years.

M53
Globular Cluster
in Coma Berenices

Visual Magnitude: 7.5
Visual Index: 4
Angular Size: 10'

Messier added this cluster to the first supplement to the famous catalog in February of 1777. Bright and condensed, this globular is easily seen in small telescopes. Partial resolution is achieved in telescopes of 6 inches, and it is easily resolved in large telescopes. A nearby cluster can be misidentified as **M53** — see *Conflict* below.

The distance is estimated at about 65,000 light-years with a total luminosity of about 200,000 Suns.

Conflict: One degree southeast is the extremely loose globular cluster **NGC 5053**. It cannot be confused with **M53** if you remember that **M53** has a compact bright center that requires a large aperture telescope to resolve; i.e., if you can easily resolve the center of the cluster, you are on **NGC 5053**.

The Year-Round Messier Marathon Field Guide

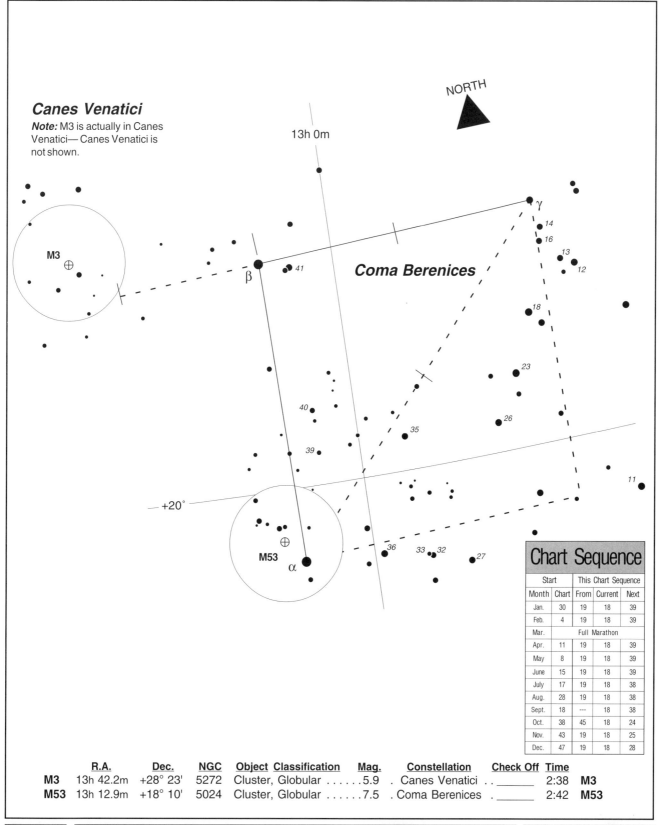

NORTH

Canes Venatici

Note: M3 is actually in Canes Venatici— Canes Venatici is not shown.

13h 0m

M3 ⊕

β

41

Coma Berenices

γ

14
16
13
12
18
23
26
35
40
39
36   33 32   27
11

+20°

M53 ⊕

α

Chart Sequence			
Start		This Chart Sequence	
Month	Chart	From	Current	Next
Jan.	30	19	18	39
Feb.	4	19	18	39
Mar.	Full Marathon			
Apr.	11	19	18	39
May	8	19	18	39
June	15	19	18	39
July	17	19	18	38
Aug.	28	19	18	38
Sept.	18	---	18	38
Oct.	38	45	18	24
Nov.	43	19	18	25
Dec.	47	19	18	28

	R.A.	Dec.	NGC	Object Classification	Mag.	Constellation	Check Off	Time	
M3	13h 42.2m	+28° 23'	5272	Cluster, Globular	5.9	. Canes Venatici . .	_____	2:38	**M3**
M53	13h 12.9m	+18° 10'	5024	Cluster, Globular	7.5	. Coma Berenices	_____	2:42	**M53**

Galaxy

Open Cluster

Globular Cluster

Planetary Nebula

Diffuse Nebula

One Power Finder Chart
Circle = 4°

The Year-Round Messier Marathon Field Guide

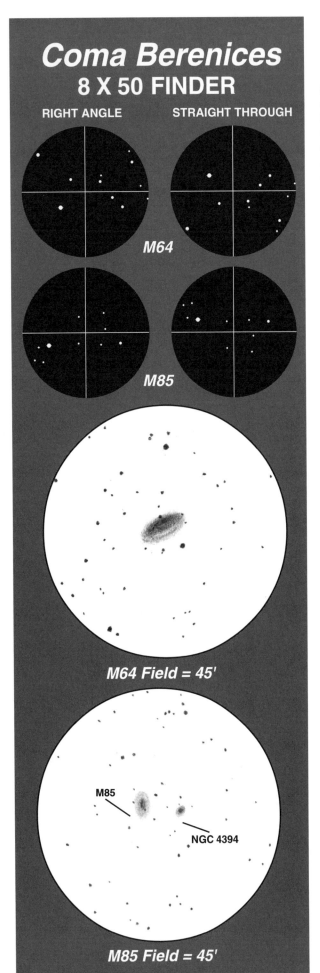

Coma Berenices
8 X 50 FINDER

RIGHT ANGLE   STRAIGHT THROUGH

M64

M85

M64 Field = 45'

M85

NGC 4394

M85 Field = 45'

M64
The Black-Eye Galaxy

Visual Magnitude: 8.5
Visual Index: 2
Angular Size: 8' X 4'

Messier found this large oval spiral in March of 1780. In the Shapley-Ames catalog it is rated as one of the twelve brightest spirals. It is a spectacular sight in telescopes of large aperture at high magnification. Its central feature is a dust lane along the north and east side of the central oval mass giving it its "black-eye" nickname. The dust lane can definitely be resolved in telescopes of 6 to 8 inches and may be glimpsed in instruments as small as 4 inches.

Its distance is estimated at 30 million light-years with a true diameter of 48,000 light-years. It blazes with an energy about 31 billion times that of the sun.

M85
Spiral Galaxy
in Coma Berenices

Visual Magnitude: 9.1
Visual Index: 4
Angular Size: 8' X 6'

Although actually located within the borders of the constellation Coma Berenices, this galaxy is a member of the Virgo cluster of galaxies. Many Messier Marathon charts and lists group this object with those in the Virgo sequence. However, I have found that this galaxy is much easier to locate and identify by using Coma Berenices as the "finder constellation" and locating it independently from those in the Virgo group (see **Marathon Chart 28-a** for the Virgo Galaxy Cluster.) This object was discovered by Messier's associate Méchain in 1781 and described by Messier later in the same year. It is a well-defined oval.

Its distance is estimated at about 44 million light-years. Estimates of the diameter put it at about 40,000 light-years with a total mass of 100 billion suns.

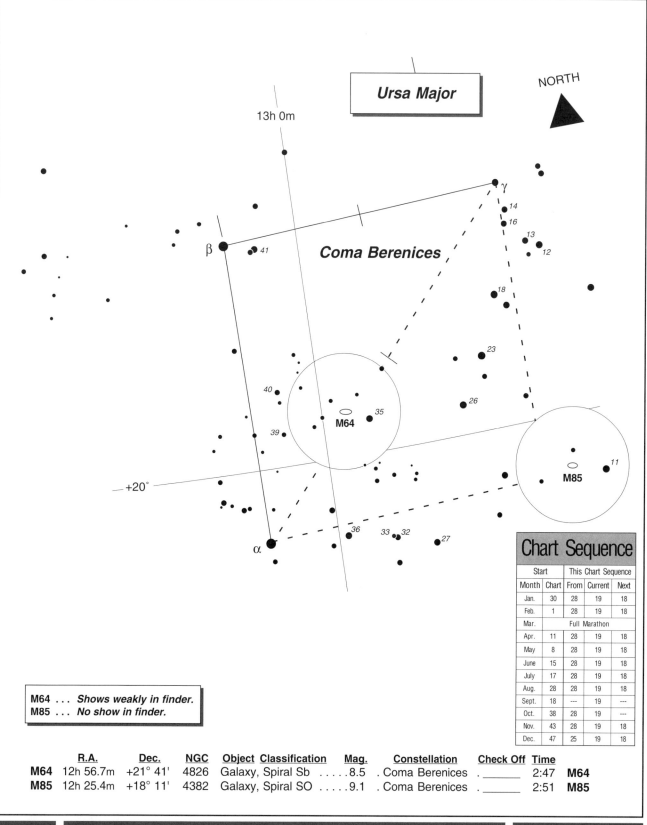

Ursa Major

NORTH

13h 0m

γ

14

16

13

12

18

β

41

Coma Berenices

23

40

26

M64

35

39

M85

11

+20°

36

33

32

27

α

M64 ... *Shows weakly in finder.*
M85 ... *No show in finder.*

Chart Sequence

Start		This Chart Sequence		
Month	Chart	From	Current	Next
Jan.	30	28	19	18
Feb.	1	28	19	18
Mar.	Full Marathon			
Apr.	11	28	19	18
May	8	28	19	18
June	15	28	19	18
July	17	28	19	18
Aug.	28	28	19	18
Sept.	18	---	19	---
Oct.	38	28	19	---
Nov.	43	28	19	18
Dec.	47	25	19	18

	R.A.	Dec.	NGC	Object Classification	Mag.	Constellation	Check Off	Time	
M64	12h 56.7m	+21° 41'	4826	Galaxy, Spiral Sb 8.5	. Coma Berenices	. _____	2:47	**M64**
M85	12h 25.4m	+18° 11'	4382	Galaxy, Spiral SO 9.1	. Coma Berenices	. _____	2:51	**M85**

Galaxy | Open Cluster | Globular Cluster | Planetary Nebula | Diffuse Nebula

One Power Finder Chart
Circle = 4°

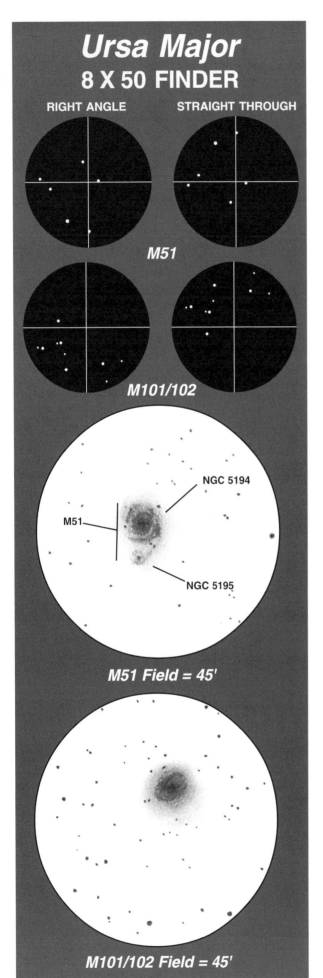

Ursa Major
8 X 50 FINDER

RIGHT ANGLE   **STRAIGHT THROUGH**

M51

M101/102

NGC 5194

M51

NGC 5195

M51 Field = 45'

M101/102 Field = 45'

M51
Double Galaxy
Whirlpool Galaxy

Visual Magnitude: 8.4
Visual Index: 3
Angular Size: 10' X 5'

The famous Whirlpool galaxy was discovered by Messier in October of 1773. It is most remarkable for its companion galaxy (**NGC 5195**), which appears to be attached to one of the spiral arms. This galaxy is easily seen in small telescopes and binoculars.

Its distance is estimated to be 35 million light-years. Estimates of its diameter range up to 100,000 light-years.

M101/M102
Spiral Galaxy
in Ursa Major

Visual Magnitude: 7.9
Visual Index: 4
Angular Size: 22' X 20'

M101 is a face-on "pinwheel" type galaxy. Larger telescopes can detect a hint of the spiral structure. The most notable aspect of this object is not its appearance but its double Messier number designation of **M101/102**.

Although the mystery was resolved by Méchain, his correction was overlooked until 1947! **M102** was a duplicate observation of **M101** — only a mistake! It has recently been proposed that the designation **M102** be assigned to **NGC 5866**, a galaxy in Draco (see **M102** Alternate, **Marathon Chart 24**).

M101 is placed at a distance of close to 35 million light-years. It is about 90,000 light-years in diameter and has a calculated mass of about 16 billion suns.

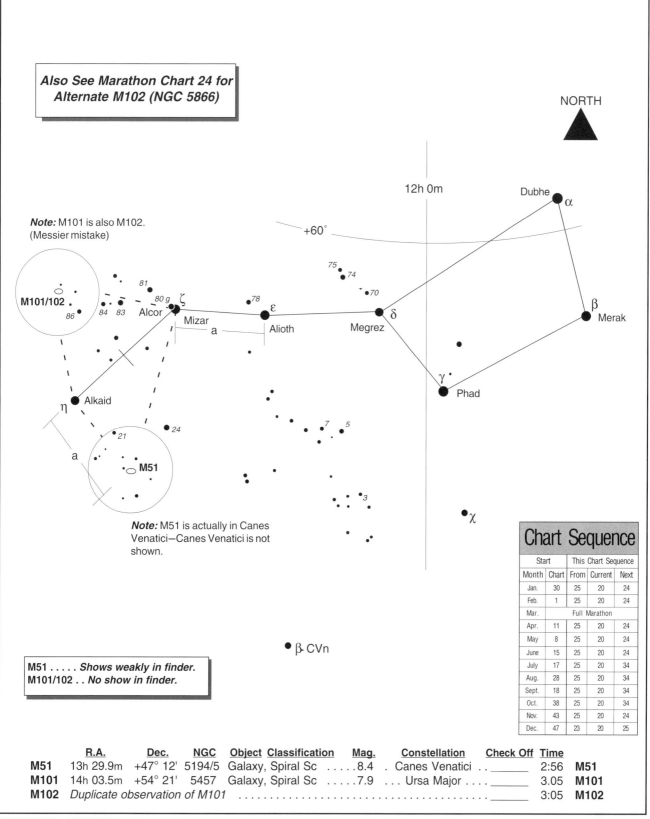

Also See Marathon Chart 24 for Alternate M102 (NGC 5866)

NORTH

12h 0m

+60°

Note: M101 is also M102. (Messier mistake)

Dubhe — α

75 74
      70

M101/102

81
80 g ζ
84 83 Alcor
86

78 ε

δ
Megrez

β
Merak

Mizar
a Alioth

γ
Phad

Alkaid

η

21 24

a

M51

7 5

χ

Note: M51 is actually in Canes Venatici—Canes Venatici is not shown.

3

β-CVn

M51 . . . . . *Shows weakly in finder.*
M101/102 . . *No show in finder.*

Chart Sequence

Start		This Chart Sequence		
Month	Chart	From	Current	Next
Jan.	30	25	20	24
Feb.	1	25	20	24
Mar.		Full Marathon		
Apr.	11	25	20	24
May	8	25	20	24
June	15	25	20	24
July	17	25	20	34
Aug.	28	25	20	34
Sept.	18	25	20	34
Oct.	38	25	20	34
Nov.	43	25	20	24
Dec.	47	23	20	25

	R.A.	Dec.	NGC	Object Classification	Mag.	Constellation	Check Off	Time	
M51	13h 29.9m	+47° 12'	5194/5	Galaxy, Spiral Sc	. . . . .8.4	. Canes Venatici . .	_____	2:56	M51
M101	14h 03.5m	+54° 21'	5457	Galaxy, Spiral Sc	. . . . .7.9	. . . Ursa Major	_____	3.05	M101
M102	*Duplicate observation of M101*			. . . .			_____	3:05	M102

Galaxy | Open Cluster | Globular Cluster | Planetary Nebula | Diffuse Nebula

One Power Finder Chart
Circle = 4°

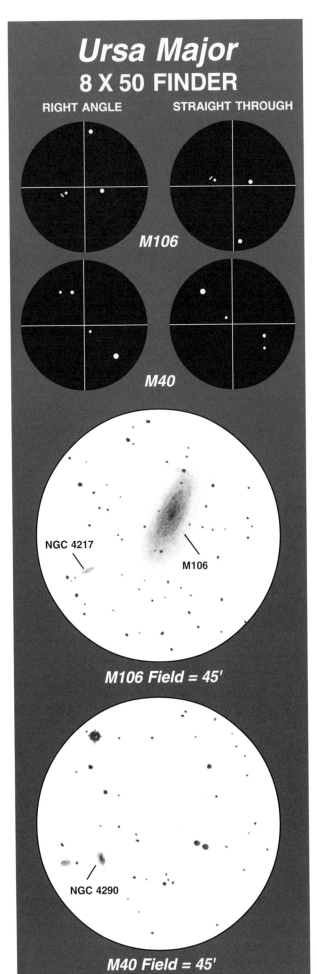

Ursa Major
8 X 50 FINDER

RIGHT ANGLE   STRAIGHT THROUGH

M106

M40

NGC 4217

M106

M106 Field = 45'

NGC 4290

M40 Field = 45'

 M106
Spiral Galaxy
in Canes Venatici

Visual Magnitude: 8.4
Visual Index: 4
Angular Size: 20' X 7'

This is another of Méchain's discoveries which was not found in time to be included in the last supplement to Messier's catalog. If the old "Ferret of Comets" had lived long enough, the numbers from 104 to 109 might have been included. It is a large spindle galaxy that is easily seen in small telescopes and binoculars. See *Conflict* below.

Its distance is given at 25 million light-years and it has a mass of about 100 billion suns.

 Conflict: There are a number of smaller galaxies within 1° of **M106**. The only one likely to cause an identification problem is **NGC 4217** — a fairly dim (magnitude 11.2) spindle-shaped galaxy less than 1° west and slightly south of **M106**. **M106** has a distinct oval shape and is considerably larger than **NGC 4217**.

When aligning the finder scope for **M106**, a slight position error will put you on **NGC 4217**. If this happens, a slight move to the east — about "one-half an eyepiece view" — will put you on **M106**.

M40
Double Star

Visual Magnitude: 9.0/9.3
Visual Index: None Listed
Angular Size: 50" Separation

M40 is a double star. Messier's listing of this object concluded his cataloging of objects for 1764. Earlier astronomers had reported a *nebulosity* at the location, and Messier was looking for, "...the nebula which is above the back of the Great Bear. ..." He was *not* looking for comets, but seeking to round-out his unpublished list with the 40th object. What is more instructive is his comment; "It is presumed that Hevelius mistook these two stars for a nebula. ..." This removes all doubt that Messier saw anything other than two faint stars. The nearby galaxy, **NGC 4290**, is magnitude 12.7 and will not be visible in smaller telescopes.

The Year-Round Messier Marathon Field Guide

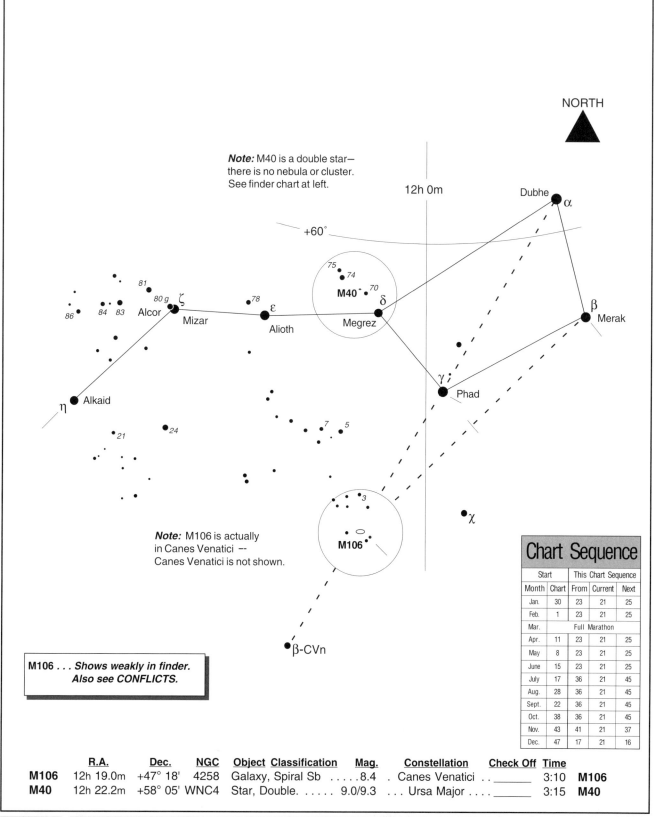

NORTH

Note: M40 is a double star— there is no nebula or cluster. See finder chart at left.

12h 0m

+60°

Dubhe • α

75
74
M40 • 70
δ

81
80 g ζ
Alcor
86 84 83
Mizar

78
ε
Alioth

Megrez

β Merak

γ Phad

η Alkaid

21 • 24 •

7 5

3

• χ

Note: M106 is actually in Canes Venatici -- Canes Venatici is not shown.

M106

M106 . . . Shows weakly in finder. Also see CONFLICTS.

• β-CVn

Chart Sequence			
Start		This Chart Sequence	
Month	Chart	From	Current	Next
Jan.	30	23	21	25
Feb.	1	23	21	25
Mar.	Full Marathon			
Apr.	11	23	21	25
May	8	23	21	25
June	15	23	21	25
July	17	36	21	45
Aug.	28	36	21	45
Sept.	22	36	21	45
Oct.	38	36	21	45
Nov.	43	41	21	37
Dec.	47	17	21	16

	R.A.	Dec.	NGC	Object Classification	Mag.	Constellation	Check Off	Time	
M106	12h 19.0m	+47° 18'	4258	Galaxy, Spiral Sb 8.4	.	Canes Venatici . . _____		3:10	M106
M40	12h 22.2m	+58° 05'	WNC4	Star, Double. 9.0/9.3	. . .	Ursa Major . . . . _____		3:15	M40

 Galaxy
 Open Cluster
 Globular Cluster
 Planetary Nebula
 Diffuse Nebula

One Power Finder Chart Circle = 4°

The Year-Round Messier Marathon Field Guide
117

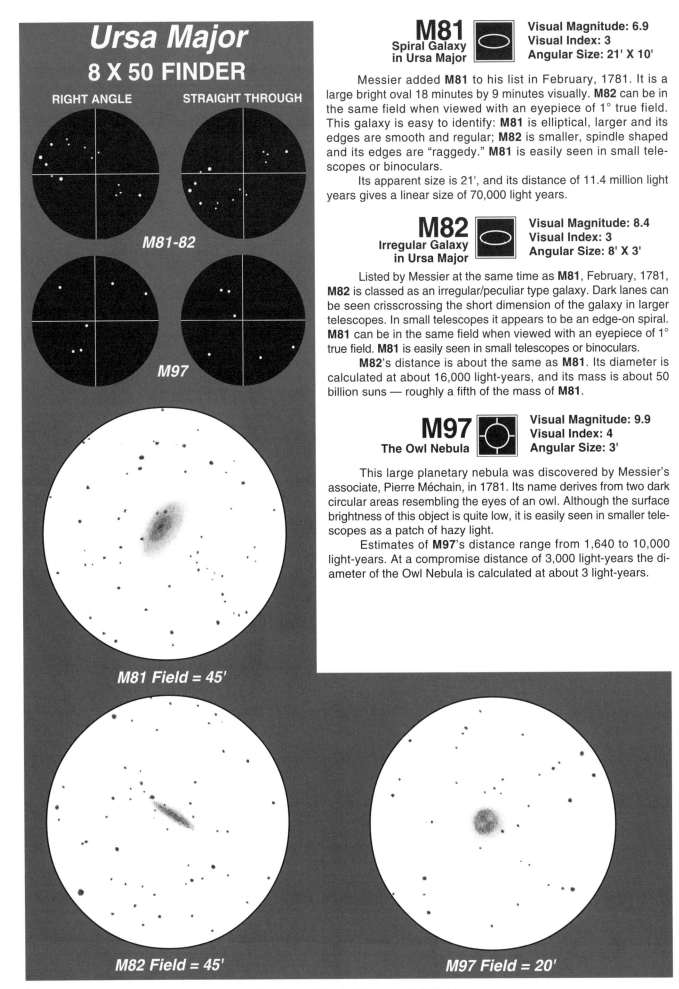

Ursa Major
8 X 50 FINDER

RIGHT ANGLE   STRAIGHT THROUGH

M81-82

M97

M81 Field = 45'

M82 Field = 45'

M97 Field = 20'

M81
Spiral Galaxy in Ursa Major

Visual Magnitude: 6.9
Visual Index: 3
Angular Size: 21' X 10'

Messier added **M81** to his list in February, 1781. It is a large bright oval 18 minutes by 9 minutes visually. **M82** can be in the same field when viewed with an eyepiece of 1° true field. This galaxy is easy to identify: **M81** is elliptical, larger and its edges are smooth and regular; **M82** is smaller, spindle shaped and its edges are "raggedy." **M81** is easily seen in small telescopes or binoculars.

Its apparent size is 21', and its distance of 11.4 million light years gives a linear size of 70,000 light years.

M82
Irregular Galaxy in Ursa Major

Visual Magnitude: 8.4
Visual Index: 3
Angular Size: 8' X 3'

Listed by Messier at the same time as **M81**, February, 1781, **M82** is classed as an irregular/peculiar type galaxy. Dark lanes can be seen crisscrossing the short dimension of the galaxy in larger telescopes. In small telescopes it appears to be an edge-on spiral. **M81** can be in the same field when viewed with an eyepiece of 1° true field. **M81** is easily seen in small telescopes or binoculars.

M82's distance is about the same as **M81**. Its diameter is calculated at about 16,000 light-years, and its mass is about 50 billion suns — roughly a fifth of the mass of **M81**.

M97
The Owl Nebula

Visual Magnitude: 9.9
Visual Index: 4
Angular Size: 3'

This large planetary nebula was discovered by Messier's associate, Pierre Méchain, in 1781. Its name derives from two dark circular areas resembling the eyes of an owl. Although the surface brightness of this object is quite low, it is easily seen in smaller telescopes as a patch of hazy light.

Estimates of **M97**'s distance range from 1,640 to 10,000 light-years. At a compromise distance of 3,000 light-years the diameter of the Owl Nebula is calculated at about 3 light-years.

The Year-Round Messier Marathon Field Guide

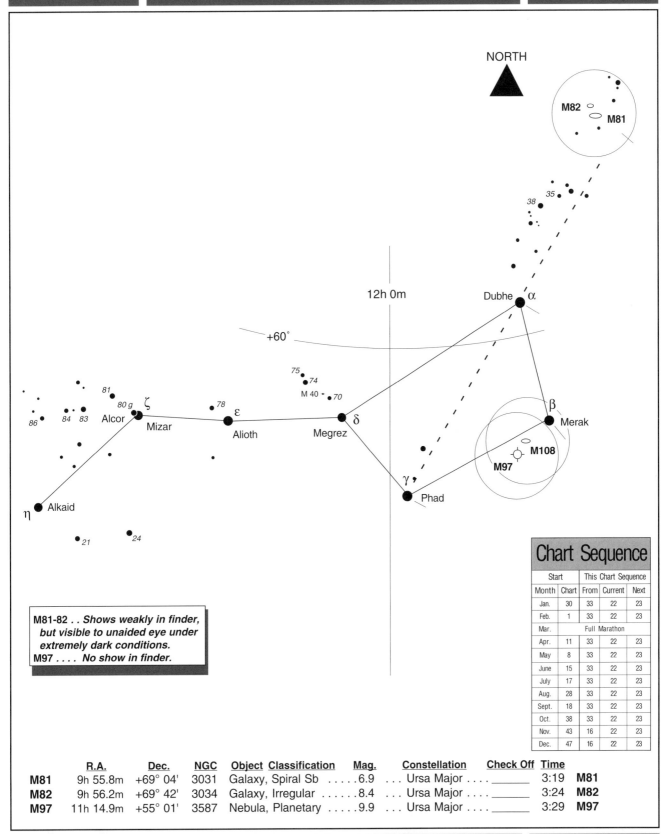

NORTH

M82 M81

38 35

12h 0m

Dubhe α

+60°

75
74
M 40 70

81
80 g ζ
86 84 83 Alcor
Mizar
78 ε
Alioth
δ
Megrez

β
Merak

M108
M97

γ
Phad

η Alkaid

21 24

M81-82 . . Shows weakly in finder,
but visible to unaided eye under
extremely dark conditions.
M97 . . . . No show in finder.

Chart Sequence

	Start		This Chart Sequence	
Month	Chart	From	Current	Next
Jan.	30	33	22	23
Feb.	1	33	22	23
Mar.		Full Marathon		
Apr.	11	33	22	23
May	8	33	22	23
June	15	33	22	23
July	17	33	22	23
Aug.	28	33	22	23
Sept.	18	33	22	23
Oct.	38	33	22	23
Nov.	43	16	22	23
Dec.	47	16	22	23

	R.A.	Dec.	NGC	Object Classification	Mag.	Constellation	Check Off	Time	
M81	9h 55.8m	+69° 04'	3031	Galaxy, Spiral Sb 6.9		. . . Ursa Major . . . . _____		3:19	M81
M82	9h 56.2m	+69° 42'	3034	Galaxy, Irregular 8.4		. . . Ursa Major . . . . _____		3:24	M82
M97	11h 14.9m	+55° 01'	3587	Nebula, Planetary 9.9		. . . Ursa Major . . . . _____		3:29	M97

 Galaxy
 Open Cluster
 Globular Cluster
 Planetary Nebula
 Diffuse Nebula

One Power
Finder Chart
Circle = 4°

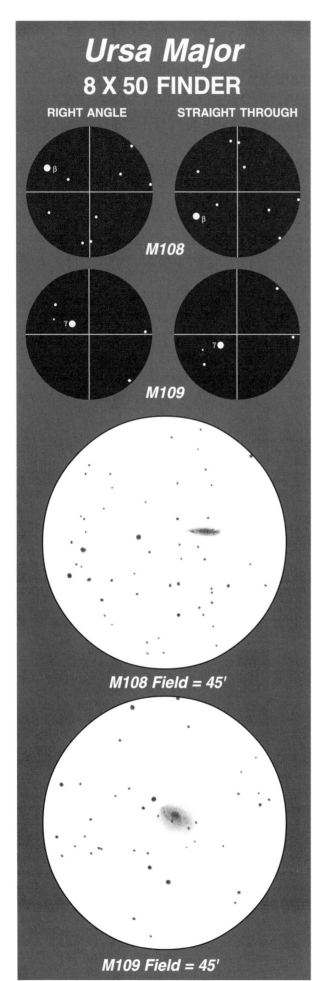

Ursa Major
8 X 50 FINDER

RIGHT ANGLE **STRAIGHT THROUGH**

M108

M109

M108 Field = 45'

M109 Field = 45'

M108
Spiral Galaxy in Ursa Major

Visual Magnitude: 10.0
Visual Index: 5
Angular Size: 8' X 1'

M108 is yet another of the objects added to the Messier Catalog in recent years. This galaxy is seen nearly edge-on. It is fairly bright and will appear somewhat "spotty" or mottled in larger telescopes. In smaller telescopes it will appear as a small "cut" of light with a brighter middle section. There is no central bulge.

Its distance is about 35 million light-years, and it has a mass of about 14 billion suns.

M109
Spiral Galaxy in Ursa Major

Visual Magnitude: 9.8
Visual Index: 5
Angular Size: 6' X 4'

The final discovery of Pierre Méchain, **M109** was added to the Messier list by Owen Gingerich in 1953. Its oval appearance is unmistakable. It is very close to γ-Ursae Majoris — Phad — the southernmost star in the bottom of the Dipper's pan. When using an eyepiece with a 1° field, it is best to move the star out of the viewing field as the glare will overpower the relatively dim galaxy. Only the brighter central portion of the galaxy will be discernible in smaller telescopes.

Its distance is about 38 million light years.

The Year-Round Messier Marathon Field Guide

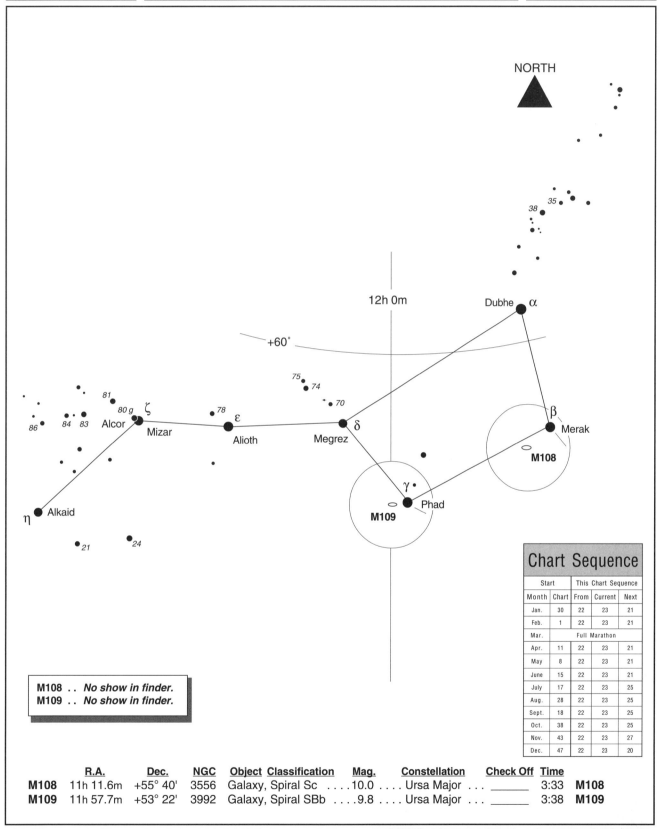

NORTH

12h 0m

+60°

Dubhe • α

75 • 74 • 70

81 • 80 g • ζ
86 • 84 • 83 • Alcor • Mizar • 78 • ε • Alioth • δ • Megrez

η • Alkaid

21 • 24 •

β • Merak
M108

γ • Phad
M109

| M108 . . **No show in finder.** |
| M109 . . **No show in finder.** |

Chart Sequence

Start		This Chart Sequence		
Month	Chart	From	Current	Next
Jan.	30	22	23	21
Feb.	1	22	23	21
Mar.		Full Marathon		
Apr.	11	22	23	21
May	8	22	23	21
June	15	22	23	21
July	17	22	23	25
Aug.	28	22	23	25
Sept.	18	22	23	25
Oct.	38	22	23	25
Nov.	43	22	23	27
Dec.	47	22	23	20

	R.A.	Dec.	NGC	Object Classification	Mag.	Constellation	Check Off	Time	
M108	11h 11.6m	+55° 40'	3556	Galaxy, Spiral Sc	10.0	Ursa Major	_____	3:33	M108
M109	11h 57.7m	+53° 22'	3992	Galaxy, Spiral SBb	9.8	Ursa Major	_____	3:38	M109

Galaxy   Open Cluster   Globular Cluster   Planetary Nebula   Diffuse Nebula

One Finder Chart
Circle = 4°

Ursa Major

8 X 50 FINDER

RIGHT ANGLE   STRAIGHT THROUGH

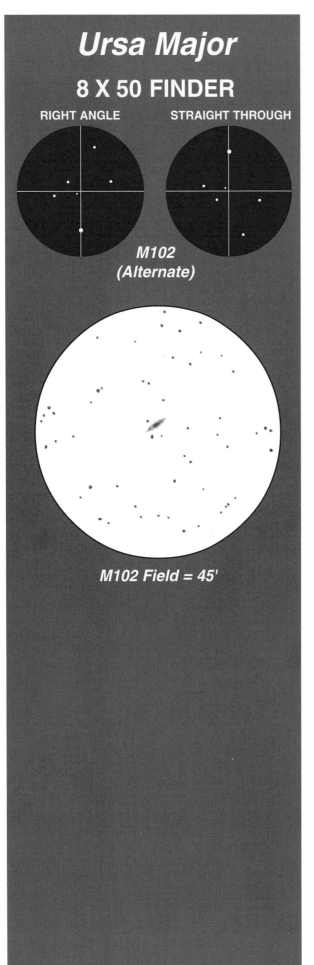

M102
(Alternate)

M102 Field = 45'

M102

Elliptical Galaxy in Draco
(Alternate) NGC 5866

Visual Magnitude: 9.9
Visual Index: Not Listed
Angular Size: 2.8' X 1'

Owen Gingerich has suggested this galaxy as a replacement for the nonexistent **M102** in Ursa Major. Therefore it is presented as an "alternate" to be used by those wishing to "find something" for **M102** rather than record the number when **M101** is observed. According to Gingerich, Méchain discovered and reported this galaxy to Messier, but the old "Ferret of Comets" never checked it and therefore it was never added to the famous list.

The galaxy is edge-on with a prominent central bulge, giving it a lens shape. In larger telescopes, a dark lane is revealed in front of the bulge.

Its distance is about 30 million light-years.

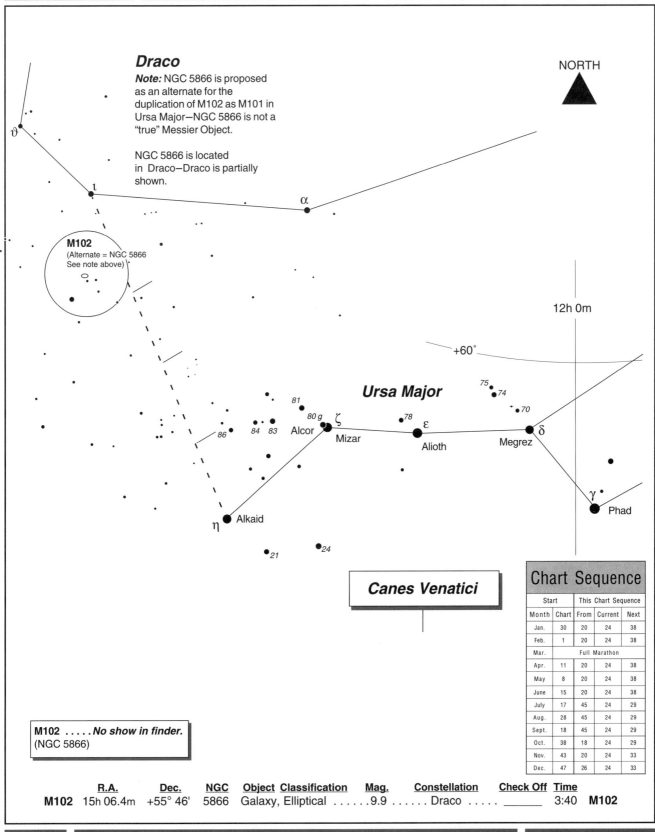

NORTH

Draco

Note: NGC 5866 is proposed as an alternate for the duplication of M102 as M101 in Ursa Major—NGC 5866 is not a "true" Messier Object.

NGC 5866 is located in Draco—Draco is partially shown.

ϑ

ι

α

M102
(Alternate = NGC 5866
See note above)

12h 0m

+60°

75 74

70

Ursa Major

81

80 g   ζ   78   ε   δ
84 83 Alcor   Alioth   Megrez
86   Mizar

γ
Phad

η   Alkaid

21   24

Canes Venatici

Chart Sequence

Start		This Chart Sequence		
Month	Chart	From	Current	Next
Jan.	30	20	24	38
Feb.	1	20	24	38
Mar.	Full Marathon			
Apr.	11	20	24	38
May	8	20	24	38
June	15	20	24	38
July	17	45	24	29
Aug.	28	45	24	29
Sept.	18	45	24	29
Oct.	38	18	24	29
Nov.	43	20	24	33
Dec.	47	26	24	33

M102 . . . . . *No show in finder.*
(NGC 5866)

	R.A.	Dec.	NGC	Object Classification	Mag.	Constellation	Check Off	Time	
M102	15h 06.4m	+55° 46'	5866	Galaxy, Elliptical	9.9	Draco	_____	3:40	**M102**

Galaxy

Open
Cluster

Globular
Cluster

Planetary
Nebula

Diffuse
Nebula

One Power
Finder Chart

Circle = 4°

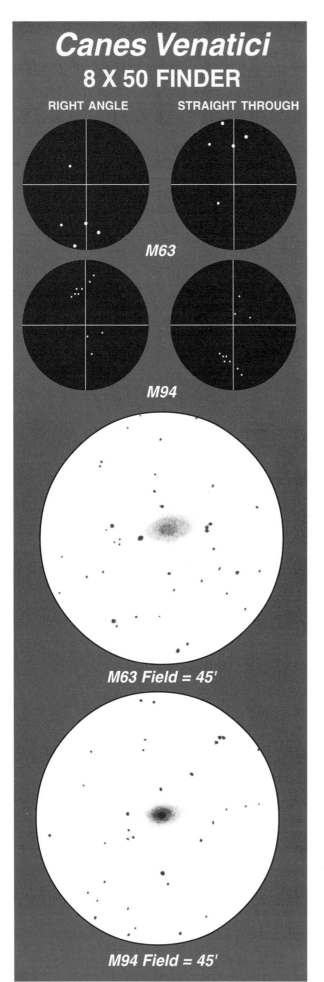

Canes Venatici
8 X 50 FINDER

RIGHT ANGLE   STRAIGHT THROUGH

M63

M94

M63 Field = 45'

M94 Field = 45'

M63
The Sunflower Galaxy

Visual Magnitude: 8.6
Visual Index: 4
Angular Size: 10' X 5'

Discovered by Méchain in 1779 and observed by Messier shortly thereafter, **M63** is a bright multiple arm oval galaxy easily located near 20 Canum Venaticorum. It is oriented about 30° from the edge-on position which explains its oval appearance. Its multiple arms account for the "sunflower" designation. **M63** is easily seen in small telescopes and binoculars. Larger telescopes will reveal some texture in this object. It is about 35 million light-years distant and has an estimated diameter of 90,000 light-years.

M94
**Spiral Galaxy
in Canes Venatici**

Visual Magnitude: 8.2
Visual Index: 3
Angular Size: 5' X 3.5'

Bright and compact with a circular form, it was discovered by Méchain in 1781. This galaxy has a bright central core measuring about 30 seconds in diameter. Its distance is estimated at close to 20 million light-years, and its diameter is placed at 33,000 light-years. It is easily seen in small telescopes and binoculars. Large aperture instruments will reveal a bright nucleus and some mottling.

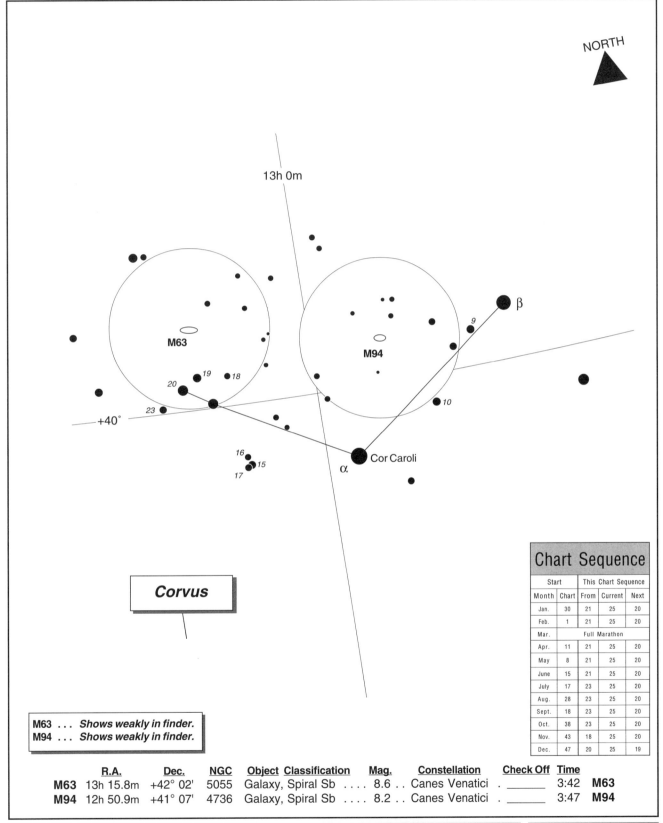

NORTH

13h 0m

M63

M94

β

9

19 18

20

23

+40°

10

16
15
17

α Cor Caroli

Corvus

Chart Sequence

Start		This Chart Sequence		
Month	Chart	From	Current	Next
Jan.	30	21	25	20
Feb.	1	21	25	20
Mar.		Full Marathon		
Apr.	11	21	25	20
May	8	21	25	20
June	15	21	25	20
July	17	23	25	20
Aug.	28	23	25	20
Sept.	18	23	25	20
Oct.	38	23	25	20
Nov.	43	18	25	20
Dec.	47	20	25	19

M63 . . . *Shows weakly in finder.*
M94 . . . *Shows weakly in finder.*

	R.A.	Dec.	NGC	Object Classification	Mag.	Constellation	Check Off	Time	
M63	13h 15.8m	+42° 02'	5055	Galaxy, Spiral Sb	8.6	. . Canes Venatici	. _____	3:42	**M63**
M94	12h 50.9m	+41° 07'	4736	Galaxy, Spiral Sb	8.2	. . Canes Venatici	. _____	3:47	**M94**

Galaxy

Open Cluster

Globular Cluster

Planetary Nebula

Diffuse Nebula

**One Power
Finder Chart**
Circle = 4°

The Year-Round Messier Marathon Field Guide

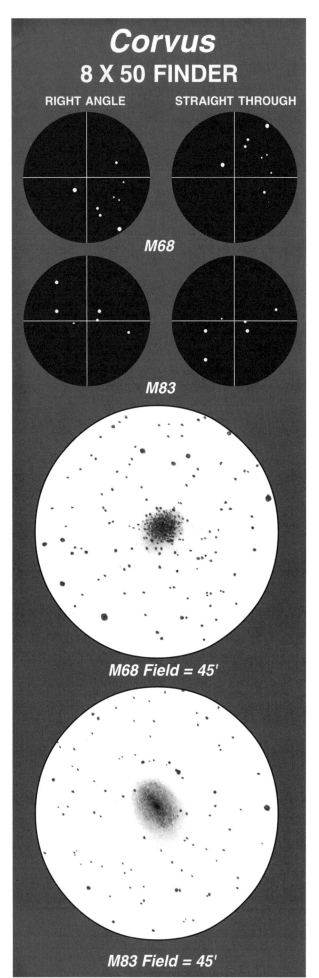

Corvus
8 X 50 FINDER

RIGHT ANGLE STRAIGHT THROUGH

M68

M83

M68 Field = 45'

M83 Field = 45'

M68
Globular Cluster in Hydra

Visual Magnitude: 7.7
Visual Index: 4
Angular Size: 2.9'

Discovered by Messier in 1780, this globular reveals some detail to telescopes of 6-inch aperture. Its distance is estimated at about 46,000 light-years. Its diameter is approximately 100 light-years. Larger telescopes will resolve many of this globular's over 100,000 member stars. It is easily seen in small telescopes and binoculars.

M83
Spiral Galaxy in Hydra

Visual Magnitude: 7.6
Visual Index: 2
Angular Size: 10' X 9.5'

Messier added this large galaxy to his list on February 17, 1781. Actually located in Hydra, Corvus is used as the "finder constellation." This large but amorphous galaxy is hard to locate because there are not any prominent nearby stars to use for reference. Study **Marathon Chart 26** carefully. Use the spatial relationships noted to locate this object. As galaxies go, this one is bright and easy to see in small instruments and binoculars. According to Burnham, **M83** is one of the 25 brightest galaxies in the heavens. The distance to **M83** is determined to be about 20 million light-years. Its diameter is estimated at 60,000 light-years.

The Year-Round Messier Marathon Field Guide

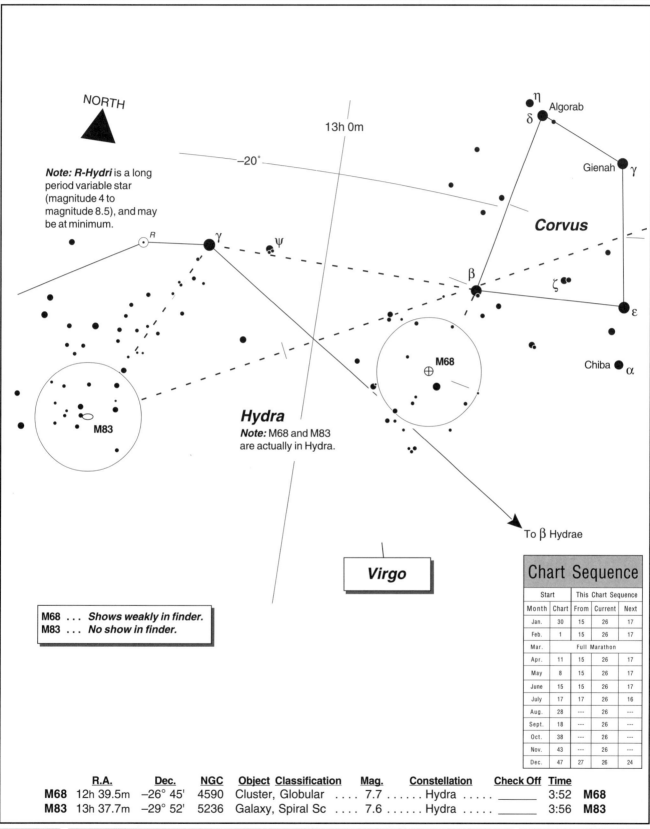

NORTH

Note: *R-Hydri* is a long period variable star (magnitude 4 to magnitude 8.5), and may be at minimum.

13h 0m

−20°

η
δ • Algorab

Gienah • γ

Corvus

β

ζ

ε

Chiba • α

R

γ

ψ

M68
⊕

Hydra
Note: M68 and M83 are actually in Hydra.

M83

To β Hydrae

Virgo

M68 . . . *Shows weakly in finder.*
M83 . . . *No show in finder.*

Chart Sequence

Start		This Chart Sequence		
Month	Chart	From	Current	Next
Jan.	30	15	26	17
Feb.	1	15	26	17
Mar.		Full Marathon		
Apr.	11	15	26	17
May	8	15	26	17
June	15	15	26	17
July	17	17	26	16
Aug.	28	---	26	---
Sept.	18	---	26	---
Oct.	38	---	26	---
Nov.	43	---	26	---
Dec.	47	27	26	24

	R.A.	Dec.	NGC	Object Classification	Mag.	Constellation	Check Off	Time	
M68	12h 39.5m	−26° 45'	4590	Cluster, Globular	7.7	Hydra	_____	3:52	**M68**
M83	13h 37.7m	−29° 52'	5236	Galaxy, Spiral Sc	7.6	Hydra	_____	3:56	**M83**

Galaxy

Open Cluster

Globular Cluster

Planetary Nebula

Diffuse Nebula

One Power Finder Chart
Circle = 4°

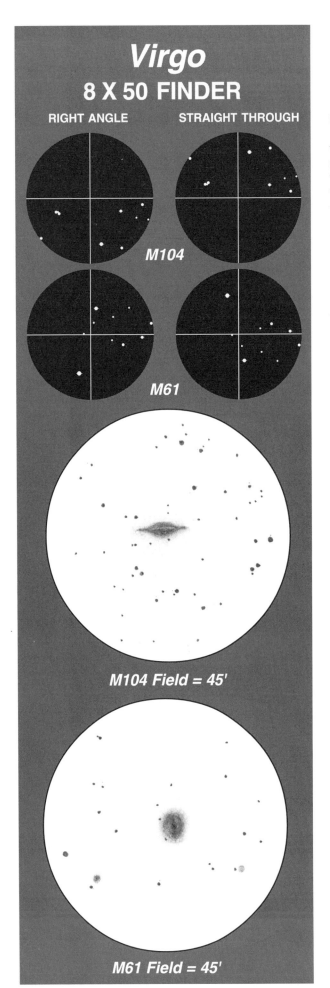

Virgo
8 X 50 FINDER

RIGHT ANGLE   **STRAIGHT THROUGH**

M104

M61

M104 Field = 45'

M61 Field = 45'

M104
The Sombrero Galaxy

Visual Magnitude: 8.0
Visual Index: 2
Angular Size: 7.1' X 4.4'

The Sombrero Galaxy was discovered by Méchain in May of 1781. Although not in Messier's final supplement, it was recorded in his own hand on a copy of the "Connaissance des Temps," 1784. The Sombrero is a spectacular object when seen in larger telescopes. The dust lane which surrounds the galaxy can be glimpsed in instruments as small as 6 inches when conditions are very nearly perfect. Small telescopes will have no difficulty in revealing the presence of the galaxy, but no detail will be seen. The Sombrero is estimated to be about 50 million years distant and 130,000 light-years in diameter.

M61
Spiral Galaxy in Virgo

Visual Magnitude: 9.7
Visual Index: 4
Angular Size: 6' X 6'

Recorded by Messier in April of 1779, **M61** reveals some detail within its compact form in telescopes of 8 inches and up. Smaller telescopes will see a moderately bright elliptical shape. **M61** is estimated to be about 50,000 light-years in diameter.

The Year-Round Messier Marathon Field Guide

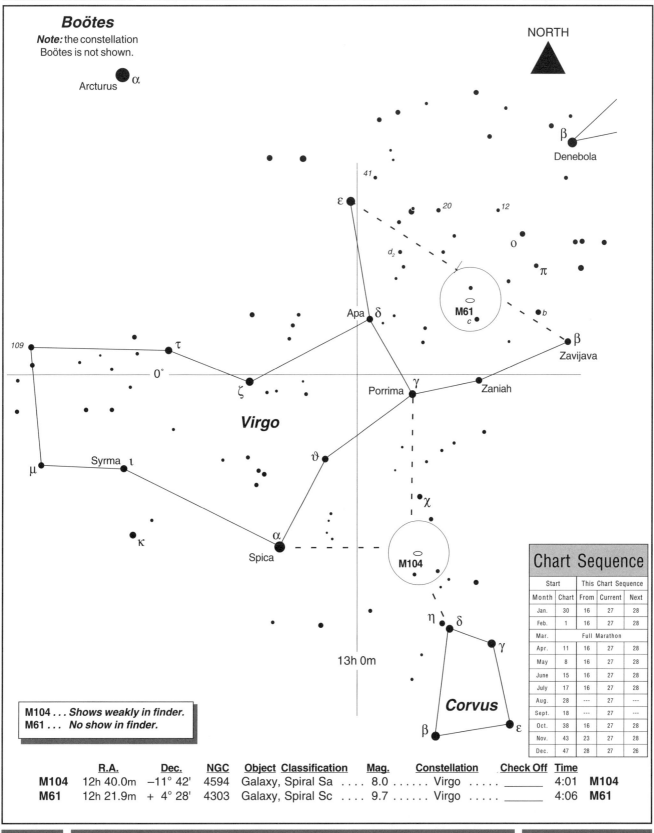

Boötes

Note: the constellation Boötes is not shown.

Arcturus • α

NORTH

Denebola β

41

ε

20

12

o

π

d₂

Apa δ

M61
c

b

β
Zavijava

109

τ

0°

ζ

Porrima γ

Zaniah

Virgo

Syrma ι

μ

ϑ

χ

κ

α
Spica

M104

13h 0m

η δ

γ

Corvus

β ε

| M104 . . . Shows weakly in finder. |
| M61 . . . No show in finder. |

Chart Sequence

Start		This Chart Sequence		
Month	Chart	From	Current	Next
Jan.	30	16	27	28
Feb.	1	16	27	28
Mar.		Full Marathon		
Apr.	11	16	27	28
May	8	16	27	28
June	15	16	27	28
July	17	16	27	28
Aug.	28	---	27	---
Sept.	18	---	27	---
Oct.	38	16	27	28
Nov.	43	23	27	28
Dec.	47	28	27	26

	R.A.	Dec.	NGC	Object Classification	Mag.	Constellation	Check Off	Time	
M104	12h 40.0m	−11° 42'	4594	Galaxy, Spiral Sa	8.0	Virgo	_____	4:01	**M104**
M61	12h 21.9m	+ 4° 28'	4303	Galaxy, Spiral Sc	9.7	Virgo	_____	4:06	**M61**

Galaxy	Open Cluster	Globular Cluster	Planetary Nebula	Diffuse Nebula

One Power Finder Chart
Circle = 4°

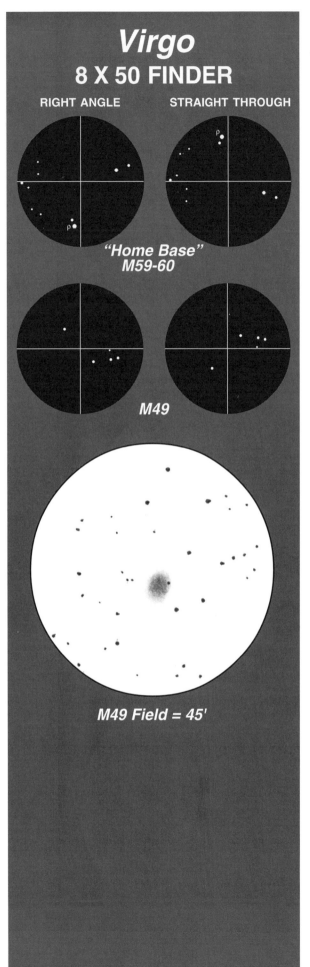

Virgo
8 X 50 FINDER

RIGHT ANGLE **STRAIGHT THROUGH**

"Home Base"
M59-60

M49

M49 Field = 45'

The Virgo Cluster

"The difficulty of locating and identifying the Virgo cluster objects is highly overrated," to quote Joe Neu — and I agree. **Marathon Charts 28-a,b,c,d** are drawn with 1° grids; the "eyepiece circles" are also 1°. It is not hard to see how many eyepiece views it will take to get from one object to the next. It is a "can't miss" road map.

If you get lost, return to *home base* and start over again. Use **M86-84** as a secondary *home base* — it is easy to identify these galaxies because they, like **M60** and **M59**, can be placed in the same eyepiece field.

Home Base is the readily identifiable pair of galaxies, M59 and M60.

M49 **Elliptical Galaxy** **in Virgo**		**Visual Magnitude: 8.4** **Visual Index: 4** **Angular Size: 8' X 7'**

Bright and easy to locate, this galaxy was discovered by Messier in February of 1771. Its distance is estimated at 42 million light-years, and its diameter is estimated at 50,000 light-years. It is nearly round when seen in an eyepiece. It is easily seen in small telescopes and binoculars.

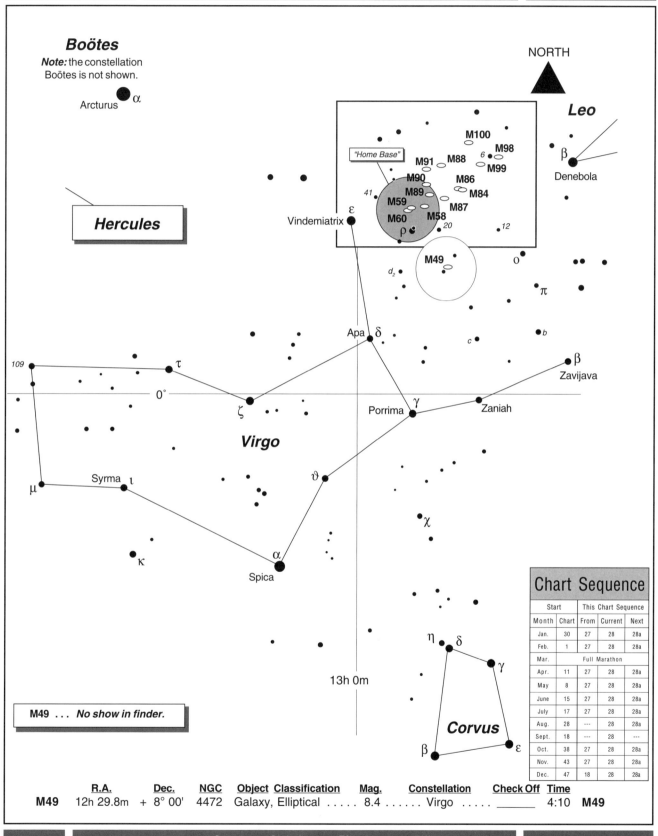

Boötes

Note: the constellation Boötes is not shown.

Arcturus α

NORTH

Leo

M100

M98

"Home Base"   M91 M88   6   M99

M90   M86

M89   M84

41   M59   M87

Vindemiatrix ε   M60 M58

ρ   20

M49   12

Hercules   d₂   o

π

Apa δ   c   b

109   τ

0°   β Zavijava

ζ   Porrima γ   Zaniah

Virgo

Syrma ι   ϑ

μ   χ

α

κ   Spica

13h 0m

M49 . . . *No show in finder.*

η δ

γ

Corvus

β   ε

Chart Sequence

Start		This Chart Sequence		
Month	Chart	From	Current	Next
Jan.	30	27	28	28a
Feb.	1	27	28	28a
Mar.		Full Marathon		
Apr.	11	27	28	28a
May	8	27	28	28a
June	15	27	28	28a
July	17	27	28	28a
Aug.	28	---	28	28a
Sept.	18	---	28	---
Oct.	38	27	28	28a
Nov.	43	27	28	28a
Dec.	47	18	28	28a

	R.A.	Dec.	NGC	Object Classification	Mag.	Constellation	Check Off	Time	
M49	12h 29.8m	+ 8° 00'	4472	Galaxy, Elliptical	8.4	Virgo	_____	4:10	M49

 Galaxy   Open Cluster   Globular Cluster   Planetary Nebula   Diffuse Nebula

One Power Finder Chart
Circle = 4°

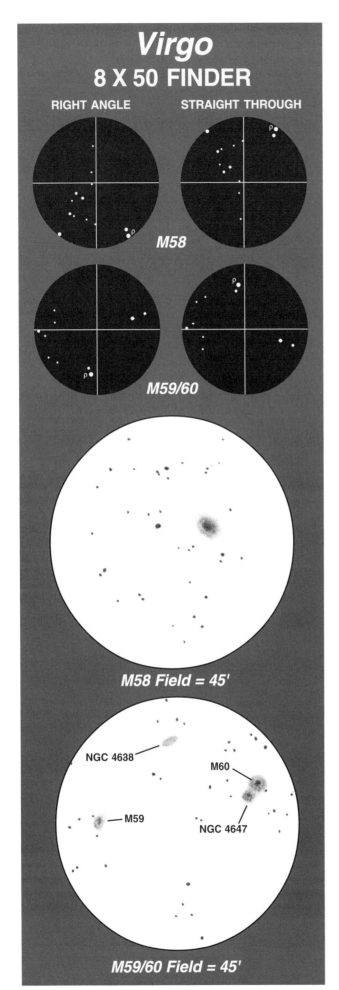

Virgo
8 X 50 FINDER

RIGHT ANGLE   **STRAIGHT THROUGH**

M58

M59/60

M58 Field = 45'

NGC 4638

M60

M59

NGC 4647

M59/60 Field = 45'

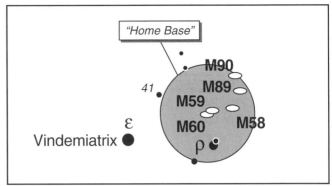

"Home Base"

M90

M89

41   M59

M60   M58

Vindemiatrix   ε

ρ

Start your journey by locating M59/60, a distinctive field easily found from the star Vindemiatrix and tucked in between 41 and ρ Virginis.

M58
Spiral Galaxy in Virgo

Visual Magnitude: 9.7
Visual Index: 4
Angular Size: 5.5' X 4.6'

Recorded by Messier in April of 1779, **M58** reveals some detail within its compact form in telescopes of 8 inches and up. Smaller telescopes will see a moderately bright elliptical shape. The distance to **M58** is estimated at about 42 million light-years and the diameter at about 50,000 light-years.

M59
Elliptical Galaxy in Virgo

Visual Magnitude: 9.6
Visual Index: 4
Angular Size: 4.6' X 3.6'

Fainter and smaller than the "run of the mill" Messier discoveries in the Virgo cluster, **M59** was discovered by Messier in April of 1779. **M60** can be seen in the same field when using an eyepiece of 1° true field. Easy identification is made by placing **M60** in the same field of view; **M59** is the fainter and smaller of the two, and it has an oval shape. It is about 42 million light-years distant. Its diameter is calculated to be about 24,000 light-years.

M60
Elliptical Galaxy in Virgo

Visual Magnitude: 8.8
Visual Index: 4
Angular Size: 7' X 6'

M60 was discovered at the same time as **M59**, in April of 1779 as Messier observed the comet of that year. **NGC 4647** may be visible in telescopes of large aperture 2.5' to the northwest. **M59** can be seen in the same field when using an eyepiece of 1° true field. **M60's** distance is estimated at 42 million light-years, and its diameter is estimated at 25,000 light-years.

   The Year-Round Messier Marathon Field Guide

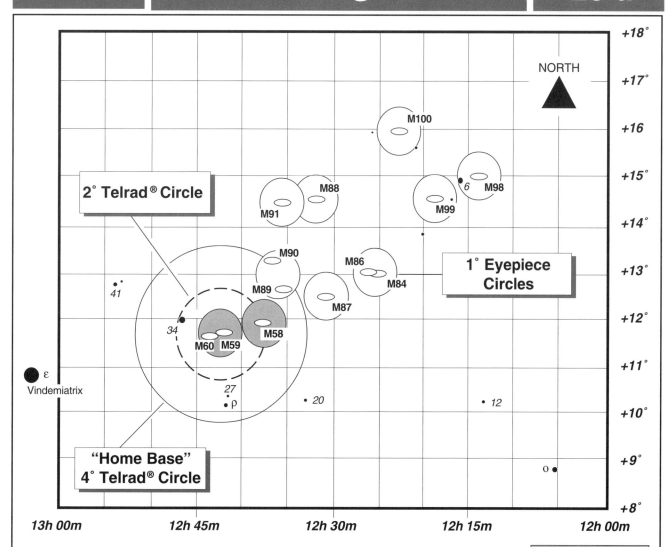

2° Telrad® Circle

M100

M88

6 M98

M91

M99

1° Eyepiece Circles

M90

M86

M89

M84

41

M87

34

M58

M60 M59

ε
Vindemiatrix

27
ρ

20

12

"Home Base"
4° Telrad® Circle

o

13h 00m	12h 45m	12h 30m	12h 15m	12h 00m

+18°
+17°
+16
+15°
+14°
+13°
+12°
+11°
+10°
+9°
+8°

Chart Sequence

Start		This Chart Sequence		
Month	Chart	From	Current	Next
Jan.	30	27	28a	28b
Feb.	1	27	28a	28b
Mar.		Full Marathon		
Apr.	11	27	28a	28b
May	8	27	28a	28b
June	15	27	28a	28b
July	17	27	28a	28b
Aug.	28	---	28a	28b
Sept.	18	---	28a	28b
Oct.	38	27	28a	28b
Nov.	43	27	28a	28b
Dec.	47	18	28a	28b

	R.A.	Dec.	NGC	Object Classification	Mag.	Constellation	Check Off	Time	
M58	12h 37.7m	+11° 49'	4579	Galaxy, Spiral Sb	9.7	Virgo	_____	4:15	M58
M59	12h 42.0m	+11° 39'	4621	Galaxy, Elliptical	9.6	Virgo	_____	4:20	M59
M60	12h 43.7m	+11° 33'	4649	Galaxy, Elliptical	8.8	Virgo	_____	4:24	M60

Virgo Galaxy Cluster Finder Chart

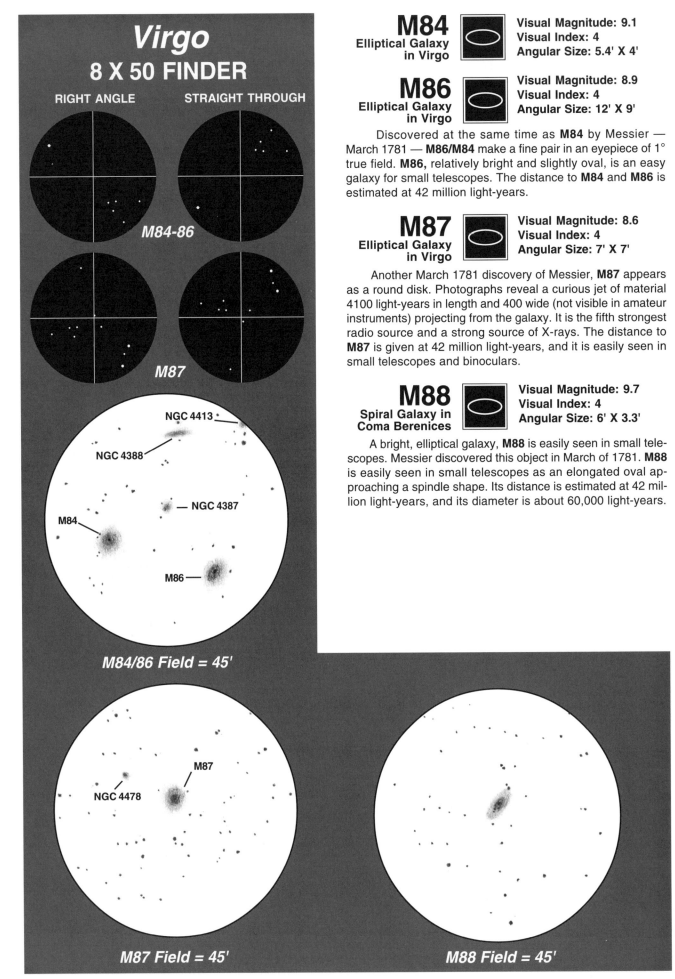

Virgo
8 X 50 FINDER

RIGHT ANGLE   STRAIGHT THROUGH

M84-86

M87

NGC 4413
NGC 4388
NGC 4387
M84
M86

M84/86 Field = 45'

M87
NGC 4478

M87 Field = 45'

M88 Field = 45'

M84
Elliptical Galaxy in Virgo

Visual Magnitude: 9.1
Visual Index: 4
Angular Size: 5.4' X 4'

M86
Elliptical Galaxy in Virgo

Visual Magnitude: 8.9
Visual Index: 4
Angular Size: 12' X 9'

Discovered at the same time as **M84** by Messier — March 1781 — **M86/M84** make a fine pair in an eyepiece of 1° true field. **M86,** relatively bright and slightly oval, is an easy galaxy for small telescopes. The distance to **M84** and **M86** is estimated at 42 million light-years.

M87
Elliptical Galaxy in Virgo

Visual Magnitude: 8.6
Visual Index: 4
Angular Size: 7' X 7'

Another March 1781 discovery of Messier, **M87** appears as a round disk. Photographs reveal a curious jet of material 4100 light-years in length and 400 wide (not visible in amateur instruments) projecting from the galaxy. It is the fifth strongest radio source and a strong source of X-rays. The distance to **M87** is given at 42 million light-years, and it is easily seen in small telescopes and binoculars.

M88
Spiral Galaxy in Coma Berenices

Visual Magnitude: 9.7
Visual Index: 4
Angular Size: 6' X 3.3'

A bright, elliptical galaxy, **M88** is easily seen in small telescopes. Messier discovered this object in March of 1781. **M88** is easily seen in small telescopes as an elongated oval approaching a spindle shape. Its distance is estimated at 42 million light-years, and its diameter is about 60,000 light-years.

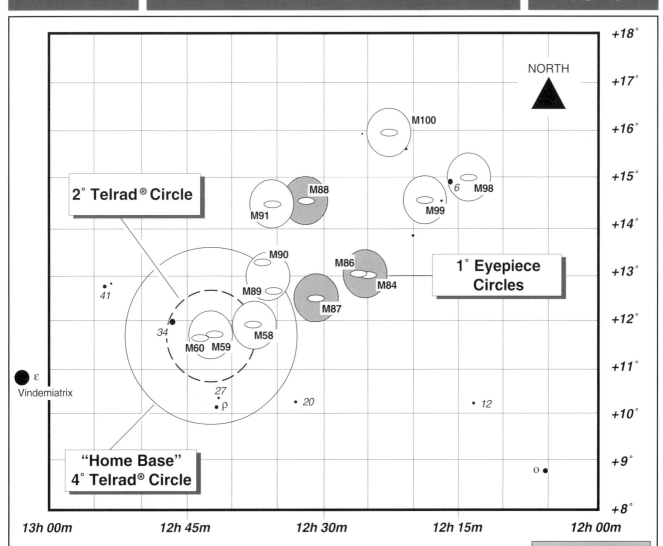

2° Telrad® Circle

M100

NORTH

+18°
+17°
+16°
+15°
+14°
+13°
+12°
+11°
+10°
+9°
+8°

M88

M91

6 M98

M99

1° Eyepiece
Circles

M90

M86

M89

M84

M87

41

34

M58

M60 M59

ε
Vindemiatrix

27
ρ

20

12

ο

"Home Base"
4° Telrad® Circle

13h 00m   12h 45m   12h 30m   12h 15m   12h 00m

Chart Sequence

Start		This Chart Sequence		
Month	Chart	From	Current	Next
Jan.	30	27	28b	28c
Feb.	1	27	28b	28c
Mar.	Full Marathon			
Apr.	11	27	28b	28c
May	8	27	28b	28c
June	15	27	28b	28c
July	17	27	28b	28c
Aug.	28	---	28b	28c
Sept.	18	---	28b	28c
Oct.	38	27	28b	28c
Nov.	43	27	28b	28c
Dec.	47	18	28b	28c

	R.A.	Dec.	NGC	Object Classification	Mag.	Constellation	Check Off	Time	
M84	12h 25.1m	+12° 53'	4374	Galaxy, Elliptical	9.1	Virgo	_____	4:33	M84
M86	12h 26.2m	+12° 57'	4406	Galaxy, Elliptical	8.9	Virgo	_____	4:33	M86
M87	12h 30.8m	+12° 23'	4486	Galaxy, Ellip/Pec.	8.6	Virgo	_____	4:38	M87
M88	12h 32.0m	+14° 25'	4501	Galaxy, Spiral Sb	9.7	Coma Berenices	_____	4:43	M88

Virgo Galaxy Cluster Finder Chart

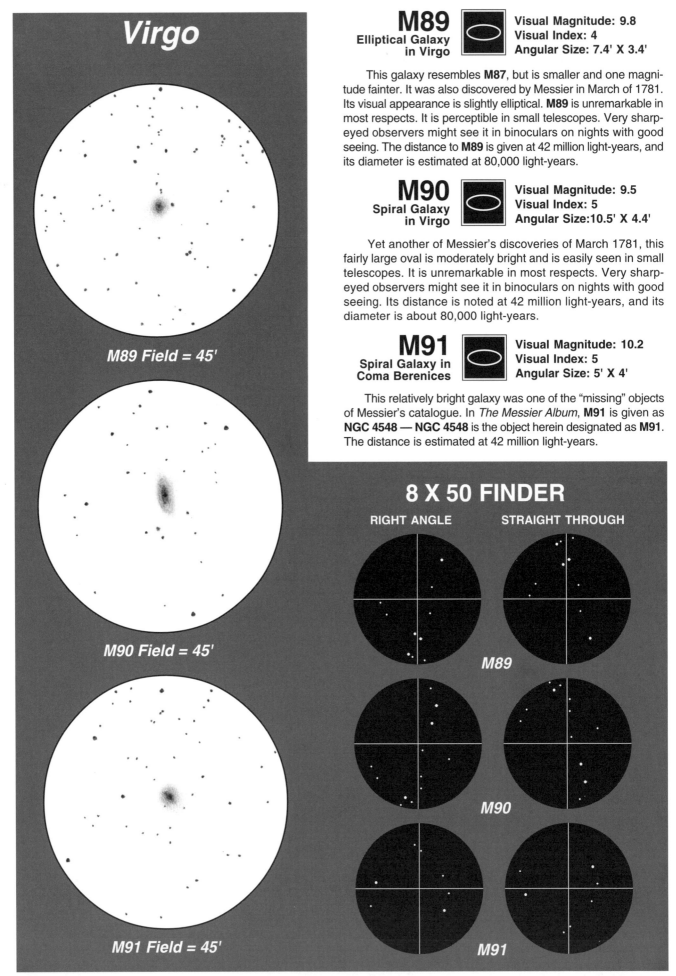

Virgo

M89
Elliptical Galaxy in Virgo

Visual Magnitude: 9.8
Visual Index: 4
Angular Size: 7.4' X 3.4'

This galaxy resembles **M87**, but is smaller and one magnitude fainter. It was also discovered by Messier in March of 1781. Its visual appearance is slightly elliptical. **M89** is unremarkable in most respects. It is perceptible in small telescopes. Very sharp-eyed observers might see it in binoculars on nights with good seeing. The distance to **M89** is given at 42 million light-years, and its diameter is estimated at 80,000 light-years.

M90
Spiral Galaxy in Virgo

Visual Magnitude: 9.5
Visual Index: 5
Angular Size:10.5' X 4.4'

Yet another of Messier's discoveries of March 1781, this fairly large oval is moderately bright and is easily seen in small telescopes. It is unremarkable in most respects. Very sharp-eyed observers might see it in binoculars on nights with good seeing. Its distance is noted at 42 million light-years, and its diameter is about 80,000 light-years.

M91
Spiral Galaxy in Coma Berenices

Visual Magnitude: 10.2
Visual Index: 5
Angular Size: 5' X 4'

This relatively bright galaxy was one of the "missing" objects of Messier's catalogue. In *The Messier Album*, **M91** is given as **NGC 4548** — NGC 4548 is the object herein designated as **M91**. The distance is estimated at 42 million light-years.

M89 Field = 45'

M90 Field = 45'

M91 Field = 45'

8 X 50 FINDER

RIGHT ANGLE   **STRAIGHT THROUGH**

M89

M90

M91

The Year-Round Messier Marathon Field Guide

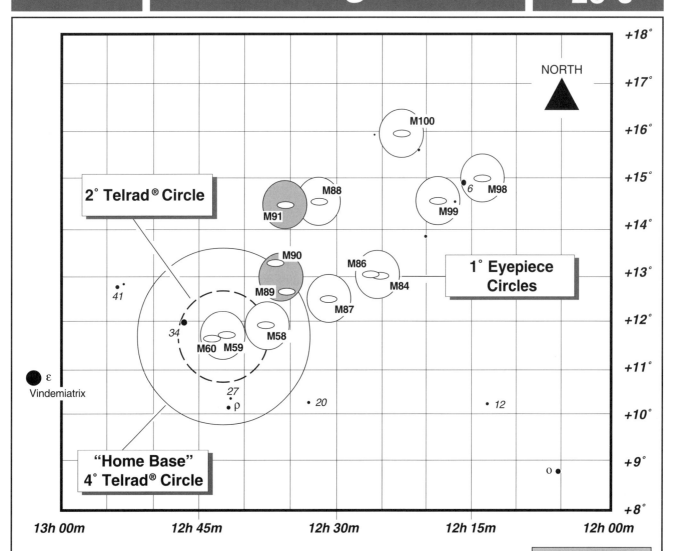

	R.A.	Dec.	NGC	Object Classification	Mag.	Constellation	Check Off	Time	
M89	12h 35.7m	+12° 33'	4552	Galaxy, Elliptical	9.8	Virgo	_____	4:47	**M89**
M90	12h 36.8m	+13° 10'	4569	Galaxy, Spiral Sb	9.5	Virgo	_____	4:52	**M90**
M91	12h 35.4m	+14° 30'	4548	Galaxy, Spiral SBb ..	10.2	..Coma Berenices .	_____	4:57	**M91**

Chart Sequence

Start		This Chart Sequence		
Month	Chart	From	Current	Next
Jan.	30	27	28c	28d
Feb.	1	27	28c	28d
Mar.		Full Marathon		
Apr.	11	27	28c	28d
May	8	27	28c	28d
June	15	27	28c	28d
July	17	27	28c	28d
Aug.	28	---	28c	28d
Sept.	18	---	28c	28d
Oct.	38	27	28c	28d
Nov.	43	27	28c	28d
Dec.	47	18	28c	28d

Virgo Galaxy Cluster Finder Chart

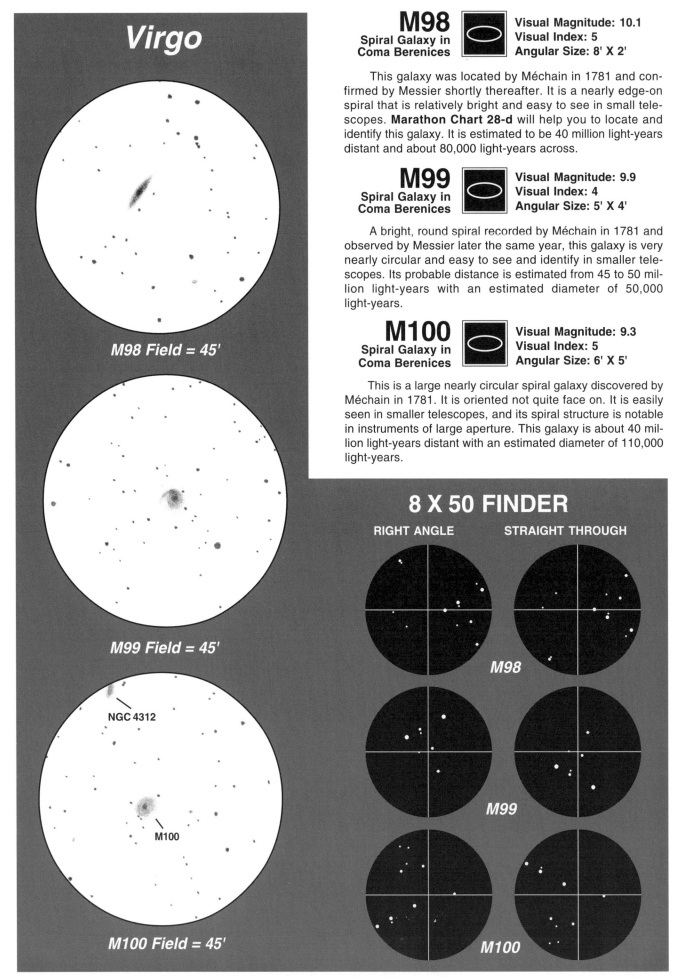

Virgo

M98 Field = 45'

M99 Field = 45'

NGC 4312

M100

M100 Field = 45'

M98
Spiral Galaxy in Coma Berenices

Visual Magnitude: 10.1
Visual Index: 5
Angular Size: 8' X 2'

This galaxy was located by Méchain in 1781 and confirmed by Messier shortly thereafter. It is a nearly edge-on spiral that is relatively bright and easy to see in small telescopes. **Marathon Chart 28-d** will help you to locate and identify this galaxy. It is estimated to be 40 million light-years distant and about 80,000 light-years across.

M99
Spiral Galaxy in Coma Berenices

Visual Magnitude: 9.9
Visual Index: 4
Angular Size: 5' X 4'

A bright, round spiral recorded by Méchain in 1781 and observed by Messier later the same year, this galaxy is very nearly circular and easy to see and identify in smaller telescopes. Its probable distance is estimated from 45 to 50 million light-years with an estimated diameter of 50,000 light-years.

M100
Spiral Galaxy in Coma Berenices

Visual Magnitude: 9.3
Visual Index: 5
Angular Size: 6' X 5'

This is a large nearly circular spiral galaxy discovered by Méchain in 1781. It is oriented not quite face on. It is easily seen in smaller telescopes, and its spiral structure is notable in instruments of large aperture. This galaxy is about 40 million light-years distant with an estimated diameter of 110,000 light-years.

8 X 50 FINDER

RIGHT ANGLE   **STRAIGHT THROUGH**

M98

M99

M100

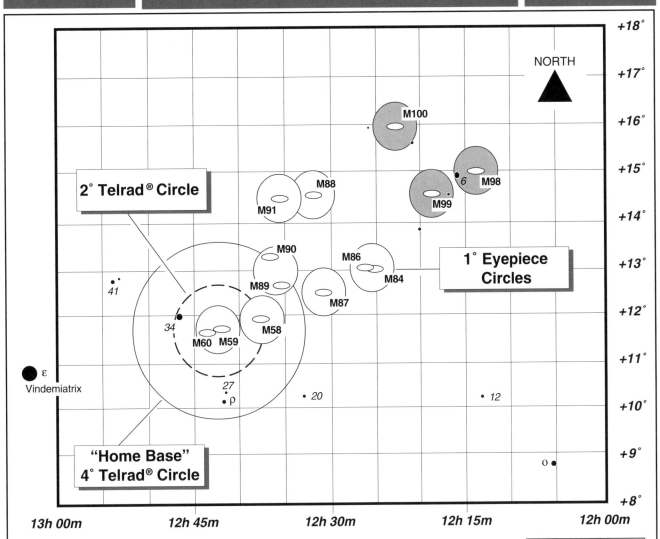

NORTH

2° Telrad® Circle

M100

M88

M98

M91

6

M99

M90

M86

1° Eyepiece Circles

M89

M84

41

M87

34

M58

M60 M59

ε
Vindemiatrix

27

20

12

ρ

"Home Base"
4° Telrad® Circle

o

13h 00m   12h 45m   12h 30m   12h 15m   12h 00m

+18°
+17°
+16°
+15°
+14°
+13°
+12°
+11°
+10°
+9°
+8°

Chart Sequence

Start		This Chart Sequence		
Month	Chart	From	Current	Next
Jan.	30	27	28d	19
Feb.	1	27	28d	19
Mar.		Full Marathon		
Apr.	11	27	28d	19
May	8	27	28d	19
June	15	27	28d	19
July	17	27	28d	19
Aug.	28	---	28d	19
Sept.	18	---	28d	--
Oct.	38	27	28d	19
Nov.	43	27	28d	19
Dec.	47	18	28d	27

	R.A.	Dec.	NGC	Object Classification	Mag.	Constellation	Check Off	Time	
M98	12h 13.8m	+14° 54'	4192	Galaxy, Spiral Sb ...	10.1	.. Coma Berenices .	_____	5:01	M98
M99	12h 18.8m	+14° 25'	4254	Galaxy, Spiral Sc	9.9	.. Coma Berenices .	_____	5:06	M99
M100	12h 22.9m	+15° 49'	4321	Galaxy, Spiral Sc	9.3	.. Coma Berenices .	_____	5:11	M100

Virgo Galaxy Cluster Finder Chart

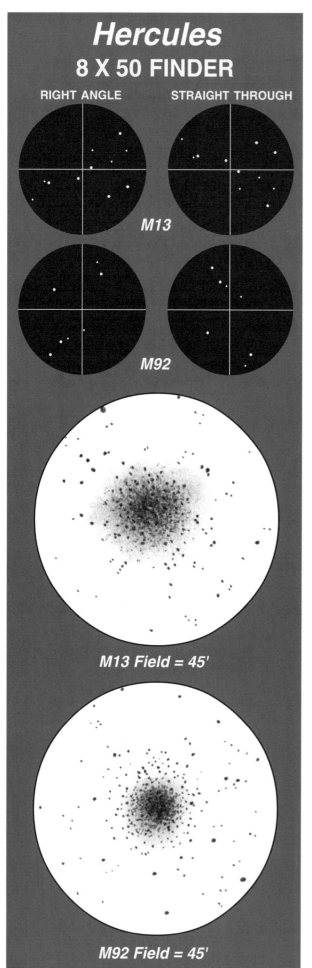

Hercules

8 X 50 FINDER

RIGHT ANGLE   STRAIGHT THROUGH

M13

M92

M13 Field = 45'

M92 Field = 45'

Visual Magnitude: 5.7
Visual Index: 3
Angular Size: 10'

One of the most spectacular sights in the northern hemisphere, the Hercules Cluster was added to Messier's original catalog in 1764. It is easily seen in small telescopes and binoculars. On nights of exceptionally good seeing, it is visible to the naked eye as a fuzzy star. The distance to **M13** is currently given at about 21,000 light-years, and the diameter is estimated at about 160 light-years. This object will take all the magnification a telescope is possible of giving — its over 1 million member stars will reveal their presence layer by layer as magnification is added.

M92

**Globular Cluster
in Hercules**

Visual Magnitude: 6.4
Visual Index: 3
Angular Size: 8.3'

Although no match for **M13** in the "spectacular category," **M92** is nonetheless truly spectacular and deserves more attention — which it would get if it were located in any other constellation. It is easily seen in small telescopes and binoculars. Its distance is estimated to be 35,000 light-years. Its diameter is about 88 light-years. Some resolution is possible in small telescopes. Binoculars will reveal a "fuzzy star."

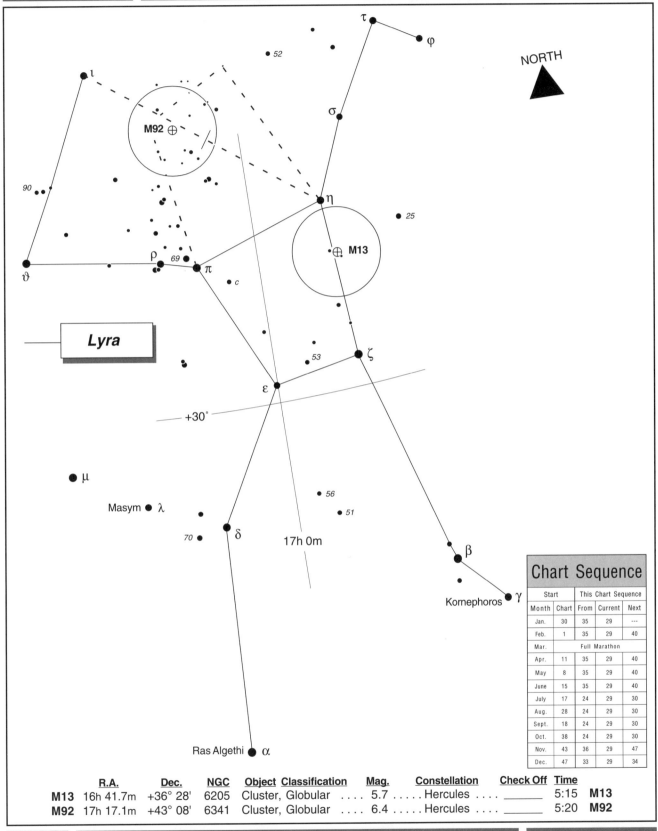

NORTH

τ
φ
52
σ
ι
M92 ⊕
90
η
25
ρ 69
π
ϑ
c
M13

Lyra

53
ζ
ε
+30°

μ
56
Masym ● λ
51
70 ●
δ
17h 0m
β
Kornephoros
γ
Ras Algethi ● α

Chart Sequence			
Start		This Chart Sequence	
Month	Chart	From	Current	Next
Jan.	30	35	29	---
Feb.	1	35	29	40
Mar.	Full Marathon			
Apr.	11	35	29	40
May	8	35	29	40
June	15	35	29	40
July	17	24	29	30
Aug.	28	24	29	30
Sept.	18	24	29	30
Oct.	38	24	29	30
Nov.	43	36	29	47
Dec.	47	33	29	34

	R.A.	Dec.	NGC	Object Classification	Mag.	Constellation	Check Off	Time	
M13	16h 41.7m	+36° 28'	6205	Cluster, Globular	5.7	..... Hercules	_____	5:15	**M13**
M92	17h 17.1m	+43° 08'	6341	Cluster, Globular	6.4	..... Hercules	_____	5:20	**M92**

Galaxy

Open Cluster

Globular Cluster

Planetary Nebula

Diffuse Nebula

One Power Finder Chart
Circle = 4°

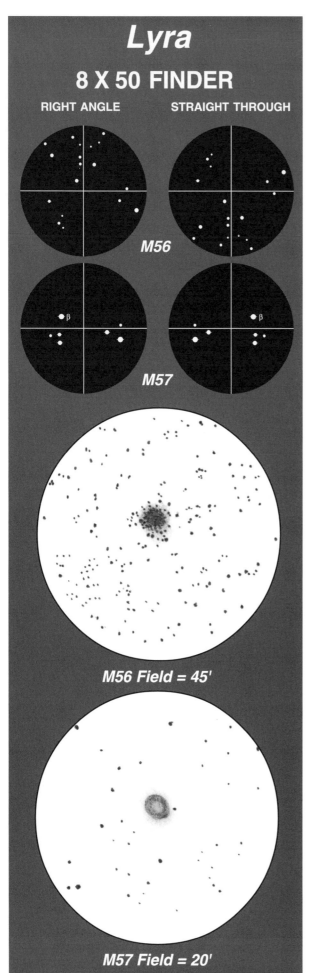

Lyra

8 X 50 FINDER

RIGHT ANGLE **STRAIGHT THROUGH**

M56

M57

M56 Field = 45'

M57 Field = 20'

M56
Globular Cluster in Lyra

Visual Magnitude: 8.3
Visual Index: 5
Angular Size: 5'

Messier discovered this globular cluster on January 19, 1779 — the same night he discovered one of his comets. Medium sized instruments will achieve some resolution around the outer edges while larger apertures will reveal much of the core. The distance is given at 46,000 light-years. The diameter is estimated at 60 light-years. **M56** is easily seen by small telescopes and binoculars.

M57
The Ring Nebula

Visual Magnitude: 8.8
Visual Index: 2
Angular Size: 1.3' X 1'

This very famous object was recorded by Messier in 1779. In small telescopes the ring will not be apparent — it will look very much like a planet, hence the name planetary nebula. In instruments of 6-inch aperture and larger, the ring appearance is quite clear. This object has a central star of about 15th visual magnitude — very difficult to see, even with very large telescopes. **M57** is currently thought to be between 1,270 and 2,000 light-years distant. The Ring's diameter is estimated to be 0.5 light-year.

The Year-Round Messier Marathon Field Guide

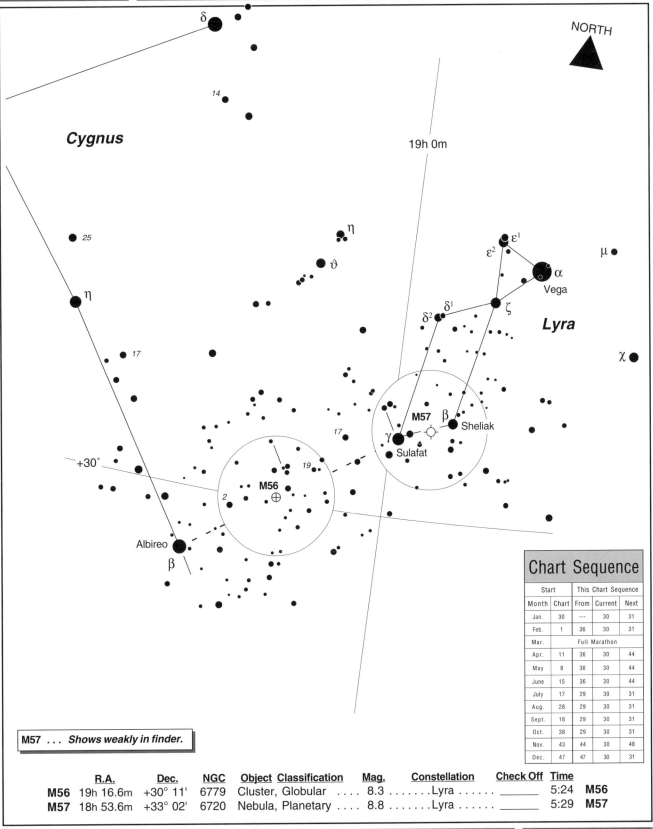

NORTH

Cygnus

19h 0m

δ

14

25

η

17

η

ϑ

ε¹

ε²

δ¹

α
Vega

μ

δ²

ζ

Lyra

χ

+30°

2

19

M56

17

M57

γ

Sulafat

β

Sheliak

Albireo

β

M57 ... *Shows weakly in finder.*

Chart Sequence

Start		This Chart Sequence		
Month	Chart	From	Current	Next
Jan.	30	---	30	31
Feb.	1	36	30	31
Mar.	Full Marathon			
Apr.	11	36	30	44
May	8	36	30	44
June	15	36	30	44
July	17	29	30	31
Aug.	28	29	30	31
Sept.	18	29	30	31
Oct.	38	29	30	31
Nov.	43	44	30	48
Dec.	47	47	30	31

	R.A.	Dec.	NGC	Object Classification	Mag.	Constellation	Check Off	Time	
M56	19h 16.6m	+30° 11'	6779	Cluster, Globular	8.3	Lyra	_____	5:24	**M56**
M57	18h 53.6m	+33° 02'	6720	Nebula, Planetary	8.8	Lyra	_____	5:29	**M57**

 Galaxy

 **Open Cluster**

 Globular Cluster

 Planetary Nebula

 Diffuse Nebula

One Power Finder Chart
Circle = 4°

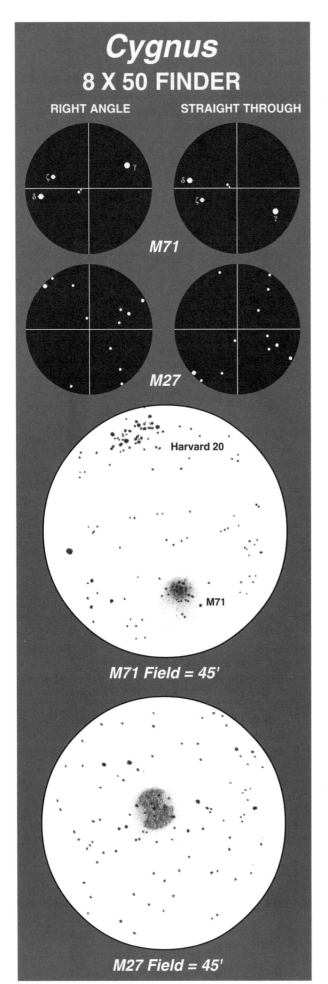

Cygnus
8 X 50 FINDER

RIGHT ANGLE   STRAIGHT THROUGH

M71

M27

Harvard 20

M71

M71 Field = 45'

M27 Field = 45'

M71

Globular Cluster in Sagitta

Visual Magnitude: 8.3
Visual Index: 4
Angular Size: 7'

Cataloged in 1780 by Messier, **M71** is a globular cluster, though for many years some authors thought this star-group might be a very compact galactic cluster (open cluster). Compare **M71** to the more typical open cluster Harvard 20 which may be seen in the same low power field of view lying 30' SSW. **M71** is about 12,000 light-years distant and about 29 light-years in diameter.

     M71 is one of the most beautiful clusters when viewed at moderate magnification because it is immersed in a rich Milky Way background.

M27

The Dumbbell Nebula

Visual Magnitude: 7.3
Visual Index: 2
Angular Size: 8'

Large and bright, this diaphanous object shows some color and detail in telescopes of moderate aperture and is easily visible in small telescopes as well as binoculars and finder scopes. The probable distance ranges between 490 and 980 light-years with a diameter of approximately 2.5 light-years. On close inspection its shape more closely resembles an hourglass than a dumbbell. It is one of the largest of the planetary nebulae and the first object of its kind to be discovered by Messier: July 1764.

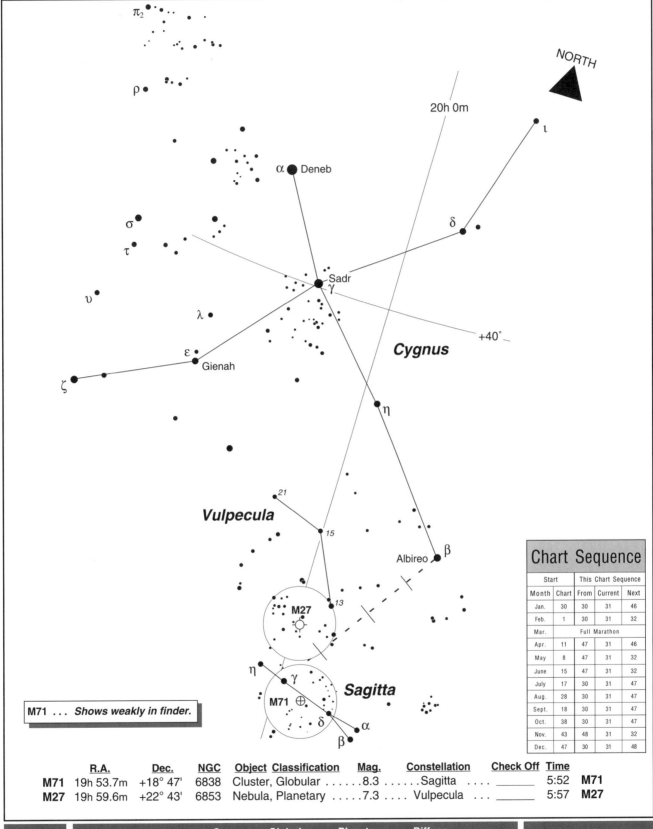

NORTH

20h 0m

α ● Deneb

δ

ι

σ

τ

υ

λ

Sadr
γ

+40°

Cygnus

ε
Gienah

ζ

η

Vulpecula

21

15

Albireo β

M27

13

η
γ

Sagitta

M71 ⊕

δ

α

β

| **M71 ... Shows weakly in finder.** |

Chart Sequence

Start		This Chart Sequence		
Month	Chart	From	Current	Next
Jan.	30	30	31	46
Feb.	1	30	31	32
Mar.		Full Marathon		
Apr.	11	47	31	46
May	8	47	31	32
June	15	47	31	32
July	17	30	31	47
Aug.	28	30	31	47
Sept.	18	30	31	47
Oct.	38	30	31	47
Nov.	43	48	31	32
Dec.	47	30	31	48

	R.A.	Dec.	NGC	Object Classification	Mag.	Constellation	Check Off	Time	
M71	19h 53.7m	+18° 47'	6838	Cluster, Globular	8.3	Sagitta	_____	5:52	M71
M27	19h 59.6m	+22° 43'	6853	Nebula, Planetary	7.3	Vulpecula	_____	5:57	M27

Galaxy	**Open Cluster**	**Globular Cluster**	**Planetary Nebula**	**Diffuse Nebula**	**One Power Finder Chart**
					Circle = 4°

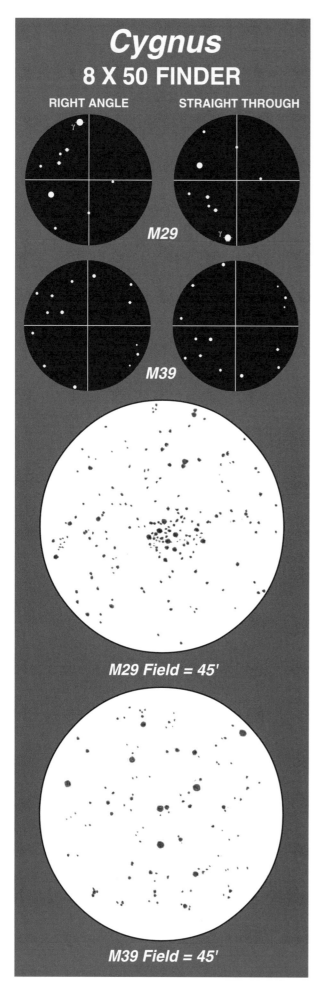

Cygnus
8 X 50 FINDER

RIGHT ANGLE | STRAIGHT THROUGH

M29

M39

M29 Field = 45'

M39 Field = 45'

M29
Open Cluster in Cygnus

Visual Magnitude: 6.6
Visual Index: 5
Angular Size: 6'

This sparse and coarse open cluster is composed of only a dozen or so members. It appears cluster-like in the finder scope, but in the eyepiece it looks like a scattering of bright background stars. For this reason it is easily overlooked, especially so for novice observers; they will have it in the eyepiece many times before finally realizing that they have found it. This is an easy object (although not very rewarding) for small telescopes and binoculars. Messier discovered it in July, 1764. The distance is estimated at 6,000 light-years. Its diameter is estimated to be 11 light-years.

M39
Open Cluster in Cygnus

Visual Magnitude: 4.6
Visual Index: 3
Angular Size: 30'

Like **M29** above, this object appears open cluster-like in the finder only. It is loose and coarse in appearance. Although it has more member stars than **M29** — estimated at about 30 — it is as undistinguished a grouping as **M29** and equally hard to recognize in the eyepiece as a cluster. This is an easy object for small telescopes and binoculars. **M39** is another of Messier's 1764 discoveries. The distance of this grouping is estimated at about 800 light-years. The diameter is about at 7 light-years.

The Year-Round Messier Marathon Field Guide   Copyright © 1997 Willmann-Bell, Inc

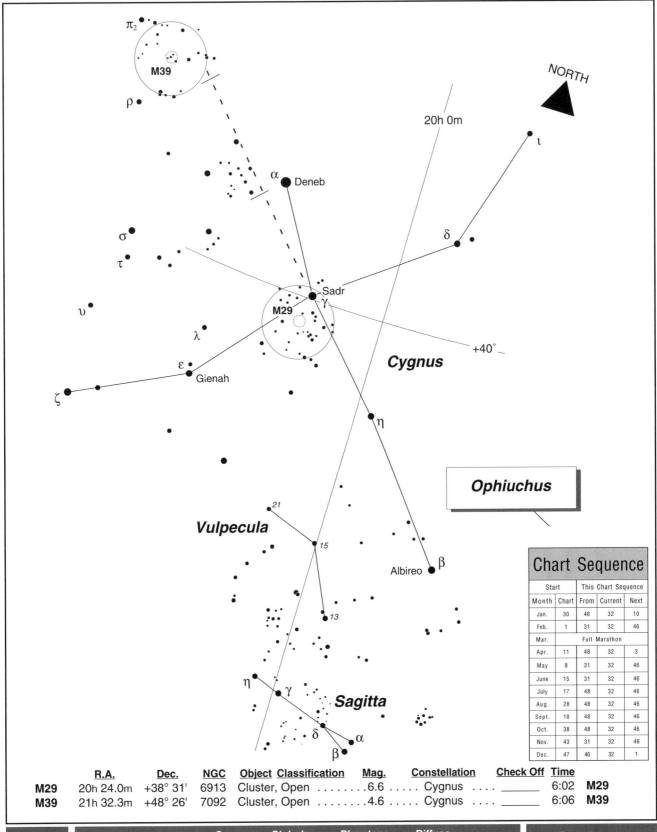

NORTH

20h 0m

α Deneb

ι

δ

π₂

M39

ρ

σ

τ

υ

λ

ε
Gienah

ζ

Sadr
M29
γ

+40°

Cygnus

η

Ophiuchus

21

Vulpecula

15

Albireo
β

13

η

γ

Sagitta

δ

α

β

Chart Sequence

Start		This Chart Sequence		
Month	Chart	From	Current	Next
Jan.	30	46	32	10
Feb.	1	31	32	46
Mar.	Full Marathon			
Apr.	11	48	32	3
May	8	31	32	46
June	15	31	32	46
July	17	48	32	46
Aug.	28	48	32	46
Sept.	18	48	32	46
Oct.	38	48	32	46
Nov.	43	31	32	46
Dec.	47	46	32	1

	R.A.	Dec.	NGC	Object Classification	Mag.	Constellation	Check Off	Time	
M29	20h 24.0m	+38° 31'	6913	Cluster, Open 6.6		Cygnus	.... _____	6:02	M29
M39	21h 32.3m	+48° 26'	7092	Cluster, Open 4.6		Cygnus	.... _____	6:06	M39

| Galaxy | Open Cluster | Globular Cluster | Planetary Nebula | Diffuse Nebula |

One Power Finder Chart

Circle = 4°

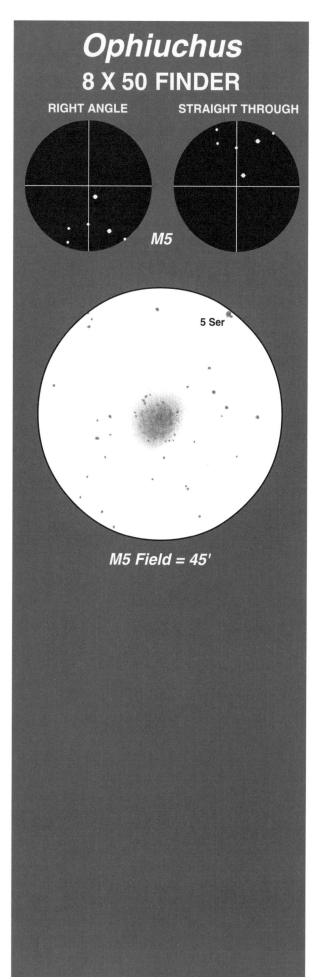

Ophiuchus
8 X 50 FINDER

RIGHT ANGLE **STRAIGHT THROUGH**

M5

5 Ser

M5 Field = 45'

M5
**Globular Cluster
in Serpens Caput**

**Visual Magnitude: 5.7
Visual Index: 2
Angular Size: 13'**

M5 was recorded by Messier in May, 1764. According to Burnham, **M5** is ranked as one of the three great show objects of the summer sky. Its distance is estimated to be about 27,000 light-years, and its diameter is given at about 100 light-years. It radiates light equal to about a quarter of a million suns. **M5** is easily seen in small telescopes and binoculars. It is partially resolved in telescopes as small as 4 inches. A notable feature is that it is not quite circular — the cluster is about ten percent longer along one axis.

Lying 20' SSE, the fine double star 5 Serpentis adds to the setting with a yellow primary and a reddish companion separated by 11".

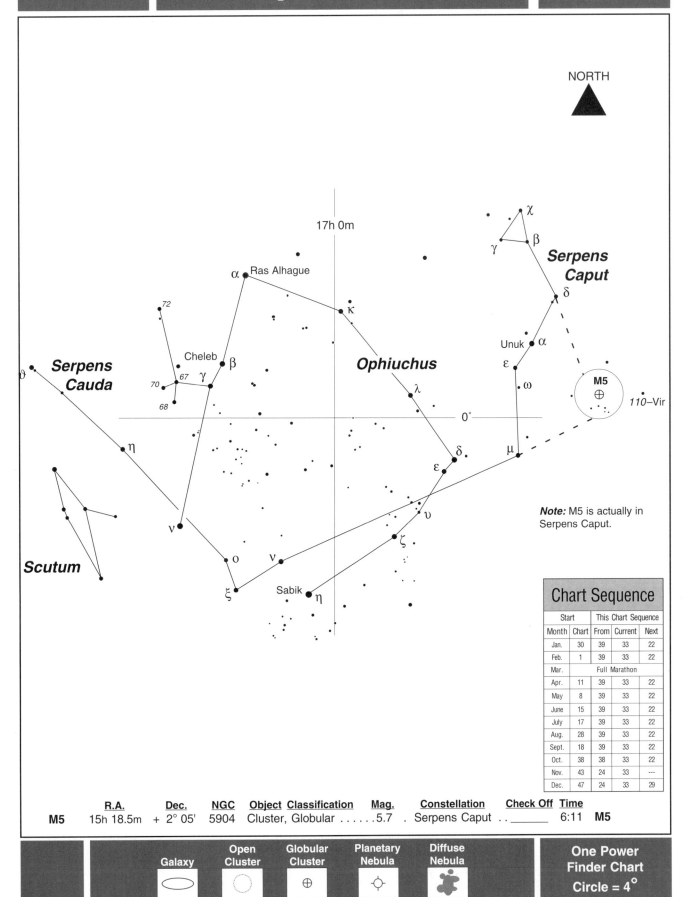

NORTH

17h 0m

α Ras Alhague

72

**Serpens
Caput**

χ

β

γ

δ

Unuk α

ε

ω

M5
⊕

110–Vir

Note: M5 is actually in
Serpens Caput.

Cheleb β

70 *67* γ

68

**Serpens
Cauda**

ϑ

Ophiuchus

λ

0°

η

δ

ε

μ

ν

υ

Scutum

o ν

ζ

ξ

Sabik η

Chart Sequence

Start		This Chart Sequence		
Month	Chart	From	Current	Next
Jan.	30	39	33	22
Feb.	1	39	33	22
Mar.	Full Marathon			
Apr.	11	39	33	22
May	8	39	33	22
June	15	39	33	22
July	17	39	33	22
Aug.	28	39	33	22
Sept.	18	39	33	22
Oct.	38	38	33	22
Nov.	43	24	33	---
Dec.	47	24	33	29

	R.A.	Dec.	NGC	Object Classification	Mag.	Constellation	Check Off	Time
M5	15h 18.5m	+ 2° 05'	5904	Cluster, Globular 5.7	.	Serpens Caput . . _____		6:11 M5

Galaxy	Open Cluster	Globular Cluster	Planetary Nebula	Diffuse Nebula

**One Power
Finder Chart**

Circle = 4°

Ophiuchus
8 X 50 FINDER

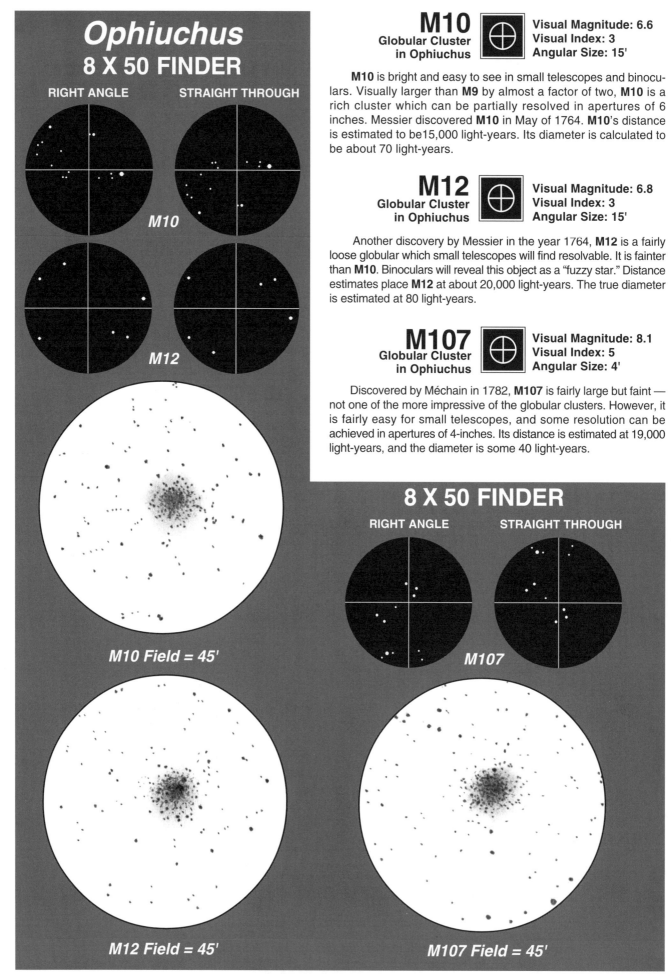

RIGHT ANGLE   **STRAIGHT THROUGH**

M10

M12

M10 Field = 45'

M12 Field = 45'

M10
Globular Cluster in Ophiuchus

Visual Magnitude: 6.6
Visual Index: 3
Angular Size: 15'

M10 is bright and easy to see in small telescopes and binoculars. Visually larger than **M9** by almost a factor of two, **M10** is a rich cluster which can be partially resolved in apertures of 6 inches. Messier discovered **M10** in May of 1764. **M10**'s distance is estimated to be 15,000 light-years. Its diameter is calculated to be about 70 light-years.

M12
Globular Cluster in Ophiuchus

Visual Magnitude: 6.8
Visual Index: 3
Angular Size: 15'

Another discovery by Messier in the year 1764, **M12** is a fairly loose globular which small telescopes will find resolvable. It is fainter than **M10**. Binoculars will reveal this object as a "fuzzy star." Distance estimates place **M12** at about 20,000 light-years. The true diameter is estimated at 80 light-years.

M107
Globular Cluster in Ophiuchus

Visual Magnitude: 8.1
Visual Index: 5
Angular Size: 4'

Discovered by Méchain in 1782, **M107** is fairly large but faint — not one of the more impressive of the globular clusters. However, it is fairly easy for small telescopes, and some resolution can be achieved in apertures of 4-inches. Its distance is estimated at 19,000 light-years, and the diameter is some 40 light-years.

8 X 50 FINDER

RIGHT ANGLE   **STRAIGHT THROUGH**

M107

M107 Field = 45'

The Year-Round Messier Marathon Field Guide

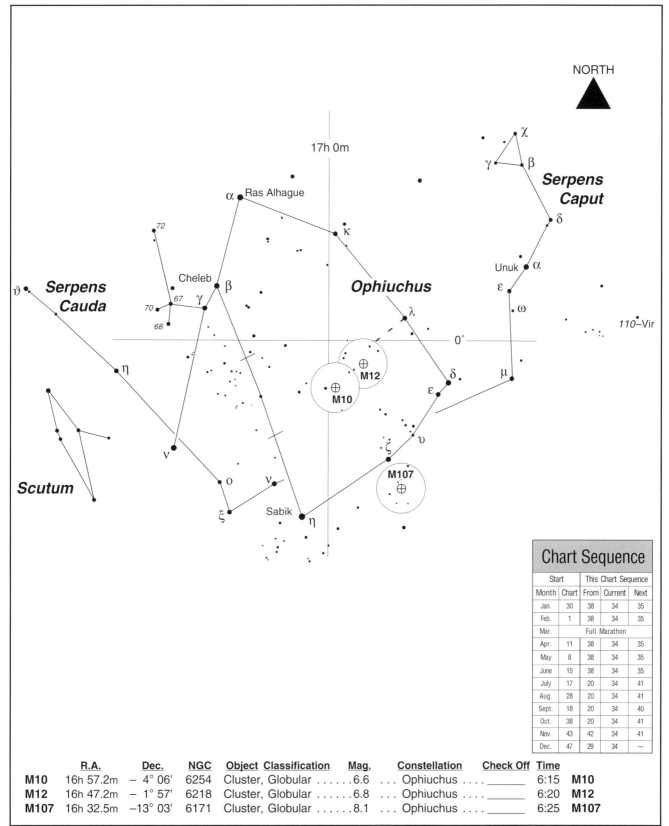

NORTH

17h 0m

Serpens
Caput

χ
γ   β

δ

Unuk   α
ε
ω

110–Vir

α Ras Alhague

κ

Ophiuchus

72

Cheleb   β
67   γ
70
68

λ

Serpens
Cauda

ϑ

0°

η

⊕
M12

⊕
M10

δ

ε

Scutum

ν

ζ   υ

ν
o   ν

ξ   Sabik
η

M107
⊕

Chart Sequence				
Start		This Chart Sequence		
Month	Chart	From	Current	Next
Jan.	30	38	34	35
Feb.	1	38	34	35
Mar.	Full Marathon			
Apr.	11	38	34	35
May	8	38	34	35
June	15	38	34	35
July	17	20	34	41
Aug.	28	20	34	41
Sept.	18	20	34	40
Oct.	38	20	34	41
Nov.	43	42	34	41
Dec.	47	29	34	---

	R.A.	Dec.	NGC	Object Classification	Mag.	Constellation	Check Off	Time	
M10	16h 57.2m	– 4° 06'	6254	Cluster, Globular	6.6	. . . Ophiuchus	_____	6:15	**M10**
M12	16h 47.2m	– 1° 57'	6218	Cluster, Globular	6.8	. . . Ophiuchus	_____	6:20	**M12**
M107	16h 32.5m	–13° 03'	6171	Cluster, Globular	8.1	. . . Ophiuchus	_____	6:25	**M107**

 Galaxy

 **Open
Cluster**

 **Globular
Cluster**

 **Planetary
Nebula**

 **Diffuse
Nebula**

 **One Power
Finder Chart**

Circle = 4°

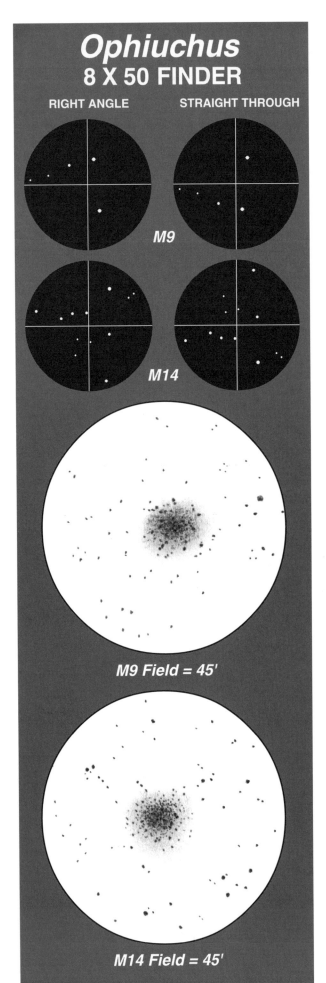

Ophiuchus
8 X 50 FINDER

RIGHT ANGLE   STRAIGHT THROUGH

M9

M14

M9 Field = 45'

M14 Field = 45'

M9
**Globular Cluster
in Ophiuchus**

**Visual Magnitude: 7.6
Visual Index: 4
Angular Size: 9'**

Quite small but bright, this globular appears to be a star in an 8X50 finder scope. It is a fuzz ball in small telescopes and binoculars. It was discovered by Messier in May of *his* marathon year of 1764. It can be partially resolved in larger telescopes. Its distance is estimated at 19,000 light-years with a diameter of 50 light-years.

M14
**Globular Cluster
in Ophiuchus**

**Visual Magnitude: 7.6
Visual Index: 4
Angular Size: 12'**

DIscovered by Messier in June 1764, this globular is remarkable for its even distribution of light across the principal diameter of the cluster. The light falls off smoothly near the outer edges. Telescopes of moderate size are required to partially resolve this cluster's outer edges. The distance to **M14** is estimated at 33,000 light-years, and the diameter at about 112 light-years.

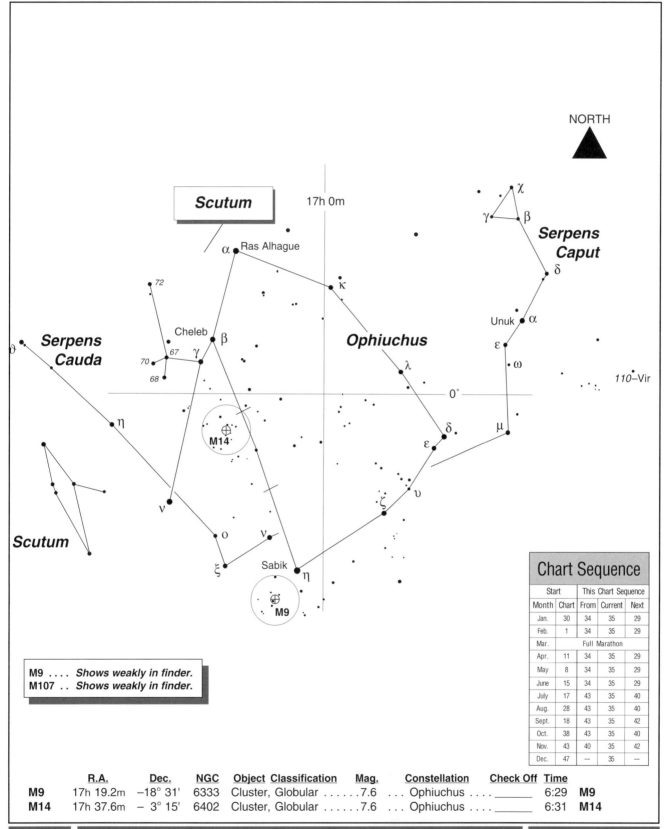

Scutum

17h 0m

NORTH

Ras Alhague

α

κ

χ

γ   β

Serpens
Caput

δ

Unuk   α

ε

ω

72

Cheleb

Serpens
Cauda

ϑ

β

67
70   γ
68

Ophiuchus

λ

110–Vir

0°

η

δ

ε

μ

ν

o   ν

ζ   υ

Scutum

ξ

Sabik   η

M14

M9

M9 .... *Shows weakly in finder.*
M107 .. *Shows weakly in finder.*

Chart Sequence

Start		This Chart Sequence		
Month	Chart	From	Current	Next
Jan.	30	34	35	29
Feb.	1	34	35	29
Mar.	Full Marathon			
Apr.	11	34	35	29
May	8	34	35	29
June	15	34	35	29
July	17	43	35	40
Aug.	28	43	35	40
Sept.	18	43	35	42
Oct.	38	43	35	40
Nov.	43	40	35	42
Dec.	47	—	35	—

	R.A.	Dec.	NGC	Object Classification	Mag.	Constellation	Check Off	Time	
M9	17h 19.2m	−18° 31'	6333	Cluster, Globular	7.6	... Ophiuchus	_____	6:29	**M9**
M14	17h 37.6m	− 3° 15'	6402	Cluster, Globular	7.6	... Ophiuchus	_____	6:31	**M14**

Galaxy	Open Cluster	Globular Cluster	Planetary Nebula	Diffuse Nebula

One Power Finder Chart
Circle = 4°

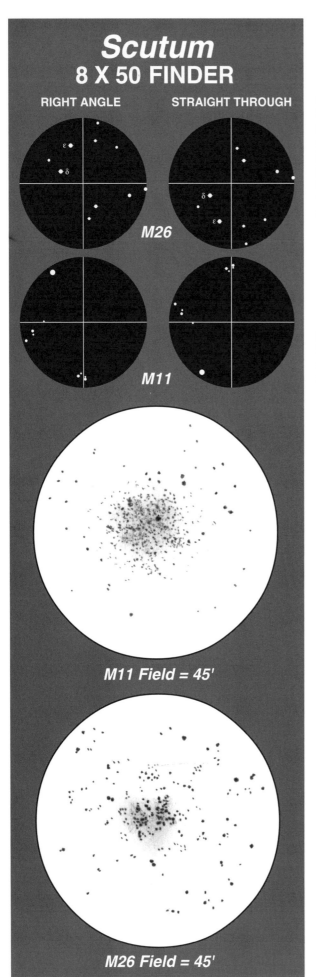

Scutum
8 X 50 FINDER

RIGHT ANGLE   **STRAIGHT THROUGH**

ε
δ

M26

M11

M11 Field = 45'

M26 Field = 45'

M11
The Wild Duck Cluster

Visual Magnitude: 5.8
Visual Index: 4
Angular Size: 12'

A rather large, concentrated open cluster which appears almost like a globular at lower magnifications, especially in smaller telescopes and binoculars, **M11** is easily mistaken for a globular cluster, especially when one is not familiar with its appearance and when using a telescope of small aperture. It can be resolved with high power in smaller telescopes, but the most rewarding views are in telescopes of moderate aperture. There are over 500 stars brighter than 14th magnitude. This is another one of Messier's 1764 discoveries. Distance estimates place this cluster at about 6,200 light-years and its diameter at approximately 21 light-years.

M26
**Open Cluster
in Scutum**

Visual Magnitude: 8.0
Visual Index: 6
Angular Size: 9'

This cluster is not very impressive, and its Milky Way background makes it appear even less so. Distance estimates place this object some 5,200 light-years distant. The estimated diameter of the group is placed at 21 light-years. A 6 to 8 inch telescope will reveal about 25 member stars.

The Year-Round Messier Marathon Field Guide

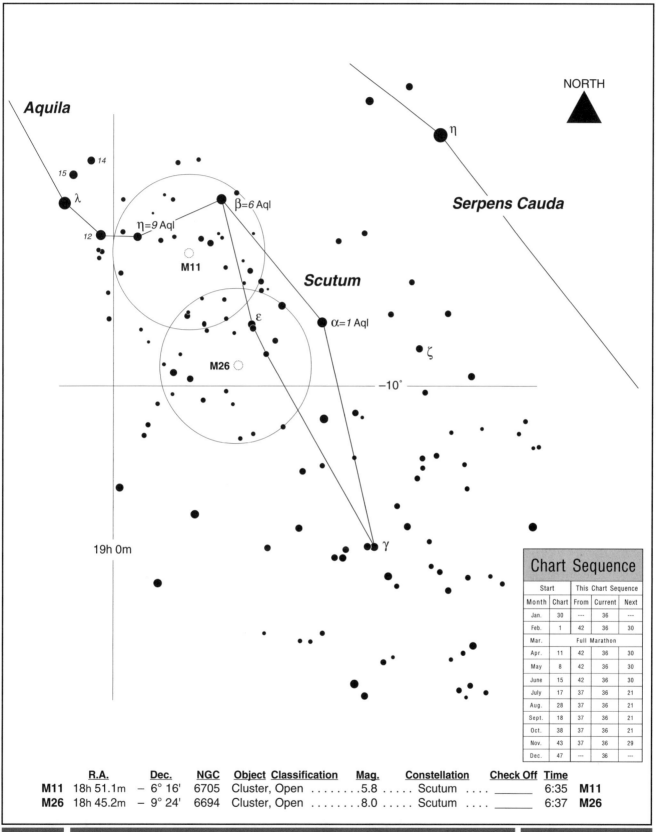

Aquila

14

15

λ

12

η=9 Aql

M11

β=6 Aql

ε

M26

Scutum

α=1 Aql

ζ

NORTH

Serpens Cauda

η

−10°

19h 0m

γ

Chart Sequence

Start		This Chart Sequence		
Month	Chart	From	Current	Next
Jan.	30	---	36	---
Feb.	1	42	36	30
Mar.		Full Marathon		
Apr.	11	42	36	30
May	8	42	36	30
June	15	42	36	30
July	17	37	36	21
Aug.	28	37	36	21
Sept.	18	37	36	21
Oct.	38	37	36	21
Nov.	43	37	36	29
Dec.	47	---	36	---

	R.A.	Dec.	NGC	Object Classification	Mag.	Constellation	Check Off	Time	
M11	18h 51.1m	− 6° 16'	6705	Cluster, Open	5.8	. . . . . Scutum	_____	6:35	**M11**
M26	18h 45.2m	− 9° 24'	6694	Cluster, Open	8.0	. . . . . Scutum	_____	6:37	**M26**

Galaxy	Open Cluster	Globular Cluster	Planetary Nebula	Diffuse Nebula	One Power Finder Chart Circle = 4°
		⊕	◇		

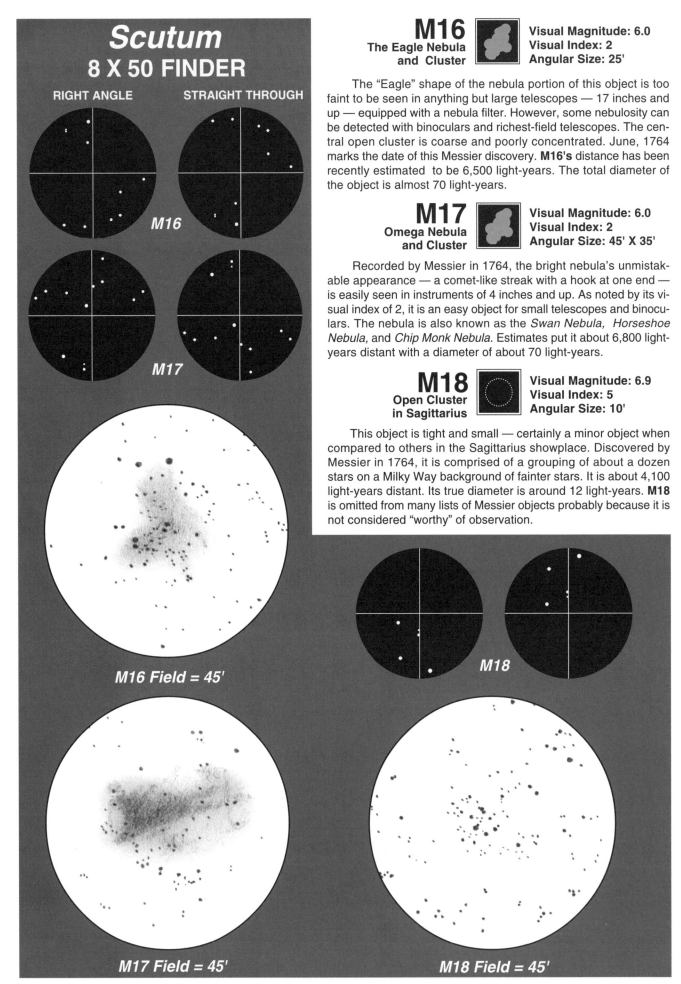

Scutum
8 X 50 FINDER

RIGHT ANGLE   **STRAIGHT THROUGH**

M16

M17

M16 Field = 45'

M17 Field = 45'

M16
The Eagle Nebula and Cluster

Visual Magnitude: 6.0
Visual Index: 2
Angular Size: 25'

The "Eagle" shape of the nebula portion of this object is too faint to be seen in anything but large telescopes — 17 inches and up — equipped with a nebula filter. However, some nebulosity can be detected with binoculars and richest-field telescopes. The central open cluster is coarse and poorly concentrated. June, 1764 marks the date of this Messier discovery. **M16's** distance has been recently estimated to be 6,500 light-years. The total diameter of the object is almost 70 light-years.

M17
Omega Nebula and Cluster

Visual Magnitude: 6.0
Visual Index: 2
Angular Size: 45' X 35'

Recorded by Messier in 1764, the bright nebula's unmistakable appearance — a comet-like streak with a hook at one end — is easily seen in instruments of 4 inches and up. As noted by its visual index of 2, it is an easy object for small telescopes and binoculars. The nebula is also known as the *Swan Nebula, Horseshoe Nebula,* and *Chip Monk Nebula.* Estimates put it about 6,800 light-years distant with a diameter of about 70 light-years.

M18
Open Cluster in Sagittarius

Visual Magnitude: 6.9
Visual Index: 5
Angular Size: 10'

This object is tight and small — certainly a minor object when compared to others in the Sagittarius showplace. Discovered by Messier in 1764, it is comprised of a grouping of about a dozen stars on a Milky Way background of fainter stars. It is about 4,100 light-years distant. Its true diameter is around 12 light-years. **M18** is omitted from many lists of Messier objects probably because it is not considered "worthy" of observation.

M18

M18 Field = 45'

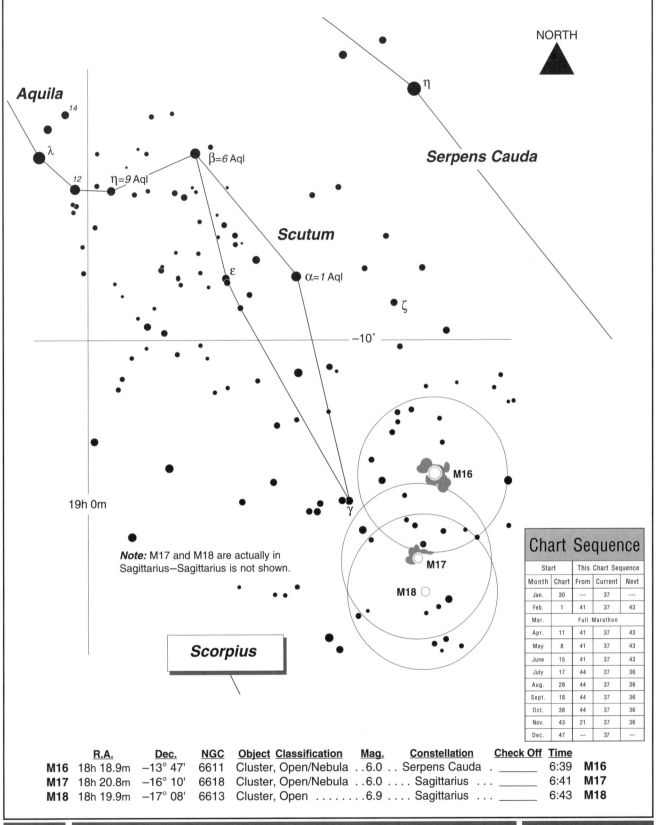

NORTH

Aquila

14

λ

12

η=*9* Aql

β=*6* Aql

Serpens Cauda

η

Scutum

ε

α=*1* Aql

ζ

−10°

19h 0m

M16

M17

M18

Note: M17 and M18 are actually in
Sagittarius—Sagittarius is not shown.

γ

Scorpius

Chart Sequence

Start		This Chart Sequence		
Month	Chart	From	Current	Next
Jan.	30	---	37	---
Feb.	1	41	37	43
Mar.	Full Marathon			
Apr.	11	41	37	43
May	8	41	37	43
June	15	41	37	43
July	17	44	37	36
Aug.	28	44	37	36
Sept.	18	44	37	36
Oct.	38	44	37	36
Nov.	43	21	37	36
Dec.	47	---	37	---

	R.A.	Dec.	NGC	Object	Classification	Mag.	Constellation	Check Off	Time	
M16	18h 18.9m	−13° 47'	6611	Cluster, Open/Nebula	..6.0 ..	Serpens Cauda	. _____	6:39	**M16**
M17	18h 20.8m	−16° 10'	6618	Cluster, Open/Nebula	..6.0	Sagittarius	... _____	6:41	**M17**
M18	18h 19.9m	−17° 08'	6613	Cluster, Open	........6.9	Sagittarius	... _____	6:43	**M18**

 Galaxy	Open Cluster	Globular Cluster	Planetary Nebula	Diffuse Nebula

One Power
Finder Chart

Circle = 4°

Scorpius

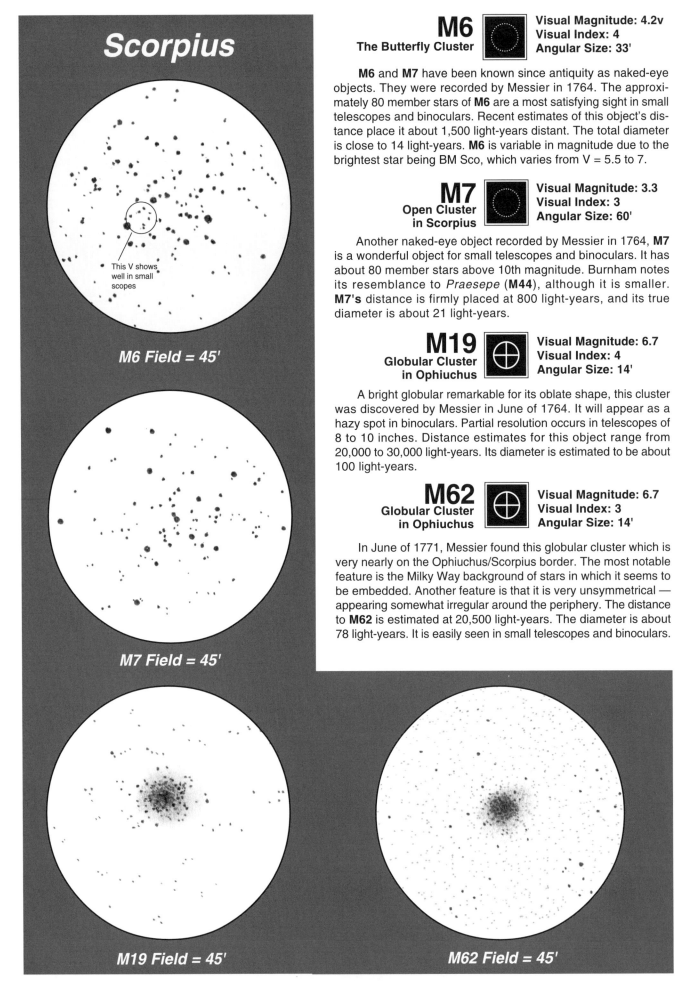

M6 Field = 45'

M7 Field = 45'

M19 Field = 45'

M62 Field = 45'

This V shows well in small scopes

M6
The Butterfly Cluster

Visual Magnitude: 4.2v
Visual Index: 4
Angular Size: 33'

M6 and **M7** have been known since antiquity as naked-eye objects. They were recorded by Messier in 1764. The approximately 80 member stars of **M6** are a most satisfying sight in small telescopes and binoculars. Recent estimates of this object's distance place it about 1,500 light-years distant. The total diameter is close to 14 light-years. **M6** is variable in magnitude due to the brightest star being BM Sco, which varies from V = 5.5 to 7.

M7
Open Cluster in Scorpius

Visual Magnitude: 3.3
Visual Index: 3
Angular Size: 60'

Another naked-eye object recorded by Messier in 1764, **M7** is a wonderful object for small telescopes and binoculars. It has about 80 member stars above 10th magnitude. Burnham notes its resemblance to *Praesepe* (**M44**), although it is smaller. **M7's** distance is firmly placed at 800 light-years, and its true diameter is about 21 light-years.

M19
Globular Cluster in Ophiuchus

Visual Magnitude: 6.7
Visual Index: 4
Angular Size: 14'

A bright globular remarkable for its oblate shape, this cluster was discovered by Messier in June of 1764. It will appear as a hazy spot in binoculars. Partial resolution occurs in telescopes of 8 to 10 inches. Distance estimates for this object range from 20,000 to 30,000 light-years. Its diameter is estimated to be about 100 light-years.

M62
Globular Cluster in Ophiuchus

Visual Magnitude: 6.7
Visual Index: 3
Angular Size: 14'

In June of 1771, Messier found this globular cluster which is very nearly on the Ophiuchus/Scorpius border. The most notable feature is the Milky Way background of stars in which it seems to be embedded. Another feature is that it is very unsymmetrical — appearing somewhat irregular around the periphery. The distance to **M62** is estimated at 20,500 light-years. The diameter is about 78 light-years. It is easily seen in small telescopes and binoculars.

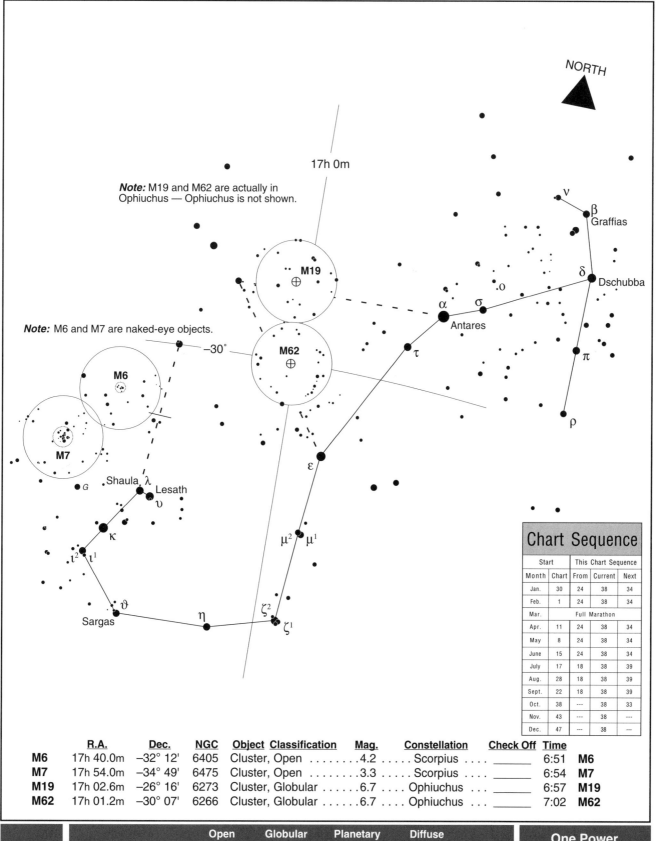

NORTH

17h 0m

Note: M19 and M62 are actually in Ophiuchus — Ophiuchus is not shown.

Note: M6 and M7 are naked-eye objects.

M19

M62

M6

M7

−30°

ν

β
Graffias

δ
Dschubba

o

α
Antares

σ

τ

π

ρ

ε

Shaula λ
Lesath
υ
G

κ

μ² μ¹

ι² ι¹

ϑ

η
ζ²
ζ¹

Sargas

Chart Sequence

Start		This Chart Sequence		
Month	Chart	From	Current	Next
Jan.	30	24	38	34
Feb.	1	24	38	34
Mar.	Full Marathon			
Apr.	11	24	38	34
May	8	24	38	34
June	15	24	38	34
July	17	18	38	39
Aug.	28	18	38	39
Sept.	22	18	38	39
Oct.	38	---	38	33
Nov.	43	---	38	---
Dec.	47	---	38	---

	R.A.	Dec.	NGC	Object Classification	Mag.	Constellation	Check Off	Time	
M6	17h 40.0m	−32° 12'	6405	Cluster, Open 4.2		Scorpius	_____	6:51	M6
M7	17h 54.0m	−34° 49'	6475	Cluster, Open 3.3		Scorpius	_____	6:54	M7
M19	17h 02.6m	−26° 16'	6273	Cluster, Globular 6.7		Ophiuchus ...	_____	6:57	M19
M62	17h 01.2m	−30° 07'	6266	Cluster, Globular 6.7		Ophiuchus ...	_____	7:02	M62

Galaxy	Open Cluster	Globular Cluster	Planetary Nebula	Diffuse Nebula	One Power Finder Chart Circle = 4°

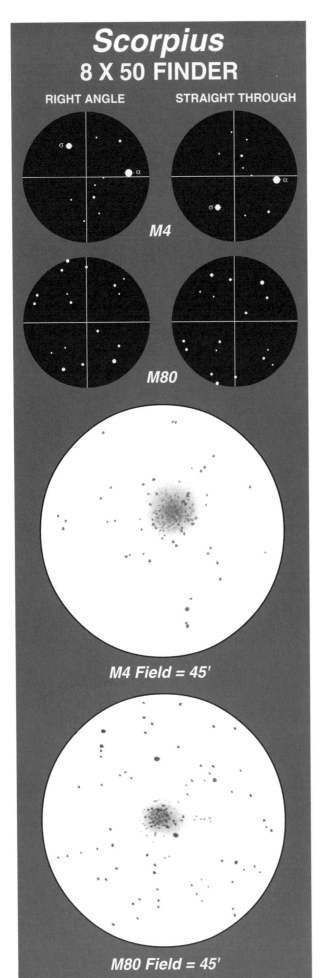

Scorpius
8 X 50 FINDER

RIGHT ANGLE   STRAIGHT THROUGH

M4

M80

M4 Field = 45'

M80 Field = 45'

M4
Globular Cluster
in Scorpius

Visual Magnitude: 5.9
Visual Index: 2
Angular Size: 26'

M4 is an easy object for small telescopes and binoculars, and a naked eye object under good seeing conditions. A 4 inch instrument will partially resolve this relatively loose but brilliant globular. This globular cluster was discovered by Messier in May, 1764. Its distance is estimated to be 6,500 light-years. Its diameter is about 52 light-years.

M80
Globular Cluster
in Scorpius

Visual Magnitude: 7.3
Visual Index: 4
Angular Size: 7'

This small but fairly bright globular cluster was evidently discovered by Messier and Méchain simultaneously — if such a thing is possible — in January, 1781. The distance to **M80** is estimated to be about 28,000 light-years, and the diameter is estimated at 72 light-years. It is very condensed and easily seen in small telescopes and binoculars. Some resolution is possible in moderately sized telescopes.

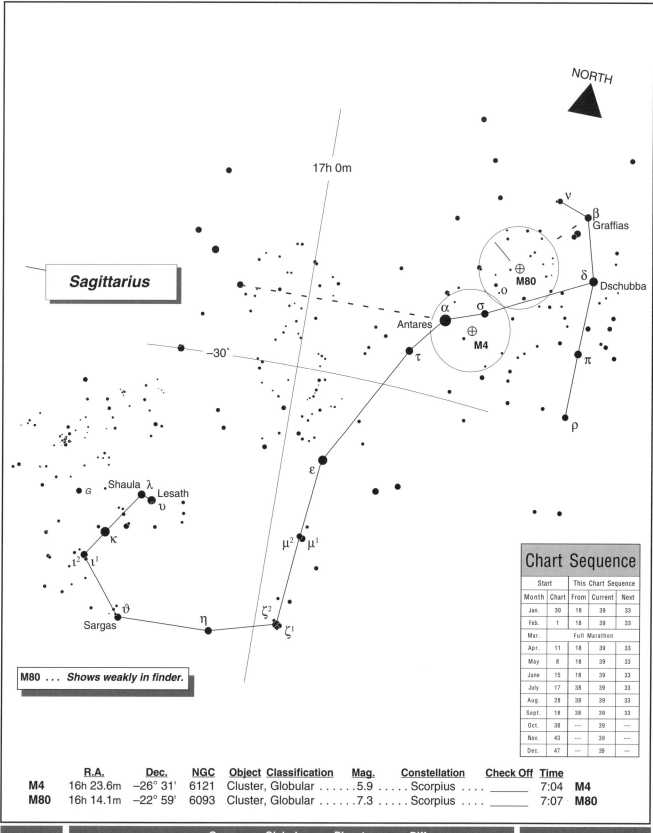

NORTH

Sagittarius

17h 0m

ν
β
Graffias

M80

δ
Dschubba

α
Antares
σ
o

M4

τ

π

ρ

ε

Shaula λ
G
Lesath
υ

κ

ι² ι¹

ϑ
Sargas
η
ζ²
ζ¹

μ² μ¹

M80 . . . *Shows weakly in finder.*

Chart Sequence				
Start		This Chart Sequence		
Month	Chart	From	Current	Next
Jan.	30	18	39	33
Feb.	1	18	39	33
Mar.	Full Marathon			
Apr.	11	18	39	33
May	8	18	39	33
June	15	18	39	33
July	17	38	39	33
Aug.	28	38	39	33
Sept.	18	38	39	33
Oct.	38	---	39	---
Nov.	43	---	39	---
Dec.	47	---	39	---

	R.A.	Dec.	NGC	Object	Classification	Mag.	Constellation	Check Off	Time	
M4	16h 23.6m	−26° 31'	6121	Cluster, Globular	......	5.9	Scorpius	...._____	7:04	**M4**
M80	16h 14.1m	−22° 59'	6093	Cluster, Globular	......	7.3	Scorpius	...._____	7:07	**M80**

Galaxy

Open Cluster

Globular Cluster

Planetary Nebula

Diffuse Nebula

One Power Finder Chart
Circle = 4°

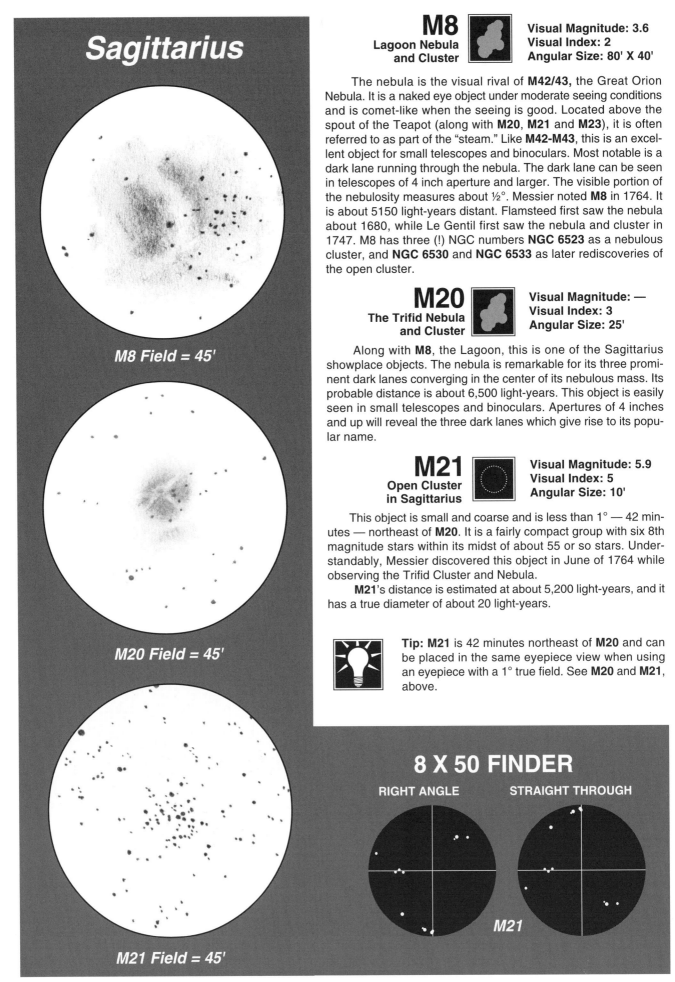

Sagittarius

M8 Field = 45'

M20 Field = 45'

M21 Field = 45'

M8
Lagoon Nebula and Cluster

Visual Magnitude: 3.6
Visual Index: 2
Angular Size: 80' X 40'

The nebula is the visual rival of **M42/43,** the Great Orion Nebula. It is a naked eye object under moderate seeing conditions and is comet-like when the seeing is good. Located above the spout of the Teapot (along with **M20, M21** and **M23**), it is often referred to as part of the "steam." Like **M42-M43,** this is an excellent object for small telescopes and binoculars. Most notable is a dark lane running through the nebula. The dark lane can be seen in telescopes of 4 inch aperture and larger. The visible portion of the nebulosity measures about ½°. Messier noted **M8** in 1764. It is about 5150 light-years distant. Flamsteed first saw the nebula about 1680, while Le Gentil first saw the nebula and cluster in 1747. M8 has three (!) NGC numbers **NGC 6523** as a nebulous cluster, and **NGC 6530** and **NGC 6533** as later rediscoveries of the open cluster.

M20
The Trifid Nebula and Cluster

Visual Magnitude: —
Visual Index: 3
Angular Size: 25'

Along with **M8,** the Lagoon, this is one of the Sagittarius showplace objects. The nebula is remarkable for its three prominent dark lanes converging in the center of its nebulous mass. Its probable distance is about 6,500 light-years. This object is easily seen in small telescopes and binoculars. Apertures of 4 inches and up will reveal the three dark lanes which give rise to its popular name.

M21
Open Cluster in Sagittarius

Visual Magnitude: 5.9
Visual Index: 5
Angular Size: 10'

This object is small and coarse and is less than 1° — 42 minutes — northeast of **M20.** It is a fairly compact group with six 8th magnitude stars within its midst of about 55 or so stars. Understandably, Messier discovered this object in June of 1764 while observing the Trifid Cluster and Nebula.

M21's distance is estimated at about 5,200 light-years, and it has a true diameter of about 20 light-years.

Tip: M21 is 42 minutes northeast of **M20** and can be placed in the same eyepiece view when using an eyepiece with a 1° true field. See **M20** and **M21,** above.

8 X 50 FINDER

RIGHT ANGLE

STRAIGHT THROUGH

M21

162

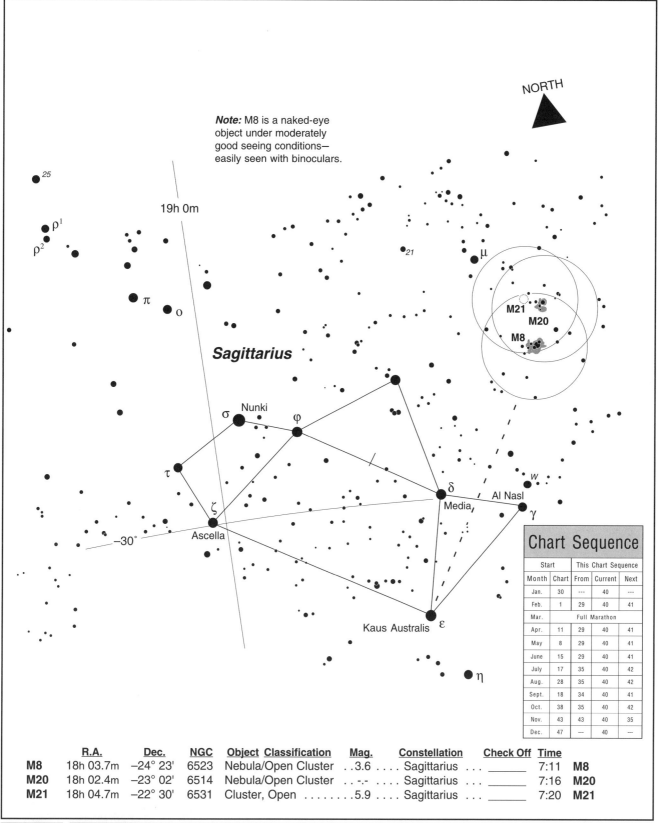

NORTH

Note: M8 is a naked-eye object under moderately good seeing conditions—easily seen with binoculars.

25

19h 0m

ρ¹
ρ²
π o

Sagittarius

21

μ

M21
M20
M8

σ Nunki φ
τ
ζ
Ascella
δ
Media
Al Nasl
w
γ
−30°

Kaus Australis ε

η

Chart Sequence

Start		This Chart Sequence		
Month	Chart	From	Current	Next
Jan.	30	---	40	---
Feb.	1	29	40	41
Mar.	Full Marathon			
Apr.	11	29	40	41
May	8	29	40	41
June	15	29	40	41
July	17	35	40	42
Aug.	28	35	40	42
Sept.	18	34	40	41
Oct.	38	35	40	42
Nov.	43	43	40	35
Dec.	47	---	40	---

	R.A.	Dec.	NGC	Object Classification	Mag.	Constellation	Check Off	Time	
M8	18h 03.7m	−24° 23'	6523	Nebula/Open Cluster	. .3.6	Sagittarius . . .	_____	7:11	**M8**
M20	18h 02.4m	−23° 02'	6514	Nebula/Open Cluster	. .-.-	Sagittarius . . .	_____	7:16	**M20**
M21	18h 04.7m	−22° 30'	6531	Cluster, Open	.5.9	Sagittarius . . .	_____	7:20	**M21**

 Galaxy
 **Open Cluster**
 Globular Cluster
 Planetary Nebula
 Diffuse Nebula

One Power Finder Chart
Circle = 4°

Sagittarius

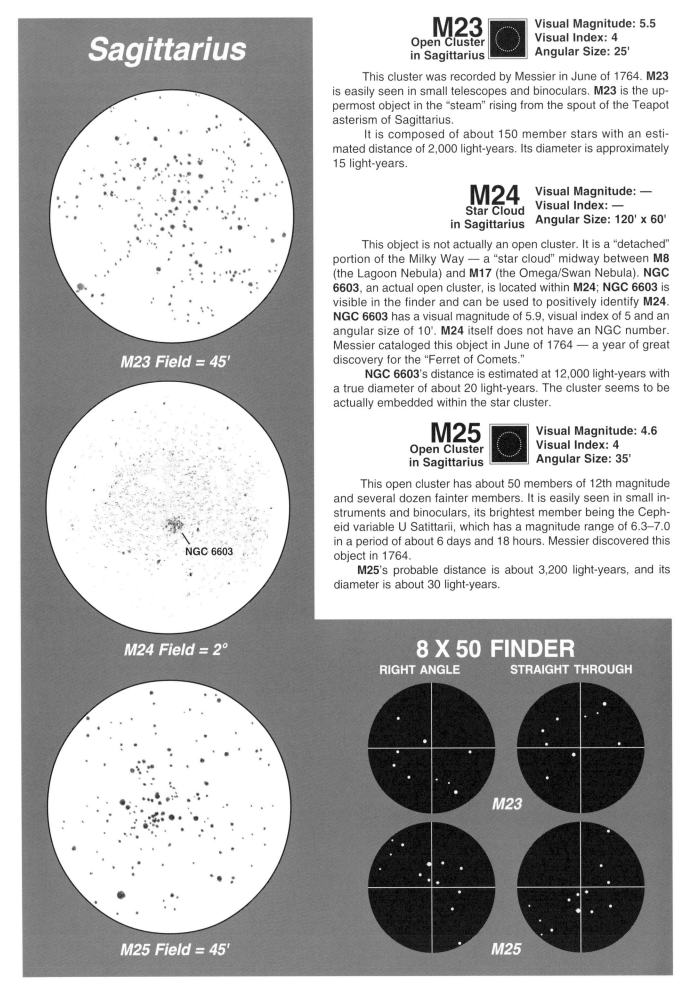

M23 Field = 45'

M24 Field = 2°

NGC 6603

M25 Field = 45'

M23
Open Cluster in Sagittarius

Visual Magnitude: 5.5
Visual Index: 4
Angular Size: 25'

This cluster was recorded by Messier in June of 1764. **M23** is easily seen in small telescopes and binoculars. **M23** is the uppermost object in the "steam" rising from the spout of the Teapot asterism of Sagittarius.

It is composed of about 150 member stars with an estimated distance of 2,000 light-years. Its diameter is approximately 15 light-years.

M24
Star Cloud in Sagittarius

Visual Magnitude: —
Visual Index: —
Angular Size: 120' x 60'

This object is not actually an open cluster. It is a "detached" portion of the Milky Way — a "star cloud" midway between **M8** (the Lagoon Nebula) and **M17** (the Omega/Swan Nebula). **NGC 6603**, an actual open cluster, is located within **M24**; **NGC 6603** is visible in the finder and can be used to positively identify **M24**. **NGC 6603** has a visual magnitude of 5.9, visual index of 5 and an angular size of 10'. **M24** itself does not have an NGC number. Messier cataloged this object in June of 1764 — a year of great discovery for the "Ferret of Comets."

NGC 6603's distance is estimated at 12,000 light-years with a true diameter of about 20 light-years. The cluster seems to be actually embedded within the star cluster.

M25
Open Cluster in Sagittarius

Visual Magnitude: 4.6
Visual Index: 4
Angular Size: 35'

This open cluster has about 50 members of 12th magnitude and several dozen fainter members. It is easily seen in small instruments and binoculars, its brightest member being the Cepheid variable U Satittarii, which has a magnitude range of 6.3–7.0 in a period of about 6 days and 18 hours. Messier discovered this object in 1764.

M25's probable distance is about 3,200 light-years, and its diameter is about 30 light-years.

8 X 50 FINDER
RIGHT ANGLE   **STRAIGHT THROUGH**

M23

M25

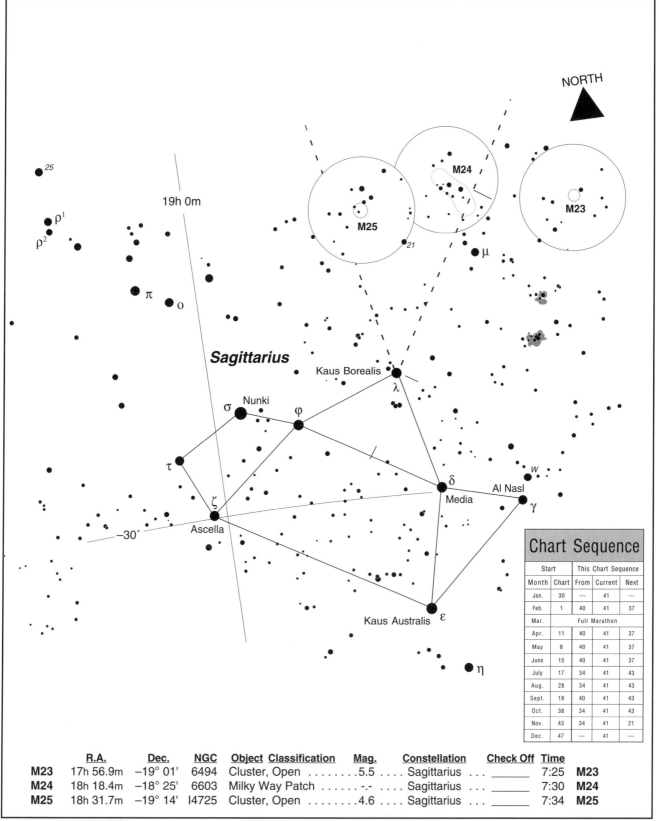

NORTH

25

ρ¹

ρ²

π

o

19h 0m

M24

M25

21

M23

μ

Sagittarius

Kaus Borealis

λ

σ Nunki

φ

τ

δ

Media

Al Nasl

w

γ

ζ

Ascella

−30°

Kaus Australis ε

η

Chart Sequence

Start		This Chart Sequence		
Month	Chart	From	Current	Next
Jan.	30	---	41	---
Feb.	1	40	41	37
Mar.		Full Marathon		
Apr.	11	40	41	37
May	8	40	41	37
June	15	40	41	37
July	17	34	41	43
Aug.	28	34	41	43
Sept.	18	40	41	43
Oct.	38	34	41	43
Nov.	43	34	41	21
Dec.	47	---	41	---

	R.A.	Dec.	NGC	Object Classification	Mag.	Constellation	Check Off	Time	
M23	17h 56.9m	−19° 01'	6494	Cluster, Open	5.5	Sagittarius	_____	7:25	M23
M24	18h 18.4m	−18° 25'	6603	Milky Way Patch	-.-	Sagittarius	_____	7:30	M24
M25	18h 31.7m	−19° 14'	I4725	Cluster, Open	4.6	Sagittarius	_____	7:34	M25

Galaxy	Open Cluster	Globular Cluster	Planetary Nebula	Diffuse Nebula	One Power Finder Chart Circle = 4°

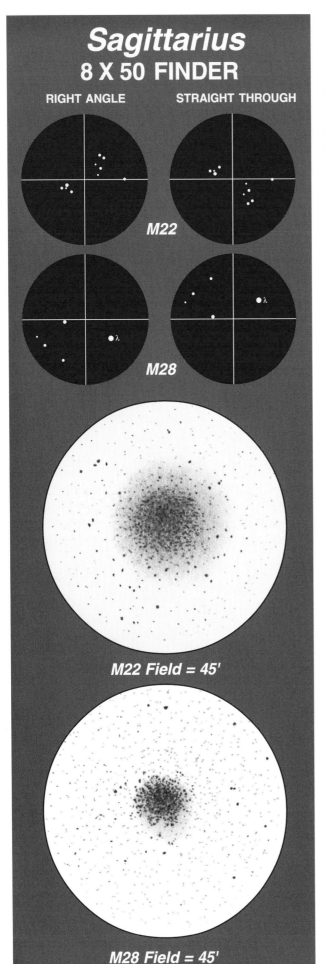

Sagittarius
8 X 50 FINDER

RIGHT ANGLE   **STRAIGHT THROUGH**

M22

M28

M22 Field = 45'

M28 Field = 45'

M22
**Globular Cluster
in Sagittarius**

Visual Magnitude: 5.1
Visual Index: 2
Angular Size: 24'

M22 is the largest and brightest Messier globular cluster; however, because of its usual low altitude, Northern Hemispere observers often consider it as second in overall interest to **M13**. **M22** is a huge, bright globular that is easily seen with the naked eye under moderately good seeing conditions. It is partially resolved in telescopes of 4 inches and composed of countless pinpoints of starlight in large aperture telescopes when using high power. It is actually brighter than **M13** but has a lower visual index. It is also easier to resolve than **M13**. Messier recorded this object in 1764.

Its distance is estimated at 9,600 light-years, and its true diameter is 70 light-years.

M28
**Globular Cluster
in Sagittarius**

Visual Magnitude: 6.8
Visual Index: 4
Angular Size: 11'

Noted by Messier in 1764, this globular is not particularly striking. It appears as a round, fuzzy spot in telescopes of small aperture and in binoculars. Large aperture is required to resolve this globular. It is, however, compact and dense with a slightly out-of-round outline.

Its distance is estimated at 19,000 light-years, and its diameter is given as about 65 light-years.

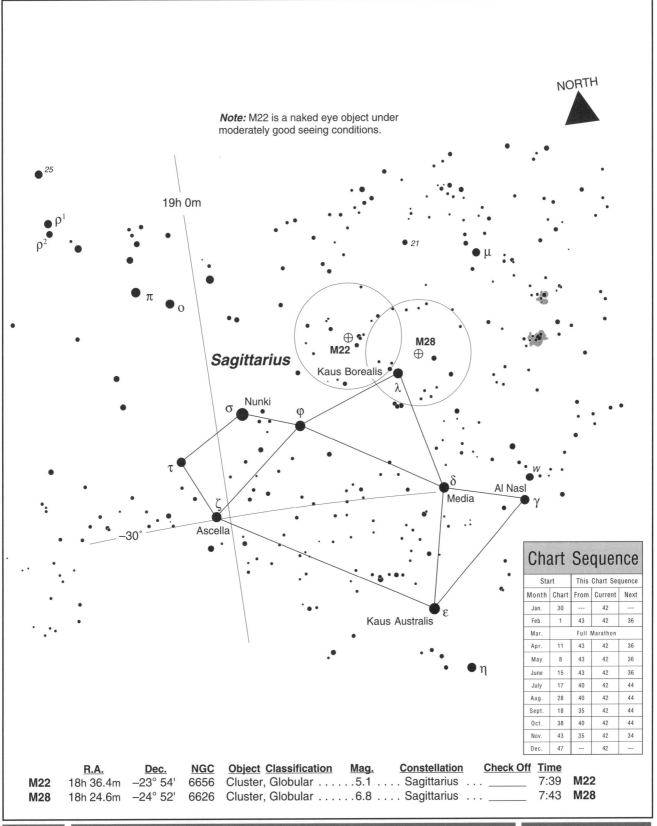

Note: M22 is a naked eye object under moderately good seeing conditions.

NORTH

19h 0m

25

ρ¹

ρ²

π

o

21

μ

Sagittarius

M22

M28

Kaus Borealis

λ

Nunki

σ

φ

τ

δ

Media

Al Nasl

w

γ

ζ

Ascella

−30°

Kaus Australis

ε

η

Chart Sequence			
Start	This Chart Sequence		
Month	Chart	From	Current	Next
Jan.	30	---	42	---
Feb.	1	43	42	36
Mar.	Full Marathon			
Apr.	11	43	42	36
May	8	43	42	36
June	15	43	42	36
July	17	40	42	44
Aug.	28	40	42	44
Sept.	18	35	42	44
Oct.	38	40	42	44
Nov.	43	35	42	34
Dec.	47	---	42	---

	R.A.	Dec.	NGC	Object Classification	Mag.	Constellation	Check Off	Time	
M22	18h 36.4m	−23° 54'	6656	Cluster, Globular	5.1	Sagittarius	_____	7:39	**M22**
M28	18h 24.6m	−24° 52'	6626	Cluster, Globular	6.8	Sagittarius	_____	7:43	**M28**

Galaxy

Open Cluster

Globular Cluster

Planetary Nebula

Diffuse Nebula

One Power Finder Chart Circle = 4°

The Year-Round Messier Marathon Field Guide

Sagittarius

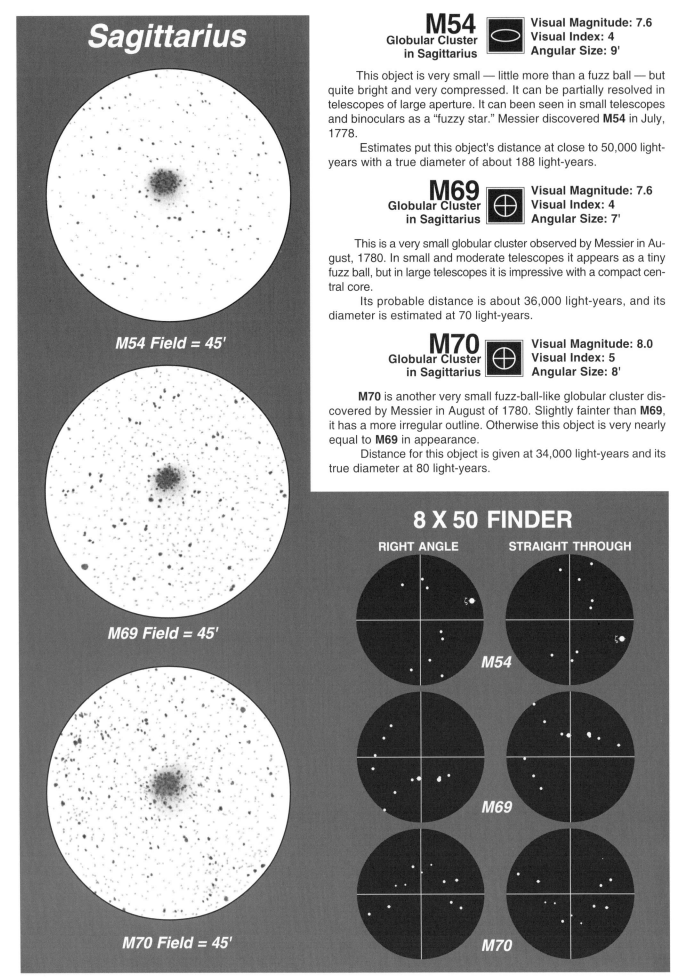

M54 Field = 45'

M69 Field = 45'

M70 Field = 45'

M54
Globular Cluster in Sagittarius

Visual Magnitude: 7.6
Visual Index: 4
Angular Size: 9'

This object is very small — little more than a fuzz ball — but quite bright and very compressed. It can be partially resolved in telescopes of large aperture. It can been seen in small telescopes and binoculars as a "fuzzy star." Messier discovered **M54** in July, 1778.

Estimates put this object's distance at close to 50,000 light-years with a true diameter of about 188 light-years.

M69
Globular Cluster in Sagittarius

Visual Magnitude: 7.6
Visual Index: 4
Angular Size: 7'

This is a very small globular cluster observed by Messier in August, 1780. In small and moderate telescopes it appears as a tiny fuzz ball, but in large telescopes it is impressive with a compact central core.

Its probable distance is about 36,000 light-years, and its diameter is estimated at 70 light-years.

M70
Globular Cluster in Sagittarius

Visual Magnitude: 8.0
Visual Index: 5
Angular Size: 8'

M70 is another very small fuzz-ball-like globular cluster discovered by Messier in August of 1780. Slightly fainter than **M69**, it has a more irregular outline. Otherwise this object is very nearly equal to **M69** in appearance.

Distance for this object is given at 34,000 light-years and its true diameter at 80 light-years.

8 X 50 FINDER

RIGHT ANGLE   **STRAIGHT THROUGH**

M54

M69

M70

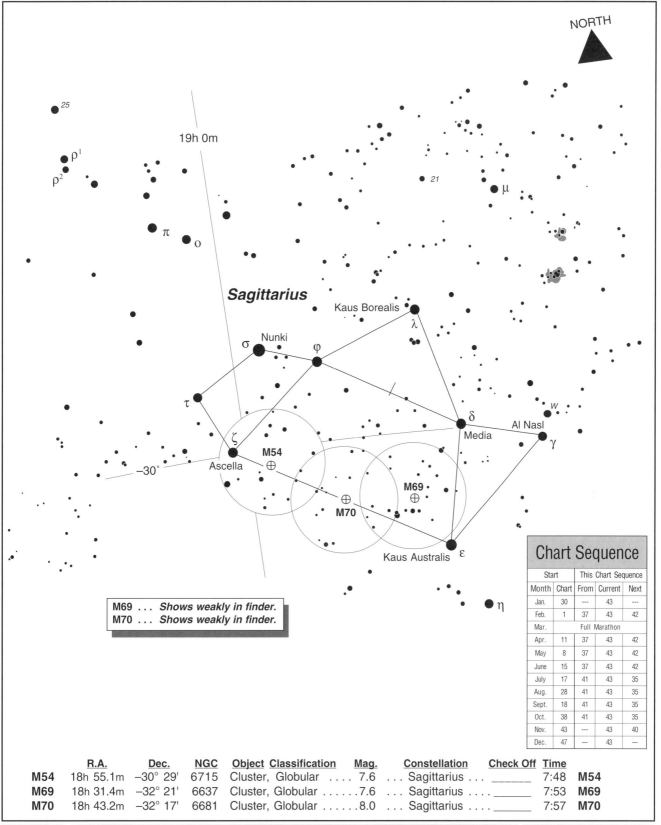

NORTH

25

19h 0m

ρ¹

ρ²

π

o

21

μ

Sagittarius

Kaus Borealis

λ

σ   Nunki

φ

τ

w

δ

Media   Al Nasl

γ

ζ

M54
⊕

Ascella

M69 ... *Shows weakly in finder.*
M70 ... *Shows weakly in finder.*

⊕
M70

M69
⊕

−30°

ε

Kaus Australis

η

Chart Sequence			
Start		This Chart Sequence	
Month	Chart	From	Current	Next
Jan.	30	---	43	---
Feb.	1	37	43	42
Mar.	Full Marathon			
Apr.	11	37	43	42
May	8	37	43	42
June	15	37	43	42
July	17	41	43	35
Aug.	28	41	43	35
Sept.	18	41	43	35
Oct.	38	41	43	35
Nov.	43	---	43	40
Dec.	47	---	43	---

	R.A.	Dec.	NGC	Object Classification	Mag.	Constellation	Check Off	Time	
M54	18h 55.1m	−30° 29'	6715	Cluster, Globular	7.6	... Sagittarius ...	_____	7:48	**M54**
M69	18h 31.4m	−32° 21'	6637	Cluster, Globular	7.6	... Sagittarius	_____	7:53	**M69**
M70	18h 43.2m	−32° 17'	6681	Cluster, Globular	8.0	... Sagittarius	_____	7:57	**M70**

Galaxy	Open Cluster	Globular Cluster	Planetary Nebula	Diffuse Nebula

One Power Finder Chart

Circle = 4°

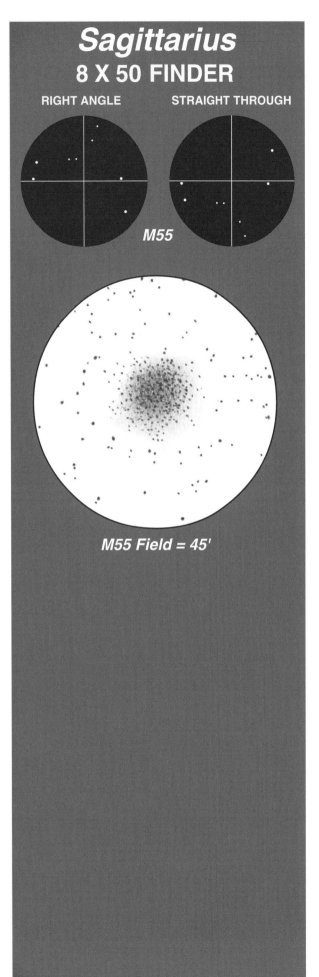

Sagittarius
8 X 50 FINDER

RIGHT ANGLE   **STRAIGHT THROUGH**

M55

M55 Field = 45'

M55
Globular Cluster
in Sagittarius

Visual Magnitude: 6.4
Visual Index: 3
Angular Size: 19'

M55 is large loose globular that is easily seen in small telescopes and binoculars, in which it is visible as a low surface brightness patch. Very large scopes will reveal more of the fainter member stars populating the central portion of this globular. Messier discovered this object in the summer of 1778.

Its distance is estimated to be a little less than 13,500 light-years, and the diameter is placed at about 95 light-years.

Sagittarius

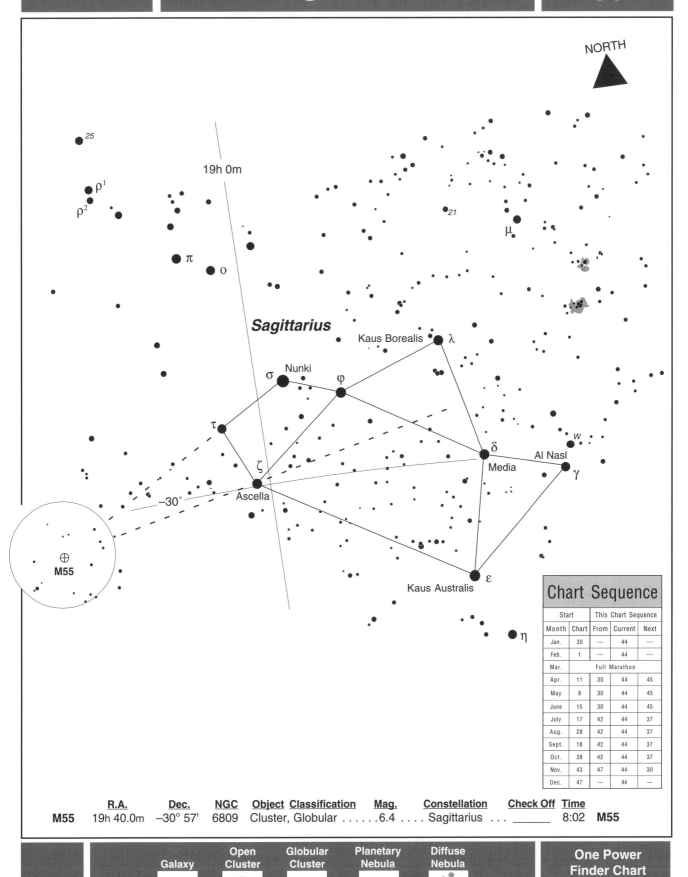

NORTH

25

ρ¹
ρ²
π
o

19h 0m

21

μ

Sagittarius

Kaus Borealis λ

σ Nunki
φ

τ

ζ
Ascella

δ
Media

w
Al Nasl
γ

−30°

⊕
M55

ε
Kaus Australis

η

Chart Sequence

Start		This Chart Sequence		
Month	Chart	From	Current	Next
Jan.	30	---	44	---
Feb.	1	---	44	---
Mar.		Full Marathon		
Apr.	11	30	44	45
May	8	30	44	45
June	15	30	44	45
July	17	42	44	37
Aug.	28	42	44	37
Sept.	18	42	44	37
Oct.	38	42	44	37
Nov.	43	47	44	30
Dec.	47	---	44	---

	R.A.	Dec.	NGC	Object Classification	Mag.	Constellation	Check Off	Time	
M55	19h 40.0m	−30° 57'	6809	Cluster, Globular 6.4		Sagittarius ...	_____	8:02	**M55**

Galaxy	Open Cluster	Globular Cluster	Planetary Nebula	Diffuse Nebula

One Power Finder Chart
Circle = 4°

The Year-Round Messier Marathon Field Guide 171

Sagittarius

8 X 50 FINDER

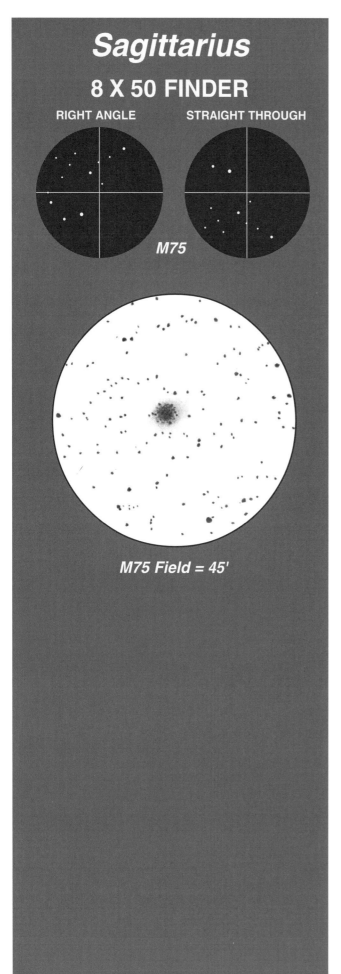

RIGHT ANGLE   **STRAIGHT THROUGH**

M75

M75 Field = 45'

M75

**Globular Cluster
in Sagittarius**

**Visual Magnitude: 8.5
Visual Index: 5
Angular Size: 6'**

First seen by Méchain in August, 1780, **M75** was confirmed by Messier two months later. **M75** is notable for its compactness and is resolved only in large telescopes. It appears as a hazy spot or fuzz ball in small telescopes and as a fuzzy star in binoculars.

Estimates of its distance place it at 59,000 light-years — possibly the most distant globular in the Messier catalog. Its diameter is calculated to be 100 light-years.

Tip: To locate **M75,** note the spatial relationships shown in the boxed figure on **Marathon Chart 45**.

Note: Small, compact and in the "boonies" on the night of the March Marathon, **M75** will be quite low on the horizon. It is difficult because it is so far away from any easily identifiable stars to help in its location. Use the inset figure on **Marathon Chart 45** to locate this slightly elusive object.

The Year-Round Messier Marathon Field Guide

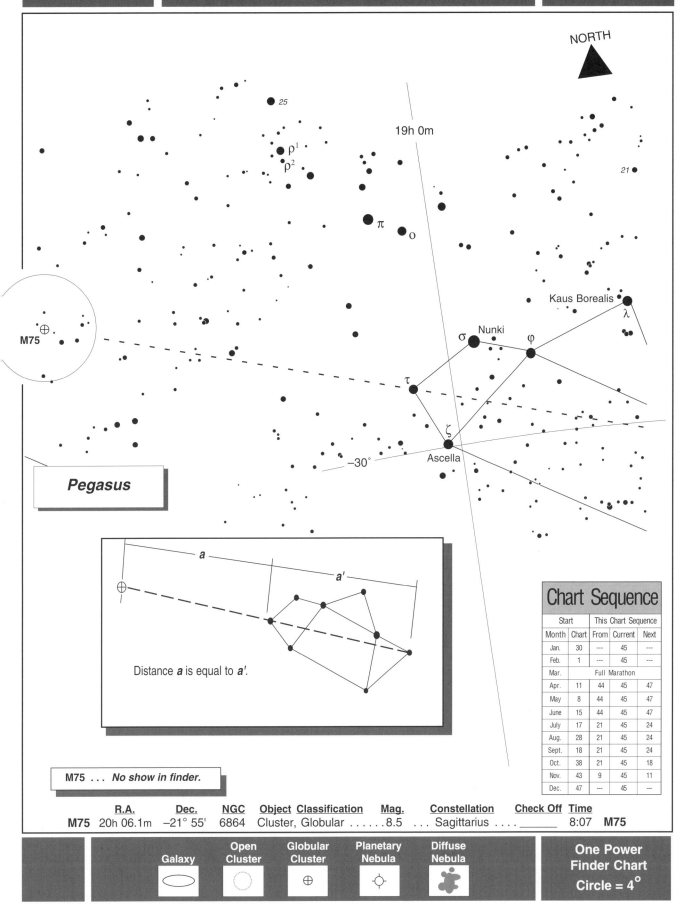

NORTH

25

ρ¹
ρ²

19h 0m

21

π   o

Kaus Borealis
λ

Nunki
σ   φ

τ

ζ
Ascella

−30°

M75

⊕

Pegasus

a
a'

Distance *a* is equal to *a'*.

M75 . . . *No show in finder.*

Chart Sequence

Start		This Chart Sequence		
Month	Chart	From	Current	Next
Jan.	30	---	45	---
Feb.	1	---	45	---
Mar.		Full Marathon		
Apr.	11	44	45	47
May	8	44	45	47
June	15	44	45	47
July	17	21	45	24
Aug.	28	21	45	24
Sept.	18	21	45	24
Oct.	38	21	45	18
Nov.	43	9	45	11
Dec.	47	—	45	—

R.A.	Dec.	NGC	Object Classification	Mag.	Constellation	Check Off	Time	
M75 20h 06.1m	−21° 55'	6864	Cluster, Globular	8.5	. . . Sagittarius	_____	8:07	**M75**

Galaxy	Open Cluster	Globular Cluster	Planetary Nebula	Diffuse Nebula

**One Power
Finder Chart
Circle = 4°**

The Year-Round Messier Marathon Field Guide

Pegasus

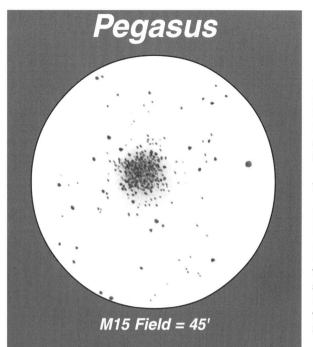

M15 Field = 45'

M15
Globular Cluster in Pegasus

Visual Magnitude: 6.0
Visual Index: 3
Angular Size: 10'

Messier added this dense, compact globular cluster to his catalog in 1764. It is a bright globular of fair size and surrenders to high magnification in larger telescopes, revealing a dense concentration of individual stellar points toward the center of its core. **M15** is easily seen in small telescopes and binoculars. It is remarkable for its brilliant core, and it is the 12th brightest of the known globular clusters. Also see *Tip*, below, and **Marathon Chart 46-a**.

Its probable distance is between 34,000 and 42,000 light-years. The diameter is estimated at 130 light-years.

Tip: M15 is fairly difficult to locate during the March Marathon night because Pegasus is not in full view. However, Enif — ε-Pegasi — is easy to find by first locating the constellation Delphinus then following a line to the horizon from Delphinus. The first bright star which is located slightly to the east of the line between the horizon and Delphinus is Enif. Delphinus, although dim, is easy to find because it is somewhat isolated without competing bright stars in the near vicinity. See **Marathon Chart 46-a**.

Pegasus

Marathon Chart 46

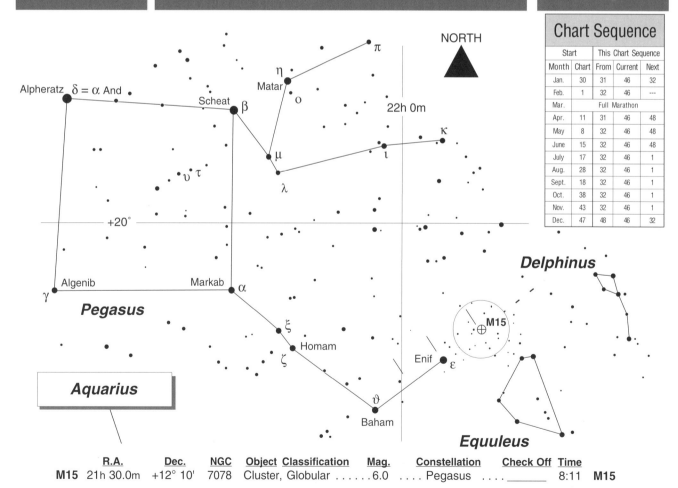

Chart Sequence

Start		This Chart Sequence		
Month	Chart	From	Current	Next
Jan.	30	31	46	32
Feb.	1	32	46	---
Mar.		Full Marathon		
Apr.	11	31	46	48
May	8	32	46	48
June	15	32	46	48
July	17	32	46	1
Aug.	28	32	46	1
Sept.	18	32	46	1
Oct.	38	32	46	1
Nov.	43	32	46	1
Dec.	47	48	46	32

	R.A.	Dec.	NGC	Object Classification	Mag.	Constellation	Check Off	Time	
M15	21h 30.0m	+12° 10'	7078	Cluster, Globular	6.0	. . . . Pegasus	_____	8:11	**M15**

 Galaxy
 Open Cluster
 Globular Cluster
 Planetary Nebula
 Diffuse Nebula

One Power Finder Chart Circle = 4°

The Year-Round Messier Marathon Field Guide

M15

EAST

SOUTHEAST

Messier Marathon "Rising Chart"—March 30th, 3:30 A.M.

The Year-Round Messier Marathon Field Guide

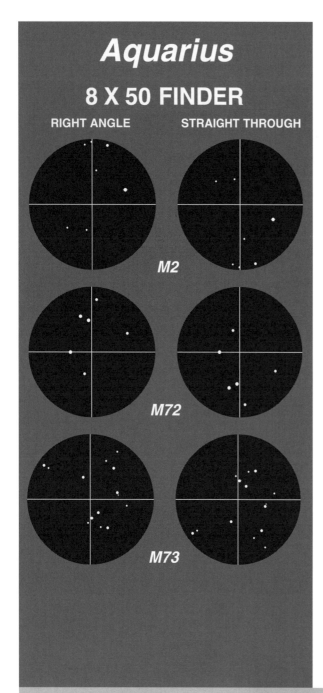

Aquarius

8 X 50 FINDER

RIGHT ANGLE   **STRAIGHT THROUGH**

M2

M72

M73

M2
Globular Cluster
in Aquarius

Visual Magnitude: 6.4
Visual Index: 3
Angular Size: 7'

Visible as a "hazy star" in binoculars, this is an easy object to resolve in telescopes of 8 inches and up. It is fairly bright and compact. **M2** is difficult to locate on March Marathon night because the constellation it is located within is not fully visible. Locate α-, β-, and μ-Aquarii using Enif in Pegasus (ε-Pegasi) as a reference. (Also see **Marathon Chart 47-a**.)

It is about 50,000 light-years distant and estimated to be 150 light-years in diameter.

M72
Globular Cluster
in Aquarius

Visual Magnitude: 9.3
Visual Index: 5
Angular Size: 3'

A very small globular, **M72** may appear as a tiny comet or planetary nebula in smaller telescopes. It can be partially resolved in telescopes of 10 inch aperture and larger. This object was discovered in August, 1780, by Méchain. See **Marathon Chart 47-a**. Also see *Tip*, below.

M72 is 60,000 light-years distant and 85 light-years across.

M73
Open Cluster
in Aquarius

Visual Magnitude: 8.9p
Visual Index: None listed
Angular Size: 1'

One of the Messier "mistakes," this object is an asterism of four stars. It is located 1.5° east and slightly south of **M72**. (See figure, below.) It was noted by Messier in October of 1780 — probably while confirming Méchain's discovery of **M72**. Although Messier noted that "...it contains a little nebulosity...," photographs show that it does not. Burnham points out that faint double or triple stars often appear fuzzy in small telescopes with poor seeing conditions. Also see *Tip*, below.

There is no distance information in any of the popular references concerning this object.

Tip: Most of Aquarius and Capricornus will be below the horizon on March Marathon night. You should have already located **M15** and **M2** and have an idea of the general area in which to locate the stars to provide the references necessary to find **M72** and **M73**. **Marathon Chart 47-a** is helpful on March Marathon night. Note that Aquila is "above" **M72** and **M73**.

Eyepiece Finder Chart for M73

M73 is an asterism consisting of four stars. There is no nebulosity associated with this small "cluster." Paul Murdin and David Allen speculate in their *Catalogue of the Universe* that it might actually be a small cluster — not just a chance visual association of four stars.

On the March Messier Marathon night, note that **M73** is rising and close to the horizon. Depending on your latitude and its southerly position, the lines of declination can be nearly vertical to the horizon at this time, and a slight move to the east and south is "down" and "to the left." If you are using an altazimuth mount, this is especially true.

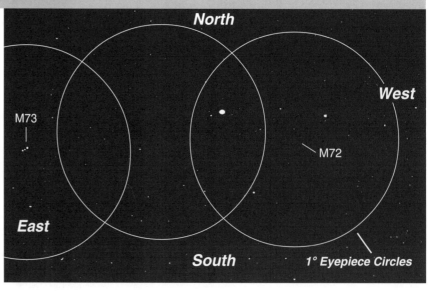

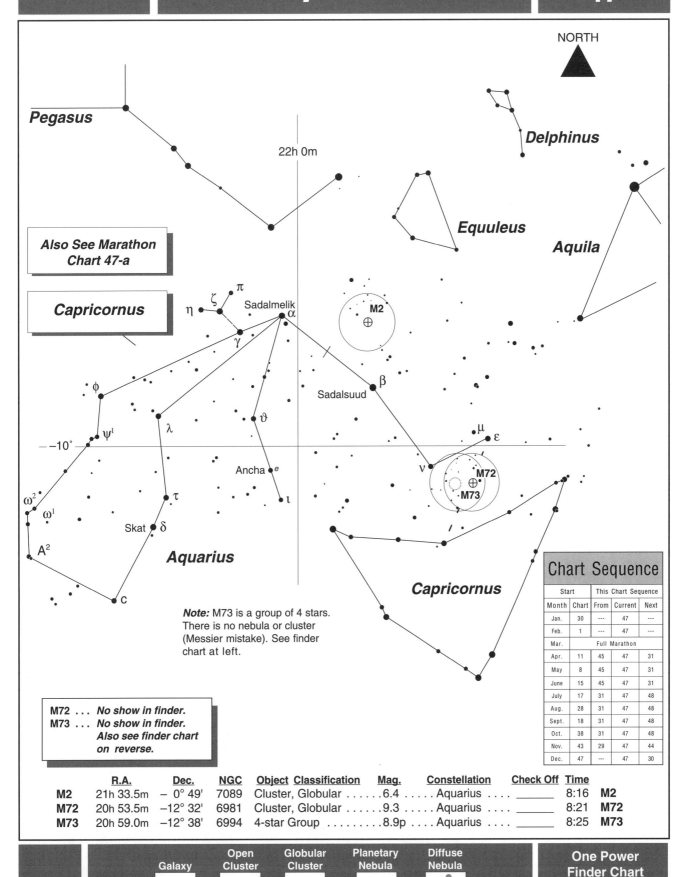

NORTH

Pegasus

Delphinus

22h 0m

Equuleus

Aquila

Also See Marathon
Chart 47-a

Capricornus

π
ζ
η   Sadalmelik
α
γ

M2

φ

ψ¹

λ
ϑ

β

Sadalsuud

–10°

Ancha e

μ
ε

ν

M72

M73

ω²
ω¹

τ

ι

A²

Skat δ

Aquarius

c

Capricornus

Note: M73 is a group of 4 stars.
There is no nebula or cluster
(Messier mistake). See finder
chart at left.

Chart Sequence			
Start		This Chart Sequence	
Month	Chart	From	Current	Next
Jan.	30	---	47	---
Feb.	1	---	47	---
Mar.	Full Marathon			
Apr.	11	45	47	31
May	8	45	47	31
June	15	45	47	31
July	17	31	47	48
Aug.	28	31	47	48
Sept.	18	31	47	48
Oct.	38	31	47	48
Nov.	43	29	47	44
Dec.	47	---	47	30

M72 . . . *No show in finder.*
M73 . . . *No show in finder.*
*Also see finder chart
on reverse.*

	R.A.	Dec.	NGC	Object Classification	Mag.	Constellation	Check Off	Time	
M2	21h 33.5m	− 0° 49'	7089	Cluster, Globular	6.4	Aquarius	_____	8:16	**M2**
M72	20h 53.5m	−12° 32'	6981	Cluster, Globular	9.3	Aquarius	_____	8:21	**M72**
M73	20h 59.0m	−12° 38'	6994	4-star Group	8.9p	Aquarius	_____	8:25	**M73**

Galaxy	Open Cluster	Globular Cluster	Planetary Nebula	Diffuse Nebula

**One Power
Finder Chart**
Circle = 4°

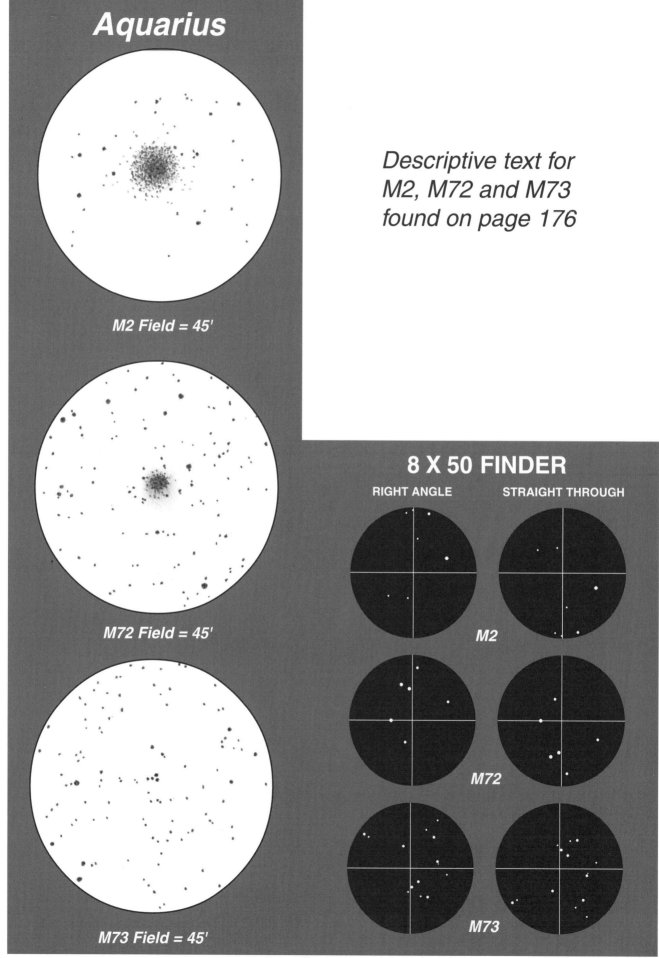

Aquarius

M2 Field = 45'

M72 Field = 45'

M73 Field = 45'

Descriptive text for M2, M72 and M73 found on page 176

8 X 50 FINDER

RIGHT ANGLE   **STRAIGHT THROUGH**

M2

M72

M73

The Year-Round Messier Marathon Field Guide

M2

M72

M73

EAST

SOUTHEAST

Messier Marathon "Rising Chart"—March 30th, 3:30 A.M.

The Year-Round Messier Marathon Field Guide

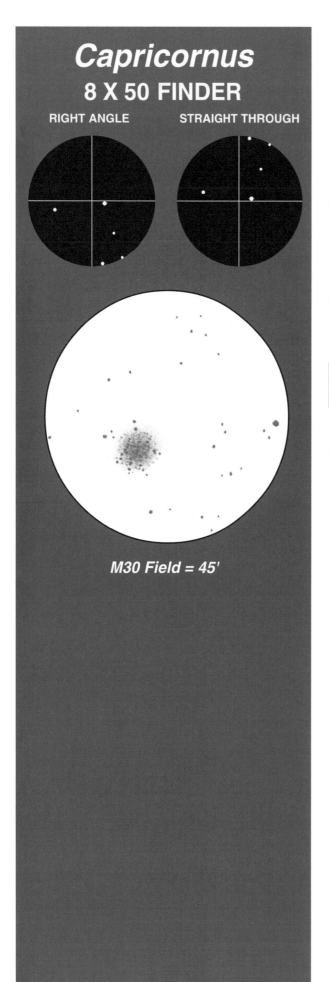

Capricornus
8 X 50 FINDER

RIGHT ANGLE   **STRAIGHT THROUGH**

M30 Field = 45'

M30
Globular Cluster
in Capricornus

Visual Magnitude: 7.3
Visual Index: 4
Angular Size: 6'

A fairly bright and dense globular discovered by Messier in August, 1764, **M30** is most notable as the last object in the March Messier Marathon. It is not particularly difficult to find or see under normal dark sky observing conditions. However, on March Marathon night, it is found in the morning's twilight, easily seen with small telescopes and binoculars under normal dark sky observing conditions. Also see *Tip*, below.

M30's distance is estimated at 40,000 light-years, and it has a diameter of about 100 light-years.

Note: M30 is a very difficult object on March Marathon night. It is the last object to be located and identified, and this must be done in morning's twilight. Under the best of conditions, this is difficult indeed. Although small (angular diameter is 1.5 minutes), it is compact and relatively bright with a visual magnitude of 7.3, making its identification under twilight conditions possible.

Tip: The best technique for locating this object on March Marathon night is to identify ζ-Capricornus and starhop, using the eyepiece, down the chain of stars shown on **Marathon Chart 48-a**. Follow the eyepiece views down to the horizon, and as each successive "hopper star" becomes visible, continue moving the telescope until you have the field containing **M30** centered. Positive identification of **M30** is possible using the three bright field stars shown in the 1° eyepiece circles on **Marathon Chart 48-a**. The brightest of these three field stars within an eyepiece of 1° true field is 41 Capricorni.

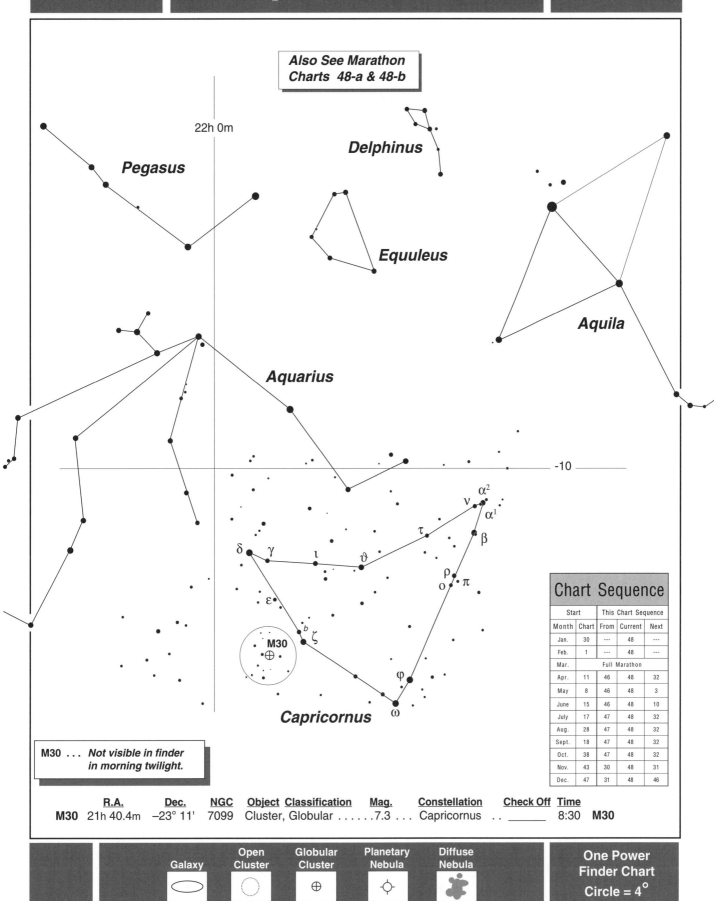

Also See Marathon
Charts 48-a & 48-b

22h 0m

Pegasus

Delphinus

Equuleus

Aquila

Aquarius

-10

ν α²
α¹
τ
β
δ γ ι ϑ
ρ
o π
ε
b ζ
M30
⊕
φ
ω

Capricornus

M30 ... *Not visible in finder in morning twilight.*

Chart Sequence

Start		This Chart Sequence		
Month	Chart	From	Current	Next
Jan.	30	---	48	---
Feb.	1	---	48	---
Mar.		Full Marathon		
Apr.	11	46	48	32
May	8	46	48	3
June	15	46	48	10
July	17	47	48	32
Aug.	28	47	48	32
Sept.	18	47	48	32
Oct.	38	47	48	32
Nov.	43	30	48	31
Dec.	47	31	48	46

	R.A.	Dec.	NGC	Object	Classification	Mag.	Constellation	Check Off	Time
M30	21h 40.4m	−23° 11'	7099	Cluster, Globular	......7.3 ...		Capricornus ..	_____	8:30 **M30**

Galaxy	Open Cluster	Globular Cluster	Planetary Nebula	Diffuse Nebula

One Power Finder Chart
Circle = 4°

Capricornus

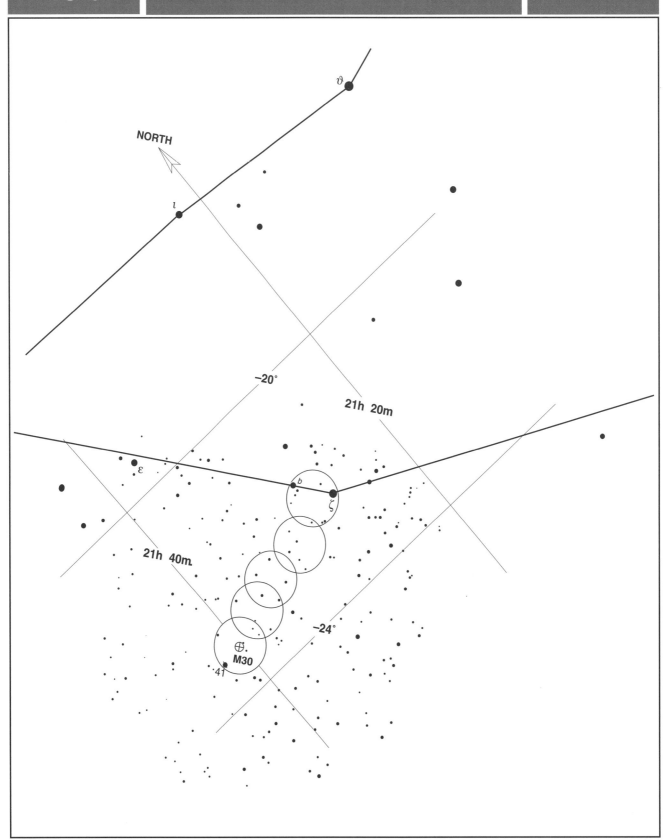

"Eyepiece Starhopper" Chart—Circles=1°

M15

M30

SOUTHEAST

Messier Marathon "Twilight Chart"—March 30th, 4:30 A.M.

The Year-Round Messier Marathon Field Guide

Appendix A | Messier's Catalog

	R.A.	Dec.	NGC	Object Classification	Mag.	Constellation	Map No.	
M1	5h 34.5m	+22° 01'	1952	Nebula (Nova Rem)	8.0	Taurus	11	M1
M2	21h 33.5m	− 0° 49'	7089	Cluster, Globular	6.4	Aquarius	47	M2
M3	13h 42.2m	+28° 23'	5272	Cluster, Globular	5.9	Canes Venatici	18	M3
M4	16h 23.6m	−26° 31'	6121	Cluster, Globular	5.9	Scorpius	39	M4
M5	15h 18.5m	+ 2° 05'	5904	Cluster, Globular	5.7	Serpens Caput	33	M5
M6	17h 40.0m	−32° 12'	6405	Cluster, Open	4.2	Scorpius	38	M6
M7	17h 54.0m	−34° 49'	6475	Cluster, Open	3.3	Scorpius	38	M7
M8	18h 03.7m	−24° 23'	6523	Nebula/Open Cluster	3.6	Sagittarius	40	M8
M9	17h 19.2m	−18° 31'	6333	Cluster, Globular	7.6	Ophiuchus	35	M9
M10	16h 57.2m	− 4° 06'	6254	Cluster, Globular	6.6	Ophiuchus	34	M10
M11	18h 51.1m	− 6° 16'	6705	Cluster, Open	5.8	Scutum	36	M11
M12	16h 47.2m	− 1° 57'	6218	Cluster, Globular	6.8	Ophiuchus	34	M12
M13	16h 41.7m	+36° 28'	6205	Cluster, Globular	5.7	Hercules	29	M13
M14	17h 37.6m	− 3° 15'	6402	Cluster, Globular	7.6	Ophiuchus	35	M14
M15	21h 30.0m	+12° 10'	7078	Cluster, Globular	6.0	Pegasus	46	M15
M16	18h 18.9m	−13° 47'	6611	Cluster, Open/Nebula	6.0	Serpens Cauda	37	M16
M17	18h 20.8m	−16° 10'	6618	Cluster, Open/Nebula	6.0	Sagittarius	37	M17
M18	18h 19.9m	−17° 08'	6613	Cluster, Open	6.9	Sagittarius	37	M18
M19	17h 02.6m	−26° 16'	6273	Cluster, Globular	6.7	Ophiuchus	38	M19
M20	18h 02.4m	−23° 02'	6514	Cluster, Open/Nebula	-.-	Sagittarius	40	M20
M21	18h 04.7m	−22° 30'	6531	Cluster, Open/Nebula	5.9	Sagittarius	21	M21
M22	18h 36.4m	−23° 54'	6656	Cluster, Globular	5.1	Sagittarius	42	M22
M23	17h 56.9m	−19° 01'	6494	Cluster, Open	5.5	Sagittarius	41	M23
M24	18h 18.4m	−18° 25'		Milky Way Patch	-.-	Sagittarius	41	M24
M25	18h 31.7m	−19° 14'	I4725	Cluster, Open	4.6	Sagittarius	41	M25
M26	18h 45.2m	− 9° 24'	6694	Cluster, Open	8.0	Scutum	36	M26
M27	19h 59.6m	+22° 43'	6853	Nebula, Planetary	7.3	Vulpecula	31	M27
M28	18h 24.6m	−24° 52'	6626	Cluster, Globular	6.8	Sagittarius	42	M28
M29	20h 24.0m	+38° 31'	6913	Cluster, Open	6.6	Cygnus	32	M29
M30	21h 40.4m	−23° 11'	7099	Cluster, Globular	7.3	Capricornus	48	M30
M31	0h 42.7m	+41° 16'	224	Galaxy, Spiral Sb	4.4	Andromeda	3	M31
M32	0h 42.7m	+40° 52'	221	Galaxy, Elliptical	8.0	Andromeda	3	M32
M33	1h 33.8m	+30° 39'	598	Galaxy, Spiral Sc	6.3	Triangulum	4	M33
M34	2h 42.0m	+42° 47'	1039	Cluster, Open	5.2	Perseus	5	M34
M35	6h 08.8m	+24° 20'	2168	Cluster, Open	5.1	Gemini	13	M35
M36	5h 36.3m	+34° 08'	1960	Cluster, Open	6.0	Auriga	12	M36
M37	5h 53.0m	+32° 33'	2099	Cluster, Open	5.6	Auriga	12	M37
M38	5h 28.7m	+35° 50'	1912	Cluster, Open	6.4	Auriga	12	M38
M39	21h 32.3m	+48° 26'	7092	Cluster, Open	4.6	Cygnus	32	M39
M40	12h 22.2m	+58° 05'	WNC4	Star, Double	9.0/9.3	Ursa Major	21	M40

	R.A.	Dec.	NGC	Object Classification	Mag.	Constellation	Map No.	
M41	6h 47.0m	−20° 44'	2287	Cluster, Open	4.5	Canis Major	9	M41
M42	5h35.3m	− 5° 23'	1976	Nebula/Open Cluster	5	Orion	7	M42
M43	5h 35.5m	− 5° 16'	1982	Nebula	7	Orion	7	M43
M44	8h 40.0m	+20° 00'	2632	Cluster, Open	3.1	Cancer	15	M44
M45	3h 47.5m	+24° 07'		Cluster, Open	1.2	Taurus	11	M45
M46	7h 41.8m	−14° 49'	2437	Cluster, Open	6.1	Puppis	8	M46
M47	7h 36.6m	−14° 29'	2422	Cluster, Open	4.4	Puppis	8	M47
M48	8h 13.8m	− 5° 48'	2548	Cluster, Open	5.8	Hydra	14	M48
M49	12h 29.8m	+ 8° 00'	4472	Galaxy, Elliptical	8.4	Virgo	28	M49
M50	7h 03.0m	− 8° 21'	2323	Cluster, Open	5.9	Monoceros	8	M50
M51	13h 29.9m	+47° 12'	5194	Galaxy, Spiral Sc	8.4	Canes Venatici	20	M51
M52	23h 24.2m	+61° 36'	7654	Cluster, Open	6.9	Cassiopeia	10	M52
M53	13h 12.9m	+18° 10'	5024	Cluster, Globular	7.5	Coma Berenices	18	M53
M54	18h 55.1m	−30° 29'	6715	Cluster, Globular	7.6	Sagittarius	43	M54
M55	19h 40.0m	−30° 57'	6809	Cluster, Globular	6.4	Sagittarius	44	M55
M56	19h 16.6m	+30° 11'	6779	Cluster, Globular	8.3	Lyra	30	M56
M57	18h 53.6m	+33° 02'	6720	Nebula, Planetary	8.8	Lyra	30	M57
M58	12h 37.7m	+11° 49'	4579	Galaxy, Spiral Sb	9.7	Virgo	28a	M58
M59	12h 42.0m	+11° 39'	4621	Galaxy, Elliptical	9.6	Virgo	28a	M59
M60	12h 43.7m	+11° 33'	4649	Galaxy, Elliptical	8.8	Virgo	28a	M60
M61	12h 21.9m	+ 4° 28'	4303	Galaxy, Spiral Sc	9.7	Virgo	27	M61
M62	17h 01.2m	−30° 07'	6266	Cluster, Globular	6.7	Ophiuchus	38	M62
M63	13h 15.8m	+42° 02'	5055	Galaxy, Spiral Sb	8.6	Canes Venatici	25	M63
M64	12h 56.7m	+21° 41'	4826	Galaxy, Spiral Sb	8.5	Coma Berenices	19	M64
M65	11h 18.9m	+13° 06'	3623	Galaxy, Spiral Sa	9.3	Leo	16	M65
M66	11h 20.3m	+13° 00'	3627	Galaxy, Spiral Sb	8.9	Leo	16	M66
M67	8h 51.3m	+11° 48'	2682	Cluster, Open	6.9	Cancer	15	M67
M68	12h 39.5m	−26° 45'	4590	Cluster, Globular	7.7	Hydra	26	M68
M69	18h 31.4m	−32° 21'	6637	Cluster, Globular	7.6	Sagittarius	43	M69
M70	18h 43.2m	−32° 17'	6681	Cluster, Globular	8.0	Sagittarius	43	M70
M71	19h 53.7m	+18° 47'	6838	Cluster, Globular	8.3	Sagitta	31	M71
M72	20h 53.5m	−12° 32'	6981	Cluster, Globular	9.3	Aquarius	47	M72
M73	20h 59.0m	−12° 38'	6994	4-star Group	8.9p	Aquarius	47	M73
M74	1h 36.7m	+15° 47'	628	Galaxy, Spiral Sc	9.4	Pisces	1	M74
M75	20h 06.1m	−21° 55'	6864	Cluster, Globular	8.5	Sagittarius	45	M75
M76	1h 42.2m	+51° 34'	650	Nebula, Planetary	10.1	Perseus	5	M76
M77	2h 42.7m	− 0° 01'	1068	Galaxy, Spiral Sb	8.9	Cetus	2	M77
M78	5h 46.7m	+ 0° 04'	2068	Nebula, Reflection	8	Orion	7	M78
M79	5h 24.2m	−24° 31'	1904	Cluster, Globular	7.8	Lepus	6	M79
M80	16h 14.1m	−22° 59'	6093	Cluster, Globular	7.3	Scorpius	39	M80
M81	9h 55.8m	+69° 04'	3031	Galaxy, Spiral Sb	6.9	Ursa Major	22	M81
M82	9h 56.2m	+69° 42'	3034	Galaxy, Irregular	8.4	Ursa Major	22	M82
M83	13h 37.7m	−29° 52'	5236	Galaxy, Spiral Sc	7.6	Hydra	26	M83
M84	12h 25.1m	+12° 53'	4374	Galaxy, Elliptical	9.1	Virgo	28b	M84
M85	12h 25.4m	+18° 11'	4382	Galaxy, Spiral SO	9.1	Coma Berenices	19	M85
M86	12h 26.2m	+12° 57'	4406	Galaxy, Elliptical	8.9	Virgo	28b	M86
M87	12h 30.8m	+12° 23'	4486	Galaxy, Ellip/Pec.	8.6	Virgo	28b	M87
M88	12h 32.0m	+14° 25'	4501	Galaxy, Spiral Sb	9.7	Coma Berenices	28b	M88
M89	12h 35.7m	+12° 33'	4552	Galaxy, Elliptical	9.8	Virgo	28c	M89
M90	12h 36.8m	+13° 10'	4569	Galaxy, Spiral Sb	9.5	Virgo	28c	M90

The Year-Round Messier Marathon Field Guide

	R.A.	Dec.	NGC	Object Classification	Mag.	Constellation	Map No.	
M91	12h 35.4m	+14° 30'	4548	Galaxy, Spiral SBb	10.7	Coma Berenices	28c	M91
M92	17h 17.1m	+43° 08'	6341	Cluster, Globular	6.4	Hercules	29	M92
M93	7h 44.6m	−23° 53'	2447	Cluster, Open	6.2	Puppis	9	M93
M94	12h 50.9m	+41° 07'	4736	Galaxy, Spiral Sb	8.2	Canes Venatici	25	M94
M95	10h 44.0m	+11° 42'	3351	Galaxy, Spiral SBb	9.7	Leo	17	M95
M96	10h 46.8m	+11° 49'	3368	Galaxy, Spiral Sb	9.2	Leo	17	M96
M97	11h 14.9m	+55° 01'	3587	Nebula, Planetary	9.9	Ursa Major	22	M97
M98	12h 13.8m	+14° 54'	4192	Galaxy, Spiral Sb	10.1	Coma Berenices	28d	M98
M99	12h 18.8m	+14° 25'	4254	Galaxy, Spiral Sc	9.9	Coma Berenices	28d	M99
M100	12h 22.9m	+15° 49'	4321	Galaxy, Spiral Sc	9.3	Coma Berenices	28d	M100
M101	14h 03.5m	+54° 21'	5457	Galaxy, Spiral Sc	7.9	Ursa Major	20	M101
M102	*Duplicate observation of M101*						24	M102
M103	1h 33.1m	+60° 42'	581	Cluster, Open	7.0	Cassiopeia	10	M103
M104	12h 40.0m	−11° 42'	4594	Galaxy, Spiral Sa	8.0	Virgo	27	M104
M105	10h 47.9m	+12° 43'	3379	Galaxy, Elliptical	9.3	Leo	17	M105
M106	12h 19.0m	+47° 18'	4258	Galaxy, Spiral Sb	8.4	Canes Venatici	21	M106
M107	16h 32.5m	-13° 03'	6171	Cluster, Globular	8.1	Ophiuchus	34	M107
M108	11h 11.6m	+55° 40'	3556	Galaxy, Spiral Sc	10.0	Ursa Major	22	M108
M109	11h 57.7m	+53° 22'	3992	Galaxy, Spiral SBb	9.8	Ursa Major	22	M109
M110	0h 42.7m	+41° 41'	205	Galaxy, Elliptical	8.8	Andromeda	3	M110

Note: All positions are equinox 2000.0

Appendix B | My Messier Log

Day / Month / Year

M1 _____/_____/_____ M1
M2 _____/_____/_____ M2
M3 _____/_____/_____ M3
M4 _____/_____/_____ M4
M5 _____/_____/_____ M5

M6 _____/_____/_____ M6
M7 _____/_____/_____ M7
M8 _____/_____/_____ M8
M9 _____/_____/_____ M9
M10 _____/_____/_____ M10

M11 _____/_____/_____ M11
M12 _____/_____/_____ M12
M13 _____/_____/_____ M13
M14 _____/_____/_____ M14
M15 _____/_____/_____ M15

M16 _____/_____/_____ M16
M17 _____/_____/_____ M17
M18 _____/_____/_____ M18
M19 _____/_____/_____ M19
M20 _____/_____/_____ M20

M21 _____/_____/_____ M21
M22 _____/_____/_____ M22
M23 _____/_____/_____ M23
M24 _____/_____/_____ M24
M25 _____/_____/_____ M25

Day / Month / Year

M26 _____/_____/_____ M26
M27 _____/_____/_____ M27
M28 _____/_____/_____ M28
M29 _____/_____/_____ M29
M30 _____/_____/_____ M30

M31 _____/_____/_____ M31
M32 _____/_____/_____ M32
M33 _____/_____/_____ M33
M34 _____/_____/_____ M34
M35 _____/_____/_____ M35

M36 _____/_____/_____ M36
M37 _____/_____/_____ M37
M38 _____/_____/_____ M38
M39 _____/_____/_____ M39
M40 _____/_____/_____ M40

M41 _____/_____/_____ M41
M42 _____/_____/_____ M42
M43 _____/_____/_____ M43
M44 _____/_____/_____ M44
M45 _____/_____/_____ M45

M46 _____/_____/_____ M46
M47 _____/_____/_____ M47
M48 _____/_____/_____ M48
M49 _____/_____/_____ M49
M50 _____/_____/_____ M50

	Day / Month / Year			Day / Month / Year	
M51	____/_____/_____	M51	M81	____/_____/_____	M81
M52	____/_____/_____	M52	M82	____/_____/_____	M82
M53	____/_____/_____	M53	M83	____/_____/_____	M83
M54	____/_____/_____	M54	M84	____/_____/_____	M84
M55	____/_____/_____	M55	M85	____/_____/_____	M85
M56	____/_____/_____	M56	M86	____/_____/_____	M86
M57	____/_____/_____	M57	M87	____/_____/_____	M87
M58	____/_____/_____	M58	M88	____/_____/_____	M88
M59	____/_____/_____	M59	M89	____/_____/_____	M89
M60	____/_____/_____	M60	M90	____/_____/_____	M90
M61	____/_____/_____	M61	M91	____/_____/_____	M91
M62	____/_____/_____	M62	M92	____/_____/_____	M92
M63	____/_____/_____	M63	M93	____/_____/_____	M93
M64	____/_____/_____	M64	M94	____/_____/_____	M94
M65	____/_____/_____	M65	M95	____/_____/_____	M95
M66	____/_____/_____	M66	M96	____/_____/_____	M96
M67	____/_____/_____	M67	M97	____/_____/_____	M97
M68	____/_____/_____	M68	M98	____/_____/_____	M98
M69	____/_____/_____	M69	M99	____/_____/_____	M99
M70	____/_____/_____	M70	M100	____/_____/_____	M100
M71	____/_____/_____	M71	M101	____/_____/_____	M101
M72	____/_____/_____	M72	M102	Duplicate of M101	M102
M73	____/_____/_____	M73	M103	____/_____/_____	M103
M74	____/_____/_____	M74	M104	____/_____/_____	M104
M75	____/_____/_____	M75	M105	____/_____/_____	M105
M76	____/_____/_____	M76	M106	____/_____/_____	M106
M77	____/_____/_____	M77	M107	____/_____/_____	M107
M78	____/_____/_____	M78	M108	____/_____/_____	M108
M79	____/_____/_____	M79	M109	____/_____/_____	M109
M80	____/_____/_____	M80	M110	____/_____/_____	M110

Bibliography

Allen, R.H., *Star Names: Their Lore and Meaning,* New York, NY, 1963: Dover Publications, Inc.

Archinal, B. A., "The Messier Marathon," *Deep Sky Monthly* No. 58, Vol. 6, No. 3, March 1982, pp. 4-9.

Becvar, A., *Atlas of the Heavens — II: Catalogue 1950.0,* 4th Ed., Prague and Cambridge, MA, 1976: Czechoslovak Academy of Sciences.

Beyer, S.L., *The Star Guide,* Boston, MA, 1986: Little, Brown and Company.

Burnham, Jr., R., *Burnham's Celestial Handbook* (3 Volumes), New York, NY, 1978: Dover Publications.

Dickinson, T., et al., *Edmund Scientific MAG 6 Sky Atlas,* Barrington, NJ, 1982: Edmund Scientific Co.

Freeman, L., *A Starhopper's Guide to Messier Objects,* Oakland, CA, 1983: Everything in the Universe.

Klein, F., *Visibility of Deep Sky Objects,* Los Altos, CA: Fred Klein.

Holyoke, E., *OBSERVE: A Guide to the Messier Objects*, Pittsburgh, PA, 1962, 1996: Astronomical League Sales.

Houston, W. S., "Deep Sky Wonders," *Sky and Telescope*, March 1979.

Kepple, G. R., *Astro Cards—The Messier Objects*, Freeport, PA, 1975: Fountain Press.

Jones, K. G., *The Search for the Nebulae,* Giles, U.K., 1975: Alpha Academic.

Jones, K. G., *Messiers Nebulae & Star Clusters*, second edition, Cambridge, U.K., 1991, Cambridge University Press.

Machholz, D., "Messier Marathon," "The Visibility of the Messier Objects Throughout the Year," "Messier Marathon Landmarks," Self Published, San Jose, CA.

Machholz, D., *Messier Marathon Observer's Guide,* Colfax, CA, 1994: MakeWood Products.

Machholz, D., "Notes on a Messier Marathon," *Night Skies*, December 1979, and *Astronomy*, March 1980.

Mallas, J. H., E. Kreimer, *The Messier Album,* Cambridge, MA, 1980: Sky Publishing Corporation.

Menzel, D., J. Pasachoff, *Field Guide of the Stars and Planets,* 2d Ed., Boston, MA, 1983: Houghton Mifflin Company.

Murdin, P., D. Allen, *Catalogue of the Universe,* New York, NY, 1979:

Crown Publishers.

Neu, J., " Papers on the Messier Marathon," Idyllwild, CA.

Olcott, W.T., *A Field Book of the Stars,* 3d Ed., Rev., New York, NY, 1935: G.P. Putnam's Sons.

O'Meara, S. J., *The Messier Objects Field Guide*, Cambridge, U.K., 1997: Cambridge University Press.

Scovil, C.E., *The AAVSO Variable Star Atlas,* Cambridge, MA, 1980: Sky Publishing Corporation.

Tirion, W., *British Astronomical Association B.A.A. Star Charts,* Hillside, NJ, 1982: Enslow Publishers.

Tirion, W., *SkyAtlas 2000.0 Deluxe Edition,* Cambridge, MA, 1985: Sky Publishing Corporation.

Tirion, W., B.N. Rappaport, and G. Lovi, *Uranometria 2000.0* (2 Volumes), Richmond, VA, 1988: Willmann-Bell, Inc.

Vehrenberg, H., *The Atlas of Deep Sky Splendors,* 4th Ed., Cambridge, MA, 1980: Sky Publishing Corporation.

Vehrenberg, H., D. Blank, *Handbook of the Constellations,* 5th Ed., Düsseldorf, W.G., 1984: Treugesell-verlag.

Index

M84, 64, 134–135
M85, 64, 112–113
M86, 64, 134–135
M87, 64, 134–136
M88, 64, 134–135
M89, 64, 136–137
M90, 64, 136–137
M91, 60–61, 64, 136–137
M92, 140–141
M93, 20, 92–93
M94, 64, 124–125
M95, 64, 108–109
M96, 64, 108–109
M97, 51–52, 60, 64, 118–119
M98, 64, 138–139, 142
M99, 64, 138–139
M100, 64, 138–139
M101, 60–61, 64, 70, 114–115, 122
M102, 57, 60–61, 64, 70, 114–115, 122–123
M103, 64, 92, 94–95
M104, 64, 128–129
M105, 64, 108–109
M106, 64, 116–117
M107, 150–151, 153
M108, 64, 120–121
M109, 64, 120–121
M110, 61, 80–81
Machholz, Don, 8–10, 13
Méchain, Pierre, 7, 61, 70, 72, 76, 84, 86, 88, 94,
    106, 108, 112, 114, 116, 118, 120, 122, 124,
    128, 138, 150, 160, 172, 176
Messier Catalog, 8, 11, 18, 60, 67, 69, 80, 96, 102,
    108, 120, 136, 172
Messier, Charles, 1, 7–8, 11, 60–61, 72, 76, 80, 82,
    84, 88, 90, 92, 94, 96, 98, 100, 102, 104,
106, 108, 110, 112, 114, 116, 118, 120, 122,
124, 126, 128, 130, 132, 134, 136, 138, 140,
142, 144, 146, 148, 150, 152, 154, 156, 158,
160, 162, 164, 166, 168, 170, 172, 174, 176,
180
Mira, 77
Monoceros, 20–21, 90–91
Murdin, Paul, 61, 176

N

Neu, Joe, 90, 130
NGC 1977, 88
NGC 1981, 88
NGC 2064, 88
NGC 2067, 88
NGC 2158, 100

NGC 2422, 61
NGC 2548, 61, 102
NGC 3384, 108
NGC 3389, 108
NGC 3628, 106
NGC 4217, 116
NGC 4312, 138
NGC 4387, 134
NGC 4388, 134
NGC 4394, 112
NGC 4413, 134
NGC 4478, 134
NGC 4548, 61
NGC 4638, 132
NGC 4647, 132
NGC 5053, 110
NGC 5195, 114
NGC 5866, 70, 114–115, 122–123
NGC 6603, 164
NGC 663, 94

O

Omega Nebula, 60, 156
Orion Nebula, 59–60, 88, 162
Orion, 11, 30, 59–60, 87–89, 162
Owl Nebula, 51, 60, 118

P

Pegasus, 63, 173–174, 176
Perseus, 84–85, 88
Phad, 120
Pinwheel Galaxy, 58, 82
Pisces, 58, 63, 72–74
Pleiades, 72, 90, 96, 156
Pliny, 104
Polaris, 27–30, 32, 40, 43
Pollux, 26, 30, 101
Pomona Valley Amateur Astronomers, 17–18
Praesepe, 104, 158
Procyon, 103
Puppis, 11, 20–21, 90–93

R

Rattley, Gerry, 9–10
Regulus, 26, 30
Reiland, Tom, 8–9
Rigel, 30
Ring Nebula, 60, 142
Riverside Telescope Maker's Conference, 52

S

Sagitta, 57, 144–145
Sagittarius, 16, 18, 25–26, 60, 63, 156–157, 161, 162–174
San Jose Amateur Astronomers, 9
Saturn, 28–29
Scorpius, 16, 18, 32, 157–161
Scutum, 57, 63, 153–157
Serpens Cadua, 157
Serpens Caput, 148–149
Seyfert galaxies, 76
Signpost Constellations, 26, 28–29
Signpost Map, 28–30
Signpost Stars, 26–27, 29–30, 32, 40, 65
Sirius, 28–30, 32
SJAA, 9
Sombrero Galaxy, 128
Spica, 28–29, 32, 40
Sunflower Galaxy, 124
Swan Nebula, 156, 164

T

Taurus, 7, 60, 95–97
Telrad, 22, 43–44, 51–53, 65, 68–69
Tirion, Wil, 69
Trapezium, 88
Trapp, Charles, 48, 98
Triangulum, 82
Trifid Nebula, 60, 162

U

Ursa Major, 25–27, 29, 45, 53, 60–61, 63, 113–123
Ursa Minor, 28

V

Vega, 28, 32
Venus, 28–29
Virgo, 11–12, 28, 70, 112, 127–139
Virgo galaxy cluster, 11, 16, 46, 61–63, 65, 112, 130–139
Vulpecula, 145

W

Webb, T.W., 59, 98
Whirlpool Galaxy, 51, 114
Wild Duck Cluster, 154
Woodside, Dorothy, 55